D. H. LAWRENCE

Literary Lives
General Editor: Richard Dutton, Senior Lecturer in English,
University of Lancaster

This series offers stimulating accounts of the literary careers of the most widely read British and Irish authors. Volumes follow the outline of writers' working lives, not in the spirit of traditional biography, but aiming to trace the professional, publishing and social contexts which shaped their writing. The role and status of 'the author' as the creator of literary texts is a vexed issue in current critical theory, where a variety of social, linguistic and psychological approaches have challenged the old concentration on writers as specially-gifted individuals. Yet reports of 'the death of the author' in literary studies are (as Mark Twain said of a premature obituary) an exaggeration. This series aims to demonstrate how an understanding of writers' careers can promote, for students and general readers alike, a more informed historical reading of their works.

Published titles

WILLIAM SHAKESPEARE
Richard Dutton

PERCY BYSSHE SHELLEY
Michael O'Neill

JOHN DONNE
George Parfitt

JOSEPH CONRAD
Cedric Watts

EMILY AND CHARLOTTE BRONTË
Tom Winnifrith and Edward Chitham

D. H. LAWRENCE
John Worthen

Further titles in preparation

D. H. Lawrence

A Literary Life

John Worthen

St. Martin's Press   New York

First published in the United States of America in 1989
Reprinted 1990

Printed in Hong Kong

ISBN 0–312–03524–1

Library of Congress Cataloging-in-Publication Data

Worthen, John
    D. H. Lawrence: a literary life / John Worthen.
        p.   cm. — (Literary lives)
    Bibliography: p.
    Includes index.
    ISBN 0–312–03524–1
    1. Lawrence, D. H. (David Herbert), 1885–1930. 2. Authors,
English—20th century—Biography.   I. Title.   II. Series: Literary
lives (New York, N. Y.)
PR6023.A93Z955 1989
823'.912—dc20
[B]   89–34364
                                                          CIP

To Conni

I hope to God I shall be able to make a living – but there, one must.

(Lawrence to Edward Garnett, 18 February 1913)

I am reading the Life. *It is interesting, but also false: far too jammy. Voltaire had made, acquired for himself, by the time he was my age, an income of £3,000 – equivalent at least to an income of twelve thousand pounds, today. How had he done it? – it means a capital of two hundred thousand pounds. Where had it come from?*

(Lawrence to Dorothy Brett, 24 November 1926)

We talked my poverty – it has got on my nerves lately. But next day had a horrible reaction . . . Definitely I hate the whole money-making world, Tom & Dick as well as en gros. But I won't be done by them either.

(Memorandum by Lawrence, 19 November 1927)

Contents

Acknowledgements		viii
Chronology 1885–1932		ix
Introduction		xx
1	Early Years	1
2	First Year as a Professional Writer: 1912–13	21
3	Success and Catastrophe: 1913–15	30
4	War: 1915–16	50
5	Poverty: 1917–19	65
6	Struggling Through: 1919–21	88
7	Living Blithely: 1922–25	114
8	Economising: 1925–27	134
9	1928	143
10	Providing: 1929–30	160
Epilogue		166
Notes		172
Further Reading		181
Index		184

Acknowledgements

Michael Black read the first draft of this book, gave me a great deal of splendidly pertinent advice and saved me from numerous errors about Lawrence, book-production and publishing. Lindeth Vasey read the manuscript on two different occasions: her marvellous eye for detail and her wide knowledge of Lawrence helped me enormously. Michael Squires greatly assisted me with the details of the publication of *Lady Chatterley's Lover*; Gerald Pollinger talked to me, wined and lunched me, and answered my questions about publishing and Lawrence from his own unique position of expertise. Richard Dutton was a thoughtful and helpful general editor. James T. Boulton allowed me access to the complete file of Lawrence's correspondence in Birmingham. I am very grateful to him, to Cambridge University Press, and to Laurence Pollinger Ltd and the Estate of Mrs Frieda Lawrence Ravagli, for permission to quote from the works and the letters of D. H. Lawrence. W. H. Clarke and George Lazarus both kindly allowed me access to their manuscript collections; Margaret Needham and Joan King answered my questions with great patience. I am also indebted to the Harry Ransom Humanities Research Center, University of Texas, to Northwestern University, to the University of Cincinatti, and to the Berg Collection, New York Public Library. The dedication, however, records the author's debt to the person who heard this book worked-out in its early stages, expounded over the washing-up as it developed, and at last tapped-out with two fingers: and who supported him financially while he wrote about another man's financial problems . . .

J. W.
Oberhausen

Chronology 1885–1932

This chronology includes a complete list of Lawrence's publications up to the end of 1919; thereafter, all his important publications are listed, and all those referred to in the text.

11 September 1885	Born in Eastwood, Nottinghamshire.
October 1892–July 1901	Pupil at Beauvale Board School; then pupil at Nottingham High School.
1902–8	Pupil teacher, teacher, and student at University College, Nottingham.
7 December 1907	'A Prelude', in *Nottinghamshire Guardian*.
October 1908	Appointed teacher at Davidson Road School, Croydon.
September 1909	Meets Ford Madox Hueffer.
November 1909	Six poems in Hueffer's *English Review*.
February 1910	'Goose Fair' in *English Review* (now edited by Austin Harrison).
April 1910	Six poems in *English Review*.
October 1910	Three poems in *English Review*.
3 December 1910	Engagement to Louie Burrows; broken off on 4 February 1912.
9 December 1910	Death of DHL's mother, Lydia Lawrence.
19 January 1911	*The White Peacock* (Duffield).
20 January 1911	*The White Peacock* (Heinemann).
June 1911	'Odour of Chrysanthemums' in *English Review*.
September 1911	'A Fragment of Stained Glass' in *English Review*.
October 1911	Meets Edward Garnett.
4 November 1911	Two poems (sent by Garnett) in *Nation*.

19 November 1911	DHL falls ill with pneumonia after weekend with Garnett; resigns his teaching post on 28 February 1912.
November 1911	Review in *English Review*.
January 1912	Review in *English Review*.
February 1912	'Second Best' in *English Review*.
Between 3 and 17 March 1912	Meets Frieda Weekley.
16 March 1912	'The Miner at Home' in *Nation*.
3 May 1912	DHL and Frieda Weekley go to Germany together.
11 May–1 June 1912	Six 'Schoolmaster' poems in *Saturday Westminster Gazette*.
23 May 1912	*The Trespasser* (Duckworth).
May 1912	*The Trespasser* (Kennerley).
June 1912	One poem in *English Review*.
3 August 1912	'French Sons of Germany' in *Saturday Westminster Gazette*.
5 August 1912	Starts journey to Italy.
10 August 1912	'Hail in the Rhineland' in *Saturday Westminster Gazette*.
September 1912–March 1913	At Gargnano, Lago di Garda, Italy.
December 1912	One poem in *Georgian Poetry 1911–1912*.
February 1913	*Love Poems* (Duckworth).
22 March 1913	'Christs in the Tirol' in *Saturday Westminster Gazette*.
March 1913	Review in *Rhythm*.
March 1913	'The Soiled Rose' in *Forum*.
April–May 1913	In Italy and Germany.
29 May 1913	*Sons and Lovers* (Duckworth).
June–August 1913	In England.
July 1913	Review in *Blue Review*.
August 1913–June 1914	In Germany, Switzerland and Italy.
16 August 1913	'The Fly in the Ointment' in *New Statesman*.
6 September 1913	'Her Turn' in *Westminster Gazette*.
13 September 1913	'A Sick Collier' in *New Statesman*.
13 September 1913	'Strike-Pay' in *Westminster Gazette*.
17 September 1913	*Sons and Lovers* (Kennerley).

September 1913	Three Italian sketches in the *English Review*.
15 November 1913	One poem in *New Statesman*.
November 1913	One poem in *Smart Set*.
1913	*Love Poems* (Kennerley).
January 1914	Eight poems in *Poetry*.
February 1914	Two poems in *English Review*.
February 1914	Reprint of *Love Poems* (Duckworth).
February 1914	'The Christening' in *Smart Set*.
March 1914	'The Shadow in the Rose Garden' in *Smart Set*.
1 April 1914	*The Widowing of Mrs Holroyd* (Kennerley).
1 April 1914	Five poems in *Egoist*.
17 April 1914	*The Widowing of Mrs Holroyd* (Duckworth).
30 June 1914	Takes J. B. Pinker as agent, signs Methuen contract for *The Rainbow*.
June 1914	'Vin Ordinaire' ['The Thorn in the Flesh'] in *English Review*.
July 1914–December 1915	In London, Buckinghamshire and Sussex.
13 July 1914	Marries Frieda Weekley in London.
18 August 1914	'With the Guns' in *Manchester Guardian*.
August 1914	'Honour and Arms' in *English Review*.
October 1914	'The White Stocking' in *Smart Set*.
26 November 1914.	*The Prussian Officer and Other Stories* (Duckworth): Garnett's title.
November 1914	'Honour and Arms' in *Metropolitan*.
December 1914	One poem in *Poetry and Drama*.
December 1914	Six poems in *Poetry*.
17 April 1915	Seven poems in *Some Imagist Poets*.
1 May 1915	One poem in *Egoist*.
30 September 1915	*The Rainbow* (Methuen).

4 October 1915	'The Crown' (i) in *The Signature*.
18 October 1915	'The Crown' (ii) in *The Signature*.
October 1915	'England, My England' in *English Review*.
1 November 1915	'The Crown' (iii) in *The Signature*.
13 November 1915	*The Rainbow* suppressed by magistrate's order.
November 1915	Expurgated *The Rainbow* (Huebsch).
November 1915	Two poems in *Georgian Poetry 1913–1915*.
30 December 1915	To Cornwall.
6 May 1916	Five poems in *Some Imagist Poets*.
1 June 1916	*Twilight in Italy* (Duckworth).
July 1916	*Amores* (Duckworth).
25 September 1916	*Amores* (Huebsch).
1916	*The Prussian Officer* (Huebsch).
1916	*Twilight in Italy* (Huebsch).
January 1917	One poem in *Egoist*.
28 February 1917	One poem in *The New Poetry*.
February 1917	One poem in *Egoist*.
March 1917	'The Thimble' in *Seven Arts*.
March 1917	'Samson and Delilah' in *English Review*.
14 April 1917	One poem in *Some Imagist Poets*.
May–August 1917	'The Reality of Peace' in *English Review*.
June 1917	One poem in *Poetry*.
July 1917	'The Mortal Coil' (*Seven Arts*).
September 1917	Three poems in *English Review*.
15 October 1917	After twenty-one months residence in Cornwall, ordered to leave by the military authorities.
October 1917–November 1919	In London, Berkshire and Derbyshire.
26 November 1917	*Look! We Have Come Through!* (Chatto and Windus).
January–February 1918	'Love' and 'Life' in *English Review*.
May 1918	Two poems in *New Paths*.
June 1918	Three poems in *English Review*.

July 1918	*Look! We Have Come Through!* (Huebsch).
October 1918	*New Poems* (Secker).
November 1918–June 1919	Eight American literature essays in *English Review*.
February 1919	Six poems in *Poetry*.
11 April 1919	'Whistling of Birds' in *Athenæum*.
April 1919	'Tickets Please' in *Strand*.
July 1919	One poem in *Monthly Chapbook*.
July 1919	Twelve poems in *Poetry*.
July 1919	Three poems in *Voices*.
August 1919	Second edition of *New Poems* (Secker).
20 November 1919	*Bay* (Beaumont).
November 1919–February 1922	In Italy, then Capri and Sicily.
27 December 1919	Breaks with J. B. Pinker as agent.
1919	'Poetry of the Present' (introduction to *New Poems*) in *Playboy* (2 issues).

*   *   *   *   *   *   *   *

16 February 1920	Takes Robert Mountsier as American agent.
April 1920	Translation of Shestov's *All Things are Possible* (Secker).
May 1920	*Touch and Go* (Daniel).
11 June 1920	*New Poems* (Huebsch).
5 June 1920	*Touch and Go* (Seltzer).
July 1920	'The Blind Man' in *English Review*.
August 1920	'The Blind Man' in *The Living Age*.
9 November 1920	*Women in Love* (Seltzer).
25 November 1920	*The Lost Girl* (Secker).
28 January 1921	*The Lost Girl* (Seltzer).
February 1921	*Movements in European History* (Oxford University Press).
February 1921	*The Widowing of Mrs Holroyd* (Seltzer).
4 April 1921	Takes Curtis Brown as English agent.

10 May 1921	*Psychoanalysis and the Unconscious* (Seltzer).
10 June 1921	*Women in Love* (Secker).
August 1921	'Wintry Peacock' in *Metropolitan*.
November 1921	Second (revised) edition of *Women in Love* (Secker).
by 2 December 1921	*The Lost Girl* awarded James Tait Black Memorial Prize.
9 December 1921	*Tortoises* (Seltzer).
12 December 1921	*Sea and Sardinia* (Seltzer).
26 February 1922	Sails from Naples to Ceylon.
March–April 1922	In Ceylon.
14 April 1922	*Aaron's Rod* (Seltzer).
15 June 1922	'Wintry Peacock' in *New Decameron III*.
June 1922	*Aaron's Rod* (Secker).
4 May–10 August 1922	In Australia.
10 August 1922	Sails from Sydney to San Francisco.
4 September 1922	Arrives in San Francisco.
September 1922–March 1923	In New Mexico.
18 October 1922	Trade edition of *Women in Love* (Seltzer).
23 October 1922	*Fantasia of the Unconscious* (Seltzer).
24 October 1922	*England, My England* (Seltzer).
24 December 1922	'Certain Americans and an Englishman' in *New York Times Magazine*.
10 January 1923	Translation of *The Gentleman from San Francisco and Other Stories* (Seltzer).
3 February 1923	Breaks with Mountsier as American agent.
23 March–9 July 1923	In Mexico.
March 1923	*The Ladybird* (containing 'The Ladybird', 'The Fox' and 'The Captain's Doll') (Secker).
11 April 1923	*The Captain's Doll* (containing 'The Ladybird', 'The Fox' and 'The

	Captain's Doll') (Seltzer).
April 1923	*Sea and Sardinia* (Secker).
April 1923	'Surgery for the Novel, or a Bomb' in *Literary Digest International Book Review*.
July 1923	*Psychoanalysis and the Unconscious* (Secker).
19 July–August 1923	In New York.
18 August 1923	Frieda sails to England.
27 August 1923	*Studies in Classic American Literature* (Seltzer).
August–November 1923	DHL travels in America and Mexico.
September 1923	*Kangaroo* (Secker, reprinted later in year).
September 1923	*Fantasia of the Unconscious* (Secker).
17 September 1923	*Kangaroo* (Seltzer).
9 October 1923	*Birds, Beasts and Flowers* (Seltzer).
13 October 1923	Translation of *Mastro-don Gesualdo* (Seltzer).
22 November 1923	DHL sails to England.
November 1923	*Birds, Beasts and Flowers* (Secker).
November 1923	Reprint of *Sons and Lovers* (Seltzer).
November 1923	Reprint of *Love Poems* (Duckworth).
December 1923–March 1924	In England, France and Germany.
January 1924	*England, My England* (Secker).
11 March 1924	Arrives (met by Seltzer) in New York.
March 1924	Takes Curtis Brown as American agent.
March–16 October 1924	In New Mexico.
June 1924	*Studies in Classic American Literature* (Secker).
28 August 1924	DHL and Mollie Skinner, *The Boy in the Bush* (Secker).
10 September 1924	Death of DHL's father, Arthur John Lawrence.
30 September 1924	DHL and Mollie Skinner, *The Boy in the Bush* (Seltzer).

September 1924	'The Border-Line' in *Smart Set*.
September 1924	'The Border-Line' in *Hutchinson's Magazine*.
1 October 1924	Introduction to *Memoirs of the Foreign Legion* (Secker).
16 October 1924	Leaves New Mexico for Mexico.
26 October 1924	'Indians and Entertainment' in *New York Times Magazine*.
October 1924	Reprint *Twilight in Italy* (Duckworth).
October 1924–25 March 1925	In Mexico.
November 1924	Reprint *The Rainbow* (Seltzer), *The Prussian Officer* (Duckworth).
January 1925	Introduction to *Memoirs of the Foreign Legion* (Knopf).
9 March 1925	Translation of *Little Novels of Sicily* (Seltzer).
29 March–September 1925	In New Mexico.
March 1925	Translation of *Mastro-don Gesualdo* (Cape).
14 May 1925	*St. Mawr* (Secker).
May 1925	Translation of *Little Novels of Sicily* (Blackwell).
5 June 1925	*St. Mawr* (Knopf).
July 1925 and January 1926	'The Woman Who Rode Away' in *Criterion*.
14 September 1925	In New York.
21 September 1925	Sails to England.
September 1925–June 1928	In England and, mainly, Italy.
7 December 1925	*Reflections on the Death of a Porcupine and Other Essays* (Centaur Press).
27 December 1925	Book review in *New York Herald Tribune*.
December 1925	Accumulated Mail' in *Borzoi 1925* (Knopf).
21 January 1926	*The Plumed Serpent* (Secker, reprinted later in year).
31 January 1926	Book review in *New York Herald Tribune*

5 February 1926	*The Plumed Serpent* (Knopf).
March 1926	Limited edition of *David* (Secker).
23 April 1926	*David* (Knopf).
19 June 1926	'Smile' in *Nation & Athenæum*.
late July 1926	To England.
July 1926	'The Rocking-Horse Winner' in *Harper's Bazaar*.
28 September 1926	'The Rocking-Horse Winner' in *The Ghost Book*.
September 1926	*Sun* (Archer).
October 1926	Reprint *Twilight in Italy* (Cape).
November 1926	*Glad Ghosts* (Benn).
February 1927	Reprint of *David* (Secker).
March 1927	Secker starts to issue pocket edition of DHL's works.
April 1927	Reprint *Sea and Sardinia* (Secker).
June 1927	*Mornings in Mexico* (Secker).
5 August 1927	*Mornings in Mexico* (Knopf).
10 September 1927	'The Nightingale' in *Spectator*.
September 1927	'The Nightingale' in *Forum*.
November 1927	Plans private publication in Florence of *Lady Chatterley's Lover*.
17 February 1928	*Selected Poems* (Benn).
February 1928	Translation of *Cavalleria Rusticana* (Cape).
March 1928	*Rawdon's Roof* (Elkin Matthews).
March 1928	Reprint of translation of *Mastro-don Gesualdo* (Cape).
8 May 1928	'The "Jeune Fille" Wants to Know' in *Evening News*.
24 May 1928	*The Woman Who Rode Away and Other Stories* (Secker).
25 May 1928	*The Woman Who Rode Away and Other Stories* (Knopf).
June 1928–March 1930	In Switzerland, Spain and (principally) in France.
June 1928	First edition (hardback) of *Lady Chatterley's Lover* (Orioli).
7 July 1928	'Laura Philippine' in *T.P.'s & Cassell's Weekly*.

12 July 1928	'Over Ernest Ladies' in *Evening News*.
2 August 1928	'Master in his own House' in *Evening News*.
3 September 1928	'Dull London' in *Evening News*.
27 September 1928	'Oh! for a new Crusade' in *Evening News*.
September 1928	*Collected Poems* (Secker).
5 October 1928	'If Women were Supreme' in *Evening News*.
13 October 1928	'Hymns in a Man's Life' in *Evening News*.
October 1928	Second edition (paperbound) of *Lady Chatterley's Lover* (Orioli).
October 1928	*Sun* (Black Sun Press).
25 November 1928	'Sex Locked Out' in *Sunday Dispatch*.
29 November 1928	'Is England still a Man's Country?' in *Daily Express*.
17 February 1929	'Myself Revealed' in *Sunday Dispatch*.
28 April 1929	'Women Don't Change' in *Sunday Dispatch*.
May 1929	Paris edition of *Lady Chatterley's Lover* (Titus).
19 June 1929	'The Real Trouble about Women' in *Daily Express*.
June 1929	*The Paintings of D. H. Lawrence* (Mandrake Press).
July 1929	Expurgated *Pansies* (Secker).
15 July 1929	*My Skirmish with Jolly Roger* (Random House).
July 1929	*Collected Poems* (Cape and Smith).
August 1929	Unexpurgated *Pansies* (Stephenson).
September 1929	*The Escaped Cock* (Black Sun Press).
14 November 1929	*Pornography & Obscenity* (Faber and Faber).
November 1929	Translation of *The Story of Doctor Manente* (Orioli).

December 1929	Reprint of *Collected Poems* (Secker).
2 March 1930	Dies at Vence, France
13 March 1930	*Nettles* (Faber and Faber).
11 April 1930	*Assorted Articles* (Knopf).
April 1930	Reprint of *David* (Secker).
April 1930	*Assorted Articles* (Secker, reprinted later in year).
17 May 1930	*The Virgin and the Gipsy* (Orioli).
24 June 1930	*A Propos of Lady Chatterley's Lover* (Mandrake).
25 November 1930	*Love Among the Haystacks* (Nonesuch).
3 June 1931	*Apocalypse* (Orioli).
26 September 1932	*The Letters of D. H. Lawrence* (Heinemann).
September 1932	*Etruscan Places* (Secker).
1 October 1932	*Last Poems* (Orioli).

Introduction

I

What should a writer do, whose wife is incapable of looking after herself financially, who is himself terminally ill and in need of money for doctors, and who suddenly makes what is, for him, a lot of money?

The answer is obvious: he should invest his money as wisely as he can. And that is exactly what the writer D. H. Lawrence did with some of his profits from the first two impressions of *Lady Chatterley's Lover*, privately published in Florence, and the third impression published in Paris. He bought stocks and shares via his literary agents in New York; by October 1929 he held shares to a total value of over $6000 and – after selling 20 shares in one corporation – was re-investing in another.[1]

The fact that he invested his money shocks his biographers. Most do not mention the fact; Harry T. Moore, who wrote the standard life, remarked that 'it seems incredible'.[2] Only Richard Aldington – himself a professional writer who lived hand-to-mouth for years – expressed himself indifferent.[3] But one glance at Lawrence's own careful 'Memorandum Book' of the costs, income and profits of *Lady Chatterley's Lover* – every cheque detailed, every bank noted – reveals the characteristic attention to the details of money of the man who had remarked, in 1913, that 'coming of hand-to-mouth poor folk, I never believe in any money that is not in my pocket'.[4] For once he had been able to ensure that the profits of his writing went straight into his pocket; and he used that money as a secure source of income for the future.

We do not sufficiently take into account the fact that writers not only write, but get paid for it: and live, and write further works – or give up, and write no more – or adapt what they write – on the strength of what they get paid. Far too often, the view of literary critics is of the author as an autonomous creator, producing his or her work independently of the money it earns, and writing according to the idealism of the creative imagination (or the commercial nexus, according to which critical language one is using). I would suggest, however, that even an author like Lawrence, who was very often idealist in his own attitude towards writing, was deeply influenced by the fact of being a man writing for his living; and that being a man dependent upon his writing sometimes dictated what he wrote and when. Moore's shock at Lawrence's investment of his earnings is, of course, provoked by the fact that the profits from a novel like *Lady Chatterley's Lover* should have been directed to such an unforseeable end; but his biography is continually reticent about what Lawrence earned, and what he did with his money; and it ignores the fact that, like all Lawrence's books, *Lady Chatterley's Lover*, too, was written with a sense of the market which would buy it and, as finally revised, it was designed (in part) to make money. Apart from the general sense that Lawrence was always rather poor, very little attention has been paid to Lawrence's increasing and diminishing earning power over the years between 1912 and 1930; when in fact even the briefest glance at his published letters shows him to have been a man continually aware of the success, or failure, of this or that work: who was intensely concerned with what agents and publishers were doing with his writings, and how well they were handling them commercially: who regularly discussed and sometimes disputed what he was paid for his writing: who actually decided, at one stage in his career, that he could run the business side of his writing better than the agent who had so far looked after it: and who did so for more than a year in England, and for the best part of a year in America a little later. This is perhaps to say no more than that Lawrence was an unusually energetic professional writer: but even that is not how he is usually seen.

The investment of his profits from *Lady Chatterley's Lover* in shares is, in fact, only another example of the financial good sense we can see throughout his career; and to be shocked by it is to underestimate Lawrence's needs. He had been a writer who, for most of his life, had earned very little, and for a good deal of it had earned only modestly. He had certainly started out with very little idea of how to earn his living. But he had been lucky in his friends; Ford Madox Hueffer had helped him enormously in getting a market for his work in 1909 and 1910, when he was still a part-time writer, and Edward Garnett took upon himself the role of an unpaid literary agent for the two crucial years after Lawrence went full-time. Unlike a writer such as James Joyce, who was nearly always short of money, whose debts pursued him around Europe and whose family became used to being turned out of their accommodation, Lawrence always made sure that he had enough money 'to keep his own life under complete control', as his wife Frieda put it.[5] Even when he and Frieda were almost destitute during 1917–18, she recalled how 'he always had enough money to buy a book he wanted, or a box of paints, or a present for somebody ... He could do miracles with the awfully little money we had.'[6] And when he finally made more money than he had ever had in his life, with *Lady Chatterley's Lover*, he invested it for the future: not, of course, his own future (there are many indications that he knew his illness was fatal): but that of Frieda, who he was sure would survive him.

II

One way of looking at Lawrence's literary career, therefore, is to see it as that of a man who – in spite of desperate poverty at times – succeeded between 1912 and 1930 in making his living by his pen, providing for those dependent upon him, and in doing what he wanted to do with his life out of the proceeds of his writing. To see him like this is not to under-rate him, but to acknowledge both the struggles and the professionalism of his life and work.

What follows will be an account not only, of course, of what he earned, but of how in a much larger sense he made his way as a writer; from the earliest years of his writing, through the start of his career as a full-time writer, through the appallingly difficult times of the war, to his ability in the early 1920s to earn in America what he needed by his pen. He ended up addressing himself both to a popular public (he wrote some striking Sunday-newspaper journalism) and to the very special public that was able to buy a novel as expensive as the limited edition of *Lady Chatterley's Lover*.

The period of the First World War was the only time when he was unable to earn what he needed: and it was towards the end of the war that he also produced the one book he ever wrote entirely for money – a history book for schools, *Movements in European History*. The war had reduced him to near destitution, and he was for a short while dependent upon his family for support, and upon any charity which his friends and fellow writers were able to give him. His school book, however, actually earned him rather little, after its initial lump-sum advance on royalties. If it was characteristic of him to take it on in order to pay his debts to his friends and family, it was also characteristic of him that the book changed while being written from hateful sweated labour to something which allowed him to write as he wanted to about the history of his own times, and the peculiar needs – as he understood them – of his own age. In spite of the unlikeliness of such a development, the book came to be, at least in part, the book he wanted to write at that particular moment, rather than the book his publisher was able to sell in very large numbers, or which would earn either his publisher or Lawrence himself the sums which school books sometimes make. It sold sufficiently – 2000 copies in the first two years, and then a reprint of another 2000 copies. His publisher did not lose by it: it was an interesting book: Lawrence earned his advance, and two other editions – an illustrated one in 1925 and a specially expurgated one for Irish schools in 1927 – earned some more. 'Basta!' as he would have said.

But it was a measure of the success of his writing life that Lawrence generally managed to write what he wanted, when he wanted, and where he wanted. He got himself into a position where he was (except during the war, and briefly late in 1927) able to do that, and simultaneously make his living. Frieda Lawrence remarked, in her book about her husband, that 'his writing was not just writing as a profession',[7] and we can guess what she meant: he never laboured for long against the grain to write when he didn't want to, even to pay his bills. His correspondence is full of remarks that he didn't feel like writing, or that it was the wrong season of the year for him to write; and although he is not usually to be trusted when he remarks that he is being lazy and not writing anything, yet he generally wrote his poems, his books, and his essays as and when he wanted to – or, as he might have said, when 'the demon' demanded. But even if the demon ruled at times, we can also see Lawrence's writing life characterised by a steady application to the business of getting published and getting paid, and of adapting himself to the needs of the market and the moment, as well as by a determination to write what he chose in spite of the protests of publishers, readers and critics.

Only the illness of his last four years prevented him travelling still further, and writing yet more books; he had expressed a desire to write a novel on each continent (but only managed three of them). In the end, it was illness alone that limited his capacity to write: he produced almost no fiction in the last two years of his life. He turned to shorter forms: to essays and poetry. And his final exploration, through *Apocalypse* and his *Last Poems*, was not of new continents but of man's relationship with the cosmos: he applied himself as a writer to the fact of his own dying and wrote about what it was like to be a human being on the point of death, still vividly and hauntingly aware of himself alive, but also looking beyond himself.

III

And yet there is another side to this same story. This is a book about a man making his way through a literary world in which he always felt alien, and where he was frequently treated as an outsider; in which, although he earned his living, he was notably unsuccessful by its standards of success. This book describes the continual problems Lawrence had: the adjustments he had to make to his work in order to be published (or to sell) at all: it also describes the problems his publishers and agents had with him, and the relatively little money he made them.

Before the First World War, a full-price new novel normally cost 6/- (though cheaper reprints would certainly come later in the case of a successful book): after the war, it rose to 9/-. An author would get a royalty (usually paid yearly) of something between 10% and 25%, depending upon his reputation and his publisher: but for many writers – and Lawrence was one of them – the advance of royalties made by a publisher upon a book's publication might well be all the money they ever got for it; certainly all they could rely upon earning. A novel would not usually start making profits for its publisher unless it sold more than 2000 copies; and of Lawrence's first three novels, only the first certainly sold more than that. The publisher of his third book, *Sons and Lovers*, actually lost money on it in the first year of sales – something not unusual even for a moderately successful book. Lawrence's advance, of £100, was therefore all he earned from it for two years. A successful serious professional writer of the period like Arnold Bennett could (in 1910) sell nearly 6000 copies in the first four months of a 'serious' novel like *Clayhanger*, having been given an advance of £300 on it by its English publisher; and he might make in all five or six times that sum with American sales, serialisations and cheap editions. A genuinely popular writer such as Compton Mackenzie could have his second novel *Carnival* reprinted five times in one year, sell 35 000 copies of a novel like *Sinister Street* (1913) in six months, and sell 30 000 copies of *Poor Relations* in three months in 1919. Mackenzie would be offered advances of between £750 and £1000 on a 25% royalty.[8]

For stories and articles in magazines, Arnold Bennett would, before the war, charge (according to the nature of the publication) up to 1/- a word; at the very least he would expect 4–6 guineas per 1000 words. (In the late 1920s he expected twice as much.) When he was paid only 2½ guineas per 1000 words by Ford Madox Hueffer for a story in the *English Review* in 1909, Bennett reckoned he had been 'done' by the editor.[9] But what was disgracefully low payment for a writer like Bennett was far more than a writer like Lawrence could expect: in 1914, when his pre-war reputation was at its height, Lawrence received only 2 guineas for a newspaper piece of 1400 words for the *Manchester Guardian*; and the *English Review* under Austin Harrison, which had offered Bennett 6 guineas per 1000 words for articles in 1911, in October 1913 only offered Lawrence £15 each for the 7400 and 8500 word stories 'Vin Ordinaire' and 'Honour and Arms' (later 'The Prussian Officer') (*Letters*, I, p. 81 n. 1).[10]

A successful writer like Bennett earned massive sums from his work: more than £11 000 in 1912 (not including the income from a West End play which made him £60 a week during its year-long run); in 1913 he was earning on average over £300 a week, and in 1920 he earned £15 783.[11] Lawrence, on the other hand, made not much more than £300 during the whole of 1914, his most financially rewarding year before the early 1920s. It was also rather easier for a writer like Lawrence to survive before the war than after it; magazine editors paid more, publishers were more generous with advances, and royalty percentages were often higher. The book-trade took a long time to recover from the war; printing and paper costs increased two- or three-fold, and the problems of the uncommercial writer like Lawrence became very acute. As late as 1929, when Bennett's reputation had somewhat declined and it was (anyway) harder to earn large sums, he was still able to earn £22 000 a year. Only the private publication of *Lady Chatterley's Lover* in 1928 made Lawrence very much money, and even that sum (over £1400 in the book's first year) was not in the Arnold Bennett league. Lawrence also started to earn money from popular journalism in 1928; the *Evening Standard* paid him £10 for a piece of 2000 words. But in 1927 they had paid Bennett £75 for review articles of the same length, his price for articles being 2/- a word:

Lawrence never got more than 6d a word.[12] Lawrence died in 1930 worth £2438; Bennett surprised many people by being worth only £36 600 on his death in 1931. (The literary agent J. B. Pinker, who had worked for them both, had left £40 000 on his death in 1922.) Lawrence survived, lived his life as he wanted, even if at times uncomfortably, and thought of Bennett as a 'sort of pig in clover'.[13] But he was never a popular writer, in spite of his agents' and publishers' regular hopes that he might start to be, and his own occasional flirtation with the idea. In general, like Conrad, he 'very consciously set himself against the public he hoped to reach out to and even transform'.[14] That was the writer he continued to be, to the end of his life.

NOTE

I have not attempted to list in this book every one of Lawrence's pieces of writing, or commercial transactions; such a compilation would require a different sort of book, and a much longer one. I have endeavoured to provide the reader with the general outlines of Lawrence's writing career, and to cover in detail the most interesting topics – such as his early breakthrough into literary success, his disastrous experience with *The Rainbow*, the problems with the publishing of *Women in Love*, his relative success in the 1920s, and finally his arrangements for the printing and publication of *Lady Chatterley's Lover* in 1928. Most of the gaps in the narrative of writings, earnings and publications can be filled by reference to Warren Roberts' *Bibliography of D. H. Lawrence*, to the published volumes of Lawrence's letters in the Cambridge Edition (see Further Reading), and to the edition of Lawrence's works from the same publisher.

1

Early Years

From our standpoint, a hundred and more years later, the fact that
David Herbert Lawrence (born 1885) became a major novelist and
major writer seems unremarkable. His status is confirmed both by
his presence on examination syllabuses for schools and universi-
ties, and by the continuing sales of his books: a new critical edition
of his works, aiming at establishing accurate texts, began to come
out in 1979. Few writers ever find their works both selling at station
bookstalls and being the subject of literary doctorates: but, like
Thomas Hardy, Lawrence is clearly a writer whom the twentieth
century has taken particularly to heart.

And thus we are in danger of ignoring the first and most
extraordinary fact about Lawrence: that his arrival at the status of
famous novelist, playwright, essayist and poet was, given his
background, extremely unlikely: it was (indeed) unprecedented.
The family into which he was born was 'upwardly mobile',
socially; whereas his father and his three uncles had all been
coalminers for most of their lives, the sons of those families –
though some became miners – also moved into a variety of
lower-middle-class jobs: as shopkeepers, tradesmen, clerks. And
the daughters also tended to marry into the lower-middle-class. If
Lawrence had not become a full-time writer, he would almost
certainly have remained the schoolteacher he trained to be, and
which he was for more than three years. It is possible to imagine
him living his life as some dynamic and unconventional headmaster, producing pamphlets about education and writing fiction as a
side-line. His younger sister Ada also trained and worked as a
teacher before her marriage, and his two brothers demonstrated
the same movement away from traditionally working-class employment: the eldest was apprenticed to a picture framer, and was
himself a craftsman, while his son in turn became a hairdresser: the
second brother was carving out for himself an exceptionally

successful career as a clerk in a London export and import firm when he died at the age of 23.

But these socially upward movements by Lawrence's elder brothers, although natural for the children of a family living in the expanding and prospering mining village of Eastwood in the last quarter of the nineteenth century, would not have included a movement into the profession of full-time writer. As Lawrence himself said with some misgiving when he was about 20, and thinking of writing for the first time – his words are reported by the great friend and companion of his adolescence, Jessie Chambers –

'It will be *poetry*.'
I took fire at that.
'Well, isn't that the very greatest thing?'
'Ah, *you* say that,' he replied. 'But what will the others say? That I'm a fool. A collier's son a poet!'[1]

Those 'others' whose opinion scared him were, almost certainly, the members of his own family. His brother George (the apprentice picture-framer) and his elder sister Emily both regarded 'writing' as trivial, his father probably thought it pointless, and his mother regarded it as a worrying waste of time for a young man who should be trying to get on in his profession. Only his sister Ada was sympathetic, and that out of her sympathy for her brother, rather than any love for writing as such; her reported opinion (at the age of 18) of Miranda's speeches in *The Tempest* as 'rubbish'[2] suggests that poetry was not one of her natural loves when she was young.

Accordingly, so far as we can tell, the members of Lawrence's family knew almost nothing about his writing for some considerable time; and they certainly did not read what he wrote. In 1928, remembering these early years, Lawrence himself recalled how 'His own family strictly "natural" looked on such performances as writing as "affectation"', and that he therefore 'wrote in secret at home'.[3] It may not perhaps have been their 'naturalness' so much as their sense of the economic folly of such a profession that made them suspicious of their brother's 'affectation'. However, as late as 1928, Lawrence felt that his family was

annoyed that I write unpleasant books that nobody really wants to read: certainly *they* don't, although they work through them, I suppose, because they still 'love' me so dearly: me, the brother Bertie, not the embarrassing D. H. Lawrence.[4]

It was the enormous change from 'the brother Bertie' to being 'the embarrassing D. H. Lawrence' which, almost single-handedly, Lawrence had to accomplish.

His early writing was, however, not only kept from his family; it was also kept from other friends. From the time he started, around 1905, until 1906, it was seen exclusively by Jessie Chambers. His closest male friend, George Neville, remembered going out more than once to the 'Haggs Farm' (the home of the Chambers family) in search of Lawrence, on hearing that he had 'crammed his papers into his pocket' and gone off there:

> I would usually find Lawrence and the 'Princess' [Neville's name for Jessie Chambers] with their heads close together and the crumpled papers spread out in front of them; but the papers soon disappeared with my arrival.[5]

Others in the Chambers family, too, had their slightly anxious suspicions that 'he must be writing a book';[6] but they, too, had as yet seen nothing – even when he had completed the first draft of his novel *The White Peacock* in 1907. Yet, all the time between 1905 and 1907, Lawrence had been showing everything he wrote to Jessie Chambers: took it to her, and then posted it to her when he went to Croydon in October 1908 to be a teacher; always expected her to read it, and to tell him what she thought of it.

But it was not even simply adolescent awkwardness about his poetry, with regard to his 'natural' family and friends, that made Lawrence secretive about it – the shyness of 'a collier's son a poet!' We cannot start to understand the young Lawrence (nor, perhaps, the older one) without realising that his background, his family, his education and his intended profession all tended to act dividedly upon him. His mother – who always presented herself to her family as someone very nearly, if not fully, middle-class, who was 'educated', who wrote fluent letters and who even wrote poetry – very badly wanted her children to 'get on' in the world in the way in which her own father and mother had so disastrously failed to do, and which she herself (marrying a collier for love) had not done either. Three of her sisters had married respectable middle-class husbands; the other two, respectable craftsmen. The professions of her sons George and Ernest as apprentice and successful clerk must have been a relief and a joy to her. Bert Lawrence's intended profession as fully qualified (and University educated) schoolmaster would probably have pleased her even more: she had herself, unqualified, taught in a 'Dame School' when young. Lawrence later remembered her ambitions for him: 'I might "get-on" in the ordinary rut, and even become a school-master at three pounds a week which would be a great rise above my father.'[7]

However, Lawrence was also his father's son, and a young man growing up in a community with an intense vitality of its own: the fact that he could speak its dialect so perfectly (in spite of his 'education' at Nottingham High School and University College), and would spend so much of his writing life recreating the life, habits, speech and personalities of his native village, demonstrates how attached (in another way) he was to the life of that community. Jessie Chambers recognised her own difference from it: a farmer's daughter, she nevertheless felt cut off by education and temperament from the community in which she grew up; she felt herself 'a "foreigner" as they would say'. But Lawrence was not a 'foreigner': he was 'bone of their bone'.

> There was no distance between him and the people amongst whom he lived; when he talked to them he spoke out of the same heritage of thought and feeling; he was like them, only greater, in a sense he contained them in himself. He had a marvellous understanding of collier folk, men and women; he knew just how they felt about things and what their reactions were, and how their thinking was not so much of the mind as, to use his own phrase, of the blood. He was quite at home with them, and they with him . . . he was one of them in an extremely close and subtle relationship.[8]

We cannot divide Lawrence simply into the man who loved his mother and followed her way, while hating his father and cutting himself off from him. His poetry-writing mother did not really approve of his writing, while his writing would eventually record with deep sympathy the community in which his father lived so vigorously and happily.

And yet it is also true, in spite of Jessie Chambers' slightly fulsome remarks, that the career of 'writer' itself set Lawrence off from his community. It was not only utterly unlikely for a collier's

son, but it confirmed that very detachment from community which
his contemporaries had observed in his behaviour from a very
early age. In spite of being 'bone of their bone', he had been the
boy who played with girls, who had refused to join in the boys'
games, who was always bookish and was jeered at as soft –
'mard-arsed' was the local term – who had been 'clever', and who
had gone (with the sons of the local shopkeepers) to Nottingham
High School, at an age where most of his contemporaries were
fretting during a last year at school before going 'down pit'. He
may have attained a 'marvellous understanding of collier folk'; he
was also blessed (and cursed) with a queer detachment from them,
born both of background and experience.

The unlikelihood, then, of 'a collier's son a poet!' is a complex
unlikelihood, given the facts, ambitions, divisions and loyalties of
the Lawrence household in Eastwood. And Lawrence himself
shared, for many years, in the embarrassment of his position.
Everything in his training and upbringing which came from his
mother's side would have encouraged him to settle down as a
professional teacher; and, after his college course, perhaps to work
for an external degree, to qualify himself still further. He was still
considering this as a possibility as late as October 1908 (*Letters*, I,
p. 85). And he did indeed work as a full-time teacher for more than
three years, in Croydon between 1908 and 1911, until he was 26
years old. James Joyce had gone off to the continent to write at the
age of 22, abandoning home and prospects; at that age, Lawrence
had not published anything at all, and had not even started his
work as a teacher.

On the other hand, he also took his writing very seriously from
the very start, and was wondering even before he finished his
college career in 1908 whether he could not earn his living by his
pen. To live by poetry and fiction was, at this stage, beyond his
ambitions; but he asked a cousin on his mother's side of the family,
Alfred Inwood (London Editor of the *Sheffield Telegraph*), about the
prospects of life as a journalist, when he was in London in
September 1908 for his teaching-job interview at Croydon. As he
wrote to a friend, 'I could write crits. – but who wants me to – who
would have 'em? How shall I squeeze my jostled, winded way into
journalism' (*Letters*, I, p. 52). Inwood offered him no opportunities
except those provided by hard work and luck; and as it turned out,
Lawrence followed his chosen (and safe) career, and stuck to his
teaching, though he later confessed that 'I *hated* it; I am no

teacher'.[9] He would earn £95 a year in Croydon; he could do what his elder brother Ernest, working in London, had often failed to do – send money regularly back home, to help support his mother in Eastwood. He could also continue to write, but only as a kind of private indulgence. We should see these years of his teaching career, while he was spending every possible spare moment writing, as another proof of his divided nature and his divided loyalties. Even when he was finally in print, and people commented to him about his work, it was (not surprisingly) 'to my embarrassment and anger. I hated being an author, in people's eyes. Especially as I was a teacher.'[10]

II

Not only was Jessie Chambers, for some years, almost the only person to see Lawrence's writing: he himself was intensely troubled by the idea of publication. Rejection was the kind of humiliation to which his divided background and nature had made him peculiarly susceptible. It is hard to say which would have been more distressing to him: the jeers of his contemporaries in Eastwood when he was a child, or the criticisms of magazine editors turning him down later. At all events, following the rejection of a poem by the Nottingham University student magazine sometime around 1906–7, Lawrence made almost no attempt to publish his work, in spite of the fact that by the time of going to Croydon in 1908 he had at least 24 poems in their final form, at least four short stories finished, at least one essay written, and (most impressive of all) two complete drafts of his long novel *The White Peacock*, which he had started in 1906, and had rewritten during 1907–8.

Even his first actual appearance in print had been shadowed in anonymity. In the late summer of every year, the local newspaper *The Nottinghamshire Guardian* would advertise its Christmas short story competition; and, in the autumn of 1907, Lawrence was provoked to go in for it by Jessie Chambers and her brother Alan, who had become a close friend of Lawrence's and so knew about his writing. Alan and Jessie may have been struck by the irony of Lawrence as a continually-writing but non-publishing author. Having decided to enter the competition, Lawrence did so on a scale that was designed to succeed; he submitted entries in all three categories offered (a story about a Legend, another about a

Happy Christmas, yet another about an Amusing Christmas). He enlisted the help of Jessie Chambers and his college friend Louie Burrows, herself an aspiring writer (and also in on the secret of Lawrence's writing), to send two of the three entries in under their own names and pseudonyms. The story submitted by 'Rosalind' – Jessie Chambers – 'A Prelude', won the 'Happy Christmas' section, and was duly printed in the newspaper under her name; there followed an embarrassing time for the whole Chambers family during which Jessie's school headmaster recorded his junior teacher's success in the school log – the secret of the authorship was never revealed to him – and her family were left unsure whether she or Lawrence had written the story. Lawrence himself wrote a letter to Jessie's sister May Holbrook denying his authorship. The eventual three-guinea cheque was, however, paid over to Lawrence by Jessie's father, so the secret finally came out within the family, at least. And the money was a substantial reward: it was almost twice what Lawrence's father would earn in a week.

It was, however, not a particularly auspicious beginning, especially as the story Lawrence had himself submitted in the belief that it was the best of the three – an early version of 'A Fragment of Stained Glass' – only got a passing mention in the paper. Although he eventually rewrote that story, and the one submitted for him by Louie Burrows – an early version of 'The White Stocking' – he never tried to recover 'A Prelude': in 1924 he referred to it as a 'a youthful story in the bad grey print of a provincial newspaper', which had 'thank God ... gone to glory in the absolute sense' (*Letters*, V, p. 86). Jessie Chambers more than once suggested to him thereafter that he might try submitting his work elsewhere; but, interestingly, his first trial of his writing after the competition was not even with someone who would publish it. He sent a piece of his writing – either an essay or a story – to G. K. Chesterton in the spring of 1908, asking for his opinion of it: he and Jessie read Chesterton's newspaper column in the *Daily News* each week. To his chagrin, after some weeks

the author's wife had returned the manuscript, saying that her husband regretted his inability to give an opinion, owing to pressure of work.

'So evidently,' said Lawrence, 'his wife acts as his amanuensis.'

I recognised only too well the chagrin that lay behind his casual words. I murmured something sympathetic and Lawrence continued in the same flat voice:

'I've tried, and been turned down, and I shall try no more. And I don't care if I never have a line published,' he concluded in a tone of finality.[11]

And, true to his word, he tried no more. Being rejected was clearly a great problem to him, and for more than a year he made no other attempt to promote his work. As late as the summer of 1909, when he had been writing for four years, and when Jessie pointed out to him that the editor of a new literary magazine which they both admired, the *English Review*, was keen on new writers submitting their work, Lawrence refused 'absolutely' to send any. Jessie Chambers remembered his insisting 'I'm not anxious to get into print. I shan't send anything. Besides they'd never take it'. She, to her eternal credit, persisted: 'How do you know unless you try?' And only then did Lawrence suddenly say:

'*You* send something. Send some of the poems, if you like.'
'Very well, which shall I send?'
'Send whatever you like. Do what you like with them, he answered.[12]

He thus made Jessie responsible for the submission, and for the rejection, if and when it came: 'if you like': 'whatever you like': 'what you like': this venture would be none of *his* doing.

Undaunted, however, in June 1909 she copied out what she thought were the best of the poems Lawrence had been sending to her from Croydon during the past year, and submitted them to the *English Review*. Ford Madox Hueffer (later Ford Madox Ford, himself a poet and novelist) had started the magazine in 1908 to publish the very best of contemporary writing: it was a quixotic ambition without financial foundation, and was taken over early in 1910 by backers who immediately removed Hueffer as editor. But for a year and a half it was an extraordinary forum of publishing: work by Henry James, Tolstoy, Conrad, Hardy and H. G. Wells had appeared in its first issue. By sending Lawrence's poems there, Jessie Chambers was sending them to the finest literary periodical in England.

The next time I saw Lawrence he said:
'Did you send those poems to the *English*?' adding immediately,
'They'll never print them.'[13]

His eagerness to know what had happened, and his desire to
escape the humiliation of rejection, seem to have been equally
strong.

But Ford Madox Hueffer had a remarkable ability to see the
strengths of new work, and not only its weakness; and he also had
a great desire to encourage new writers, especially from a background such as Lawrence's. Not only did he reply that 'something
might be done', but he asked to see Lawrence in person. And that
was really the start of Lawrence's career as a writer; he impressed
Hueffer, and the latter did his very best for his protégé: he read his
work, criticised it, talked it over with him, printed it, and encouraged him to submit it where it might be printed by others too. And
he introduced him into literary circles; within a couple of months,
Lawrence was attending literary parties in Hampstead where he
met figures like H. G. Wells, W. B. Yeats, Ezra Pound and the
editor of Dent's Everyman series of books, Ernest Rhys. Jessie
Chambers wrote how:

> A new and immensely larger life was opening out before him. A
> kind of transfiguration from obscurity and uncertainty had taken
> place. Thanks to the kind offices of Ford Madox Hueffer his
> chance of a hearing was assured. And it had all come about so
> simply, almost without effort. There was a glamour about those
> days, even something of a glitter.[14]

London's pre-war literary world was remarkably small, and Lawrence was plunged into it as a curiosity – the son of a coal-miner
who wrote poetry published by the *English Review*. He was, as a
contemporary remarked, 'from the outset a critical stranger in
middle-class aesthetic society'.[15] He received nothing but kindness
and some slightly patronising (though helpful) interest; yet he
knew how his background, and his profession as elementary
schoolmaster, cut him off from it.

Hueffer was the first person outside Lawrence's own immediate
circle to see the sprawling manuscript of *The White Peacock*:

> He read it immediately, with the greatest cheery sort of kindness

and bluff. And in his queer voice, when we were in an omnibus in London, he shouted in my ear: 'It's got every fault that the English novel can have ... But,' shouted Hueffer in the 'bus, 'you've got GENIUS.'[16]

The later Lawrence would comment, rather sourly, that 'In the early days they were always telling me I had got genius, as if to console me for not having their own incomparable advantages', though he exempted Hueffer from that particular charge. But, in spite of his criticisms of the novel, Hueffer did the most helpful thing of all: he not only suggested that Lawrence try the publisher William Heinemann with the novel, but he wrote Lawrence a letter on 15 December 1909 which he could use when submitting the novel to publishers. Unlike, for example, Methuen, Heinemann was not primarily a commercial publisher; Compton Mackenzie remembered him dismissing commercial success with one novel as 'a success with the little London clique, but of what importance is that to a publisher?'[17] Heinemann published novels he believed in: and Hueffer's letter stressed Lawrence's potential as an artist. His novel, 'properly handled',

> might have a very considerable success ... you have in you the makings of a very considerable novelist, and I should not have the least hesitation in prophesying for you a great future, did I not know how much a matter of sheer luck one's career always is. With this in view I should advise you in approaching a publisher to promise him at least the refusal of several of your future works. This means that he will be encouraged to make efforts with your first book with some confidence that if it succeeds you will not immediately abandon him for another firm.[18]

He also mentioned, as in the same vein as Lawrence's kind of long book, *Lorna Doone* and the novels of William de Morgan – novels actually published by Heinemann (and making a good deal of money for him, too). Both the advice and the comparison were designed to endear Lawrence to Heinemann: Lawrence copied out the letter and submitted the manuscript. And within a few weeks, Heinemann had agreed to publish the book; Lawrence promising some rewriting, which he did in the spring of 1910. In the summer, he and Heinemann agreed terms: they would pay him a 15%

royalty, and he would have a £50 advance upon publication; he also committed himself (as Hueffer's letter suggested he should) to offering Heinemann his next novel on the same terms (*Letters*, I, p. 161 n. 4).

After the years of hesitation, and the fears of rejection, it had been a marvellously smooth road to acceptance of his work: as Lawrence put it, in 1928:

> I was a poor boy. I *ought* to have wrestled in the fell clutch of circumstance, and undergone the bludgeonings of chance before I became a writer with a very modest income and a very questionable reputation. But I didn't. It all happened by itself and without any groans from me.[19]

Not only was the novel, so long laboured over, accepted: Hueffer, too, began to print Lawrence in the *English Review*. First came the poems Jessie had copied out, in November 1909, which – at the usual rate of a guinea a page – had paid Lawrence 5 guineas; then a story in February 1910 which probably earned him another £5.[20] And even when Hueffer had to relinquish control of the magazine early in 1910, his successor Austin Harrison wrote to Lawrence 'saying that he hopes he will continue sending his work'.[21] Harrison printed poems by Lawrence in April and October 1910, and two short stories in 1911.

And yet, even at this very early stage, there were indications of problems ahead. For one thing, Lawrence was still hardly started on the road to being a full-time writer. The promise of £50 for *The White Peacock* was all he had, and he shared the money for 'Goose Fair' in February 1910 with his friend Louie Burrows, because it had originally been *her* story. For another thing, he was thoroughly unsure about what kind of writer he was. *The White Peacock* had dealt only tangentially with the coal-mining region, and with the working-class: its main characters had been gentle-folk and yeoman farmers (though the gossip of a character like Alice Gall suggests a rather lower social class). It may well have been advice from Hueffer that made Lawrence, in the winter of 1909, write his very first pieces of fiction about the coal-mining region in which he had grown up, 'Odour of Chrysanthemums' and his play *A Collier's Friday Night*. It is striking that he seems to have written nothing similar before meeting Hueffer, and being exposed to the latter's demand that 'in the early decades of this century, we

enormously wanted authentic projections of that type of life which
hitherto had gone quite unvoiced'.[22] Lawrence also wrote two
unadorned sketches of elementary school life around December
1909, 'Lessford's Rabbits' and 'A Lesson on the Tortoise'; these,
too, may have been done at Hueffer's instigation.

Being 'a writer' was thus a particular complexity for a man of
Lawrence's background; the detachment described above had also,
as yet, prevented him from using his deep local sympathies in his
writing work. It is also significant that 'Odour of Chrysanthemums', first written in the winter of 1909, took more than eighteen
months actually to get printed in the *English Review*, and suffered
requests from Austin Harrison for cuts that led to the almost
complete rewriting of parts of it; it was unusual enough to cause
Harrison particular misgivings.

It was also the case that Hueffer himself never made any secret
(even in his letter for Lawrence to send to a publisher) of the fact
that he did not really approve of Lawrence's kind of writing,
however much he helped him. Lawrence might have genius, but
his novel had 'got every fault that the English novel can have': 'the
book, with its enormous prolixity of detail, sins against almost
every canon of art as I conceive it . . .'[23] To use the language of the
time, Lawrence's fiction lacked 'form'; the charge would dog him
for years. As late as November 1912 he was still trying to defend
himself against it; he would submit *Sons and Lovers* to his publisher
with the insistence that 'I tell you it has got form – *form*' (*Letters*, I,
p. 476). He was also seen, from the beginning, as a writer bedevil-
led by a tendency to 'erotic' writing, something that his critics
linked with what they saw as a lack of control – or (again) 'form' –
in his art: the failure of a natural (and native) genius to discipline
his native woodnotes. Even *The White Peacock* suffered pre-
publication cuts in England (though not in America): Heinemann
submitted to Lawrence a last-minute demand for changes to two
passages, and Lawrence rewrote them. A phrase describing how a
peacock – 'the dirty devil' – had 'run her muck over that angel' in a
churchyard was changed to 'the miserable brute has dirtied that
angel'; a longer passage describing the marriage of Lady Chrystabel and Annable was also rewritten. According to Annable, Lady
Chrystabel would 'have me in her bedroom while she drew Greek
statues of me'; the sentence became 'she would choose to view me
in an aesthetic light. I was Greek statues for her, bless you'; while
the sentence 'it took her three years to have a real bellyful of me'

became 'it took her three years to be really glutted with me'.[24] Words like 'have' and 'bellyful' were too much for the middle-class reading public. It was Lawrence's 'first experience of the objectionable',[25] his first brush with the censorship with which he would later become so involved.

A pre-publication copy of the novel had been rushed to Eastwood early in December 1910 for Mrs Lawrence to see in her final illness. She could do no more than glance at it; but, after the funeral:

> my father struggled through half a page, and it might as well have been Hottentot.
> 'And what dun they gi'e thee for that, lad?'
> 'Fifty pounds, father.'
> 'Fifty pounds!' He was dumbfounded, and looked at me with shrewd eyes, as if I were a swindler. 'Fifty pounds! An' tha's niver done a day's hard work in thy life.'[26]

There is work and work, of course. Rewriting the novel in the spring of 1910 had for Lawrence been 'a new labour of Hercules' (*Letters*, I, p. 158); he would tell May Holbrook on 11 October 1911 how:

> It's eleven now, at night. I've been working since 7.0, at verse, getting it ready to take to Edward Garnett on Friday ... night after night one stumbles up, half blind with work or with wastefulness – ah bosh. (*Letters*, I, p. 311)

And that, after a day's teaching at school. But through the famous anecdote about Lawrence's father we can, too, recover the extraordinary distance Lawrence had travelled from Eastwood, and from his father's world, to his position as published author. Arthur Lawrence's unease about the novel – its 'Hottentot' quality – would have been heightened by the kind of novel it was: intensely sensitive and inwardly, even morbidly, reflective. How could this be the work of a writer from Eastwood – or of 'a collier's son'?

However, the publication of (and the money from) *The White Peacock* were the first signs that Lawrence was capable of making the break from Eastwood, and from the career his education and training had mapped out for him; £50 was half a year's salary as a teacher. Yet the major problem of money remained; although he was a teacher earning £95 a year, in Croydon, what with sending money home, and his own expenses, he was desperately hard up: 'my shirts are patched, my boots are – well, not presentable' (*Letters*, I, p. 286). He had actually had to ask Heinemann for a special prior payment of part of the royalty advance due on the publication of *The White Peacock*; and was (very cordially) sent £15 in September 1910 (ibid., p. 177 n. 2). It is likely that the initial expenses of his mother's illness (first diagnosed in August 1910) necessitated his sudden appeal. He would need to earn at least £100 every year to survive, living as cheaply as possible. And he had been writing *The White Peacock* since 1906; only two novels a year, or ten to fifteen stories published, could bring in anything equivalent to what he earned at school. And that, every year, for ever. Besides which, although the death of his mother must have lightened the financial pressure he was under from home, six days before her death he had become engaged to his friend Louie Burrows, and was supposed to be saving for their marriage until he had £100 capital and an income of £120 a year (ibid., p. 223). By July 1911, the estimate had gone up: they reckoned they needed 'an assured income of £150, and a hundred quid to marry on' (ibid., p. 293). There seemed no possibility that Lawrence's writing could bring in that kind of money on a regular basis; he was not sufficiently known, and he had very few outlets for his work.

And it was not even just the lump-sum of money earned by *The White Peacock* that really mattered; Lawrence had rather hoped the novel would:

> break me an entrance into the jungle of literature; that it would give me a small but individual name by which I should be known; and that it might bring me a bit of monthly work to eke out my lamentable state. (*Letters*, I, p. 222)

It does not seem to have brought him in any reviewing work, however; and the fate of his second novel must have confirmed his doubts about his future. This book – which would become *The Trespasser*, but which was at this stage called 'The Saga of Siegmund' – was finished by August 1910, and Lawrence naturally sent it at once to Ford Madox Hueffer. The latter's opinion this time, though, had been damning:

'The book' he said 'is a rotten work of genius. It has no

construction or form – it is execrably bad art, being all variations on a theme. Also it is erotic – not that I, personally, mind that, but an erotic work *must* be good art, which this is not.' (*Letters*, I, p. 339)

Hueffer also remarked, later, that the book 'would damage your reputation, perhaps permanently' (*Letters*, I, p. 339). Heinemann also showed themselves very unsure of the book's quality. Their general editor had remarked, 'I don't care for it, but we will publish it' – but Lawrence was feeling thoroughly concerned about his 'tender reputation' (ibid., p. 276), his 'small but individual name' (ibid., p. 222). He felt that he needed to preserve that, if he were ever to become a full-time writer, and at this stage did not want to be offensive in ways that might put publishers (or readers) off. 'I don't want to be talked about in an *Anne Veronica* fashion' (ibid., p. 339), he remarked: Wells's *Ann Veronica* had been attacked as 'a dangerous novel' in 1909 (ibid., p. 339 n. 4) because of the sexual forwardness of its heroine. Lawrence therefore told Heinemann that, after all, he did not want to publish 'The Saga'; and to make up for its effective disappearance, in the autumn of 1910 he started yet another novel: 'Paul Morel': the book which would one day become *Sons and Lovers*. And he determined to stick at that 'like a broody hen at her eggs, lest my chickens hatch in a winter of public forgetfulness' (ibid., p. 276).

However, although the publication of *The White Peacock* in January 1911 – together with two more stories, this time at £10 each, in the *English Review* during the year – might seem to have marked for Lawrence the real start of his public reputation, yet 1911 was in many ways a dreadfully arid year both for his writing and for his prospects as a full-time writer. Hueffer was no longer in sympathy with him, and had – Lawrence felt – 'left me to paddle my own canoe. I *very* nearly wrecked it and did for myself' (ibid., p. 471). The reviews of *The White Peacock* turned out not particularly good; his private life was a struggle, following the death of his mother and his, in many ways, unfortunate engagement to Louie Burrows; and his writing of 'Paul Morel' went both slowly and unhappily. Almost the only bright spot was the request, in June 1911, by the young publisher Martin Secker for a volume of short stories by Lawrence. Secker had started his publishing career with a batch of novels in January 1911, and had made his reputation with *The Passionate Elopement* by one of his first authors – Compton

Mackenzie: he 'was resolved to confine his list to those whose work he personally admired',[27] and Lawrence's story 'Odour of Chrysanthemums' in the June *English Review* had caught his eye. But Lawrence could do nothing about that exciting request, having (as he confessed to Secker) too few stories: 'Because nobody wanted the things, I have not troubled to write any' (ibid., p. 275). He did, however, for a while concentrate on writing stories rather than on his novel; he had written 'The Witch à la Mode' in the spring, and now wrote both 'The Old Adam' and 'Daughters of the Vicar' in its first version, and a little later 'Love Among the Haystacks'. But none of these stories got into print; and by themselves they were not enough for a volume for Secker, either.

By September 1911, Lawrence was starting to feel desperate. He even broached the problem to Louie Burrows: she for whom he was trying to earn that 'assured income of £150' (ibid., p. 293).

> As a matter of fact, I am rather tired of school. There are so many things I want to do, and can't. I can't settle down of an evening nowadays. This week I haven't written a scrap. Should you be cross if I were to – and I don't say I shall – try to get hold of enough literary work, journalism or what not, to keep me going without school. Of course, it's a bit risky, but for myself I don't mind risk – like it. And then, if I get on with literature, I can increase my income . . . (*Letters*, I, p. 303)

But he must also have known how very doubtful that 'increase' in his income would be. Two months later, things were still worse.

> I am really very tired of school – I can*not* get on with Paul [i.e. 'Paul Morel']. I am afraid I shall have to leave – and I am afraid you will be cross with me – and I loathe to plead my cause. (*Letters*, I, p. 326)

He had got himself into a situation where giving up his teaching was effectively a way of saying he did not want to marry Louie; and yet his writing was condemned to hopeless amateurism if he continued teaching.

It was not perhaps an accident that this talk of leaving his teaching job coincided with his first contacts with Edward Garnett: Garnett 'who, somehow, introduced me to the world',[28] and who after Lawrence had '*very* nearly wrecked' his own canoe, 'like a

good angel, fished me out' (*Letters*, I, p. 471). Garnett was immensely well known in London publishing circles, and mostly well
respected: as a young publisher's reader he had effectively discovered Conrad, back in the 1890s, had encouraged John Galsworthy
and W. H. Hudson, and was at present reader for the publisher
Gerald Duckworth. He also acted as agent for some American
magazines. He had written to Lawrence in August 1911 asking for
stories for *The Century*. Lawrence sent him two, and asked for
criticism of them; and Garnett had a wonderfully sharp eye for the
strengths and weaknesses of writing. Not only did he send helpful
criticism about how to revise the early 'Daughters of the Vicar', he
made Lawrence feel (wrongly, as it turned out) that the story was
eminently publishable; and he also asked to meet Lawrence. The
latter went to see him in London early in October, and made a
deep impression on Garnett; he paid the first of many visits to
Garnett's country home, called The Cearne, a fortnight later.
Garnett was not at this stage able to do very much for his friend's
actual publications (Lawrence was, after all, contracted to William
Heinemann, and his stories were not suitable for *The Century*). But
Garnett suggested that Lawrence – now becoming known as a poet
through his publications in the *English Review* – might get Heinemann to publish a volume of his poems, 'and perhaps a vol of
plays, in Spring' (ibid., p. 316). Lawrence had, by now, three
unpublished plays. He also got two of Lawrence's poems into 'the
Nation . . . a sixpenny weekly, of very good standing' (ibid., p. 324)
– Lawrence's first magazine publication outside the *English Review*.
Garnett could give both good advice in general about the publishing world, and in particular some much-needed support and
encouragement for a writer whose career was thoroughly uncer-
tain in its direction, as Lawrence hovered on the brink of abandoning his teaching career. Garnett must have made that break seem
not only attractive but possible.

As it turned out, the final decision was taken out of Lawrence's
hands. In mid-November 1911 – incidentally while at The Cearne
for the weekend to meet the literary editor of the *Daily News*, R. A.
Scott-James, presumably with a view to getting work on the paper
– Lawrence caught a chill, developed double pneumonia, and
nearly died. Returning to teaching was out of the question. And it
was just at this moment, in December 1911, that Garnett saw 'The
Saga of Siegmund', returned at last from Heinemann. He liked it,
and told Lawrence that it would not after all damage his reputation

to publish it. He further suggested that Lawrence rewrite it for his own firm of Duckworth; although Heinemann naturally had an option clause in their contract with Lawrence, they were prepared to ignore the earlier novel and would be satisfied if they got 'Paul Morel'. This meant that Lawrence could get both his second and third novels published; and this, at the very moment when he was trying to launch out as a full-time writer. Garnett's support, practical advice and influence at Duckworths made all the difference to Lawrence's prospects.

In February 1912, Lawrence returned to Eastwood to live, after convalescing in Bournemouth for a month (and during that month getting 'The Saga' into shape for Duckworth, with its new title *The Trespasser*). With that behind him, a certainty of publication, and a future advance on royalties assured, he could concentrate upon his 'colliery novel' for Heinemann. He also, however, managed to write some short journalistic pieces, one of which ('The Miner at Home') was accepted by the *Nation* – again, probably because of Garnett's contacts. And there was still the possibility that Heinemann would take a book of his poetry; perhaps selected by the poet Walter de la Mare, now a reader at Heinemann.

This period between early December 1911 and early May 1912 is one of the magical times of Lawrence's life. In October 1911 he had been a man who could not finish his autobiographical third novel, and who seemed unable to make his long-hoped-for break into successful publication (only the *English Review* had ever published him); he was still suffering from the death of his mother, his life and financial prospects were clouded by an unhappy engagement, he was stuck in a job he could see no real prospect of leaving, and he was building up to a desperate illness. But with the illness came, too, the opportunity to start again. He could not teach at least for some months; he could no longer earn and save towards his marriage. He broke his engagement, and sent in his resignation to Croydon. And by May 1912 he had had his old novel 'The Saga' accepted for publication, 'Paul Morel' finished except for some revision, and at least a start made at journalism.

He had also, in March, met the woman with whom he would spend the rest of his life, Frieda Weekley. The 34-year-old wife of the Nottingham Professor of Modern Languages Ernest Weekley, Frieda (née von Richthofen), was the daughter of minor German aristocrats: she had three young children, and – in spite of two earlier affairs – was apparently settled into the existence of the bourgeois wife. Yet meeting Lawrence changed her life utterly. They went away together in May 1912; but her decision to stay with Lawrence was at the cost of her children (Weekley would not let them live with her again).

The period marks one of the great in-rushes of confidence into Lawrence; he told Frieda how 'You make me sure of myself, whole',[29] but his success as a writer who needed to publish must also have helped. The man who during 1911 had been trying to earn and save sufficient to support a decent marriage would find himself, at the start of May 1912, in love with a woman who loved him, and going away with her with only £11 in his pocket. Not only was he at last free to be a full-time writer, he was going to have to support Frieda; and his writing would have to do it.

III

Lawrence's early career, then, is the story of the most unexpected development of a collier's son from the Midlands into a writer who, living abroad in Italy and Germany, could just about support himself (and his wife) with his pen. He himself always stressed the ease and lack of complication in the transition: seeing, for example, Jessie Chambers as the person who 'had launched me, so easily, on my literary career, like a princess cutting a thread, launching a ship'.[30] And he was also nicely complimentary about the help he had received from Hueffer and Garnett. But from 1914 onwards, in many ways life would be much harder for him as a professional writer, and much less help forthcoming; if a publisher rejected a novel, as Heinemann effectively rejected 'The Saga', there would not normally be another publisher waiting in the wings, as Garnett and Duckworth were waiting in the winter of 1911–12.

But it is important to add to that story of an easy, uncomplex transition something of the necessary complexity of a man like Lawrence becoming a full-time writer. Not only did he have enormous financial problems; he had the particular problem of abandoning the role of self-reliant professional man, able to support a wife and family, for which his upbringing and education had fitted him. And he had the very real problem of being a boy from Eastwood who moved into the metropolitan literary world. He played all this down in his late autobiographical writing, which always presented him as straightforwardly working-class writer who – unexpectedly but luckily – discovered his *metier* without running into difficulties. The struggles he underwent were not perhaps the more usual and external ones created by poverty, reluctant publishers and rejection slips; but the internal struggles were deep and long-lasting, and were not answered simply by emergence into print. *Sons and Lovers* itself shows something of the problem in question; as we view the artistic hero, Paul Morel, making his way in the world, we may be surprised that such an autobiographical book should have chosen to present Paul as a man working as a clerk in a factory throughout his formative years. But Paul is straightforwardly working-class, as D. H. Lawrence was not, going as he did to High School and College and becoming a teacher, while simultaneously developing a literary career that at points – exemplified by parts of *The White Peacock* and a good deal of *The Trespasser* – demonstrates a 'literariness' which indicates the problem for him that the whole matter of 'literature' was. Like a good deal of the middle-class and cultured world he experienced in London, the 'literary' had a horrible but irresistible fascination for the young Lawrence; it provided him with his badge of difference from the world he had moved away from, and for a while he wore it defiantly. He also wanted to be impressive, and a high style and a literary manner were the only ways he knew. Such things became obstacles he had to learn to surpass, by writing them out of himself. But, as a result, novels like *The White Peacock* and *The Trespasser* cannot really be understood without some knowledge of the literary culture in which (and for which) Lawrence wrote them, and in which he hoped to make his way. One of the great achievements of *Sons and Lovers* would be that Lawrence found a style and a straightforward voice which showed that he was no longer either helplessly or willingly implicated in the literary pretensions of his age. His 'breakthrough' with that novel was not only into a way of understanding parents and children, but into unpretentious fictional prose.

2

First Year as a
Professional Writer: 1912–13

I

Problems, of course, remained. What would he and Frieda – with whom he went abroad on 3 May 1912 – live on? Heinemann had paid Lawrence a second instalment of £50 for royalties from *The White Peacock* in February 1912; but just as the first instalment had largely gone in the expenses of his mother's illness, so the second was almost swallowed up by the costs of his own. By early May, all he had was £11 in hand, with £25 (probably from the Heinemann money) owed him by a friend; even a second-class single fare to Germany cost £2 1s 9d. Less than a week after they had left England, Lawrence told Frieda that 'we've only enough money to run us a fortnight, and we don't know where the next will come from' (*Letters*, I, p. 394). He had the expense of hotels in Metz and Trier, and then the train to Waldbröl, where he was staying with relations; on 21 May, he only had 'about four quid' (ibid. p. 408), enough to get him down to Munich to rejoin Frieda at the end of the month. He was starting to wonder (to Garnett) whether Duckworth – like Heinemann – would give him an advance on his advance: 'give me a sub – £10. But for the Lords sake, don't ask him yet – I'd rather anything' (ibid., p. 409). Lawrence was still feeling especially indebted to Duckworth, and did not want to seem grasping or ungrateful.

Journalism and poetry for the *Westminster Gazette* (who printed two sketches and six poems) helped; and Lawrence assiduously worked away at newspaper sketches throughout the difficult time he and Frieda had in Metz, while they were bombarded with threats from Frieda's husband and family, and subsequently on his own in Trier. And that journalism, German sketches published in the *Westminster Gazette*, had earned Lawrence £25 by August, even though only two of his four sketches were taken. But in the meanwhile – apart from money which Frieda had brought with her to Germany in May – it must have been money from her family which supported her and Lawrence through the period June–August 1912; Lawrence remarked in September 1914 how Frieda 'always got money from Germany when we have been badly reduced before' (*Letters*, II, p. 213). Her sister Else probably helped them with money at least once.[1] In the end, after struggling hand-to-mouth for some months, but avoiding applying to Duckworth, Lawrence and Frieda were finally saved from penury by 'The Saga of Siegmund', which had been published at the end of May as *The Trespasser*. Lawrence received £50 in notes from Duckworth – 'the angel!' – on 16 September 1912; it was that money which supported him and Frieda for their first winter abroad.

During the summer of 1912, they had – of necessity – lived rent-free in a flat in Bavaria borrowed from Alfred Weber, the lover of Frieda's sister Else: the first of their sequence of borrowed houses and flats. There in Icking Lawrence had worked on 'Paul Morel', and on some short stories. Not for the first – nor last – time, he felt that 'I must try and make running money' (*Letters*, I, p. 430); that was their need, that summer. Lawrence's ambition, for the first two or three years of his professional career, was to make a regular income from shorter pieces, as well as to earn the considerably larger lump sums payable as advances on novels; but advances to be paid some months away never seemed very secure, and 'coming of hand-to-mouth poor folk, I never believe in any money that is not in my pocket' (ibid., p. 510). However, he very rarely realised the dream of 'running money'; none of the short stories he wrote and revised in 1912 were accepted for publication until the following summer.

One of the reasons for this was his odd situation of living abroad, but trying to place his work in England (and America) without the use of a literary agent. Walter de la Mare, whom he had got to know when de la Mare became a reader at Heinemann in the spring of 1912, was doing what he could for Lawrence both at William Heinemann and at the *Westminster Gazette*. Between the spring of 1912 and the spring of 1913 he was influential in getting the two German sketches by Lawrence printed in the magazine, a later sketch in the spring of 1913, as well as the poems. But, even more important, Edward Garnett was still, out of love and admiration for Lawrence, acting as the kind of unofficial (and unpaid) agent he had begun to be in the autumn of 1911, and which he would continue to be until the spring of 1914.

But the contacts of both de la Mare and Garnett were limited; de la Mare to the *Westminster*, while Garnett was only ever influential – apart from persuading Duckworth to accept Lawrence's second and third novels – in getting two poems, one sketch and one story by Lawrence into print. Lawrence's lack of an agent brought other disadvantages, too. Austin Harrison, at the *English Review*, had, in March 1912, been offended by Garnett offering Lawrence's work to the American magazine *The Forum* before it came to him at the *English Review* – 'he doesn't love the *Forum*' (*Letters*, I, p. 380) – and Lawrence had then tried to reassure Harrison that 'Certainly Mr Garnett is no literary agent, and I should be very sorry to think I had lost your favour' (ibid., p. 377). The truth was, as Lawrence told Garnett, that the editor 'likes to think he's a personal benefactor' (ibid., p. 380); but Harrison must have been offended in spite of Lawrence's apology, and printed only one piece by Lawrence (a poem) between February 1912 and September 1913. And this in spite of negotiating for a story of Lawrence's in April 1912, apparently agreeing to print the story 'Love Among the Haystacks' (ibid., pp. 380–1), and asking Lawrence what reviewing he wanted. He had called Lawrence in to 'jaw' him in April 1912 (ibid., p. 384), probably to explain what annoyed him.

But having thus effectively lost the support of the *English Review* at a crucial moment, Lawrence had no other place he could rely on to look favourably at his work. What he got from Garnett, in particular, was advice and support; but he was always very conscious of the danger (and embarrassment) of being a nuisance to Garnett, and asking him to do too much. And Lawrence always hated the idea of sending his work blindly to people or places he did not know; so either he had to bother Garnett to send his stories around for him, or else he had to leave them unpublished. He chose the latter; he left the publication of the stories he had written in the summer of 1912 until he himself came back to England in June 1913. As a consequence, it was almost exclusively money from his novels that he had to rely upon in the interim.

He had however been tempted in the summer of 1912 by another offer from Secker, this time to publish his novels; and he had rather naïvely asked Garnett for his advice: 'Does Duckworth really want the "Paul Morel" novel? Shall I offer Secker that? You see I must get some money from somewhere, shortly. And how I hate to

worry you' (*Letters*, I, p. 434). This was just after Garnett had
acquired the novel for Duckworth; Lawrence would have worried
Garnett far more by leaving Duckworth for another publisher. The
publisher T. Fisher Unwin also wrote asking for 'a good strong
novel' in September 1912, while the firm of Hutchinson offered
Lawrence an advance of £110 on receipt of a novel manuscript:
Garnett naturally advised against both.[2] But the offers continued to
come: Lawrence wrote to Garnett again in January 1913, shortly
after getting an offer from the literary agent J. B. Pinker to handle
his next novel:

> Do you feel, with me, a bit like the old man of the seas? If I
> weren't so scared of having no money at all, I'd tell you to shovel
> all my stuff onto Pinker, get rid of the bother of me, and leave me
> to transact with him. (*Letters*, I, p. 501)

But Garnett obviously advised him *not* to accept Pinker's offer:
Garnett was very conscious of having acquired Lawrence and his
novels for Duckworth, and he certainly didn't want Lawrence
going elsewhere. If the price for keeping Lawrence as one of
Duckworth's authors was working on Lawrence's behalf – then it
was work he was happy to do. It was in the same spirit that, in the
winter of 1912, he had taken on the job of cutting *Sons and Lovers* for
Duckworth.

Lawrence, however, continued to worry about the nuisance he
was being; in the summer of 1913, for example, when he had
written another three stories before returning to England, he told
Garnett about them, and commented:

> I might send them away, mightn't I. It is not fair for you to be
> troubled with the business. So I shall give them to you and you,
> perhaps, will suggest where they may go. (*Letters*, II, p. 21)

That is, Lawrence would do the actual writing of letters and
posting of his stories to magazines – Garnett could be saved that
much; but even after a year living by his pen Lawrence was still
totally reliant upon Garnett's advice about 'where they may go'.
He still knew very little about literary London: the disadvantage of
having always been an outsider in it now began to show. On 23
July 1913, however, Garnett forwarded one of the three stories to
the literary agent Pinker to place:

I am sending you herewith a very fine story 'Honour and Arms', by Mr D. H. Lawrence, in the hope that you will be able to place it advantageously for him.

Of course on the usual terms.

... If you succeed with this, there will be others to follow. (*Letters*, II, p. 6)

It was probably a sign that Garnett felt he could not do justice to Lawrence's work that made him send this story to Pinker – coupled with a genuine desire to get Lawrence more widely known as a writer, while Duckworth still retained him as a novelist. It was not uncommon at that date to use an agent to place particular pieces of work, while otherwise retaining a free hand; H. G. Wells, for example, like (he insisted) 'all sensible authors', refused to 'employ agents except for specific jobs'.[3] For the moment, Lawrence did not employ Pinker as the agent for the rest of his work.

But considering that Lawrence's reputation had been starting to grow from the time of his second novel, which got good reviews, it is striking that Garnett and he managed to get so few of his short stories into print. Garnett managed just one, 'The Soiled Rose' in *The Forum*, between August 1911 and the spring of 1914. Even Pinker, after the magisterial letter from Garnett in the summer of 1913, was unable to get 'Honour and Arms' published for more than a year: and then only in the *English Review*, which had known about (and had been printing) Lawrence's work since 1909. No new ground had been broken, after all; and looking back with hindsight, as we can do, that is certainly an ominous sign. Lawrence's work was not commercial, however much he may at this stage have hoped that it was; and for all its qualities it was viewed in many quarters with suspicion. It was, however, some time before the consequences of that began to reveal themselves. For the moment, with help, he could earn his living.

II

It was impossible for Lawrence and Frieda to keep their borrowed flat in Icking after August 1912, and unrealistic to expect their income to provide for them in Germany; the money and houses Frieda borrowed from her family could not be too heavily relied

upon. Returning to England unmarried, however, was equally
impossible. They took the advice of Frieda's sister Else that they
should try Italy, where living was cheap and, accordingly, on 5
August 1912, they set off with knapsacks on their backs to walk to
Italy. With the help of some buses and trains, they got there early
in September. A fortnight's precarious eking out of their funds was
followed by the arrival of the £50 from Duckworth; and it turned
out that they could afford to live wonderfully cheaply beside the
Lago di Garda. They took the bottom flat of the Villa Igea in Villa,
next to Gargnano – 'dining room, kitchen, 2 bedrooms, furnished –
big pretty rooms looking over the road on to the lake' (*Letters*, I,
p. 453); it would cost them only just over £3 a month to rent.
Money that would not have supported them in England could
bring them a decent standard of living in Italy: and for the next
three years they lived entirely by Lawrence's writing.

Thus the great blow Lawrence had suffered in June 1912 – the
most unexpected rejection by Heinemann of the 'Paul Morel' novel
– turned out to be survivable. Heinemann thought it far too explicit
sexually, and unprintable. In fact – just like *The Trespasser* – the
novel was almost immediately acquired by Duckworth, again via
the good agency of Garnett; and although Garnett was assiduous
in suggestions for its revision, the worst aspect of the rejection
must have been that it postponed still further the date when
Lawrence might expect to earn any money from his novel. But with
money coming in so appositely from *The Trespasser*, he could afford
to wait for money from (as it was after rewriting) *Sons and Lovers*.
Accordingly, the flat in the Villa Igea saw the rewriting for
Duckworth, during September–November, of the novel; Lawrence
finished it and immediately posted it off to Garnett on 18 November 1912.

We can only understand what happened then if we understand
Lawrence's financial position. Within a fortnight of sending the
novel to Garnett, he had a stern letter back saying that, after all,
Sons and Lovers would not do: it was too long and formless, and
needed cutting; and that with Lawrence's permission Garnett
would simply cut it for publication as he thought necessary.

Lawrence was in an awkward position. He liked and was deeply
grateful to Garnett, and he effectively depended upon him for his
future publishing in England, for advice of all sorts, for his present
contacts (such as they were) with magazines, and indeed for
almost all his immediate prospects. From the distance of the Lago

di Garda, it seemed that Garnett was the only man in England with the capacity (or the desire) to sustain Lawrence's literary career. And Lawrence depended upon *Sons and Lovers* in particular for his future, after the funds from *The Trespasser* ran out, as he knew they must, sometime in the spring of 1913. He had almost nothing else coming in: without *Sons and Lovers* he would be sunk. Accordingly he acquiesced to Garnett's demands:

> I sit in sadness and grief after your letter. I daren't say anything. All right, take out what you think necessary – I suppose I shall see what you've done when the proofs come, at any rate. I'm sorry I've let you in for such a job – but don't scold me too hard, it makes me wither up. (*Letters*, I, p. 481)

His meekness may strike us now as remarkable, but – for Lawrence at the end of 1912 – it was simply inevitable. He did not want to work on the book again, but he very much needed it published; and it had already been turned down once, by a sympathetic publisher.

And, anyway, Duckworth's terms for it were 'quite gorgeous' – they included an advance of £100 payable 'on day of publication', which was twice the advance that Lawrence had got either for *The White Peacock* or for *The Trespasser*. It was a sign of Duckworth's growing confidence in him. And Lawrence also trusted Garnett to know, better than he did, what would be acceptable in the book market.

None of that means that Lawrence wanted the book cut: only that he accepted, *faute de mieux*, the practical necessity of going along with what Garnett demanded. He would eventually congratulate Garnett on having done the cutting (by almost one tenth) 'jolly well' (*Letters*, I, p. 517) but a lot of damage was done to the book. Lawrence took an identical attitude in March 1913, at the proof stage, when Garnett warned him that Duckworth was uneasy about the sexual explicitness of some of the scenes in the novel – probably because of the loss of potential sales to libraries: between them, Mudies, Boots and Smiths could easily absorb 2000–3000 copies of a popular novel. Lawrence commented: 'I don't mind if Duckworth crosses out a hundred shady pages in *Sons and Lovers*. It's got to sell, I've got to live' (ibid., p. 526). And some of the scenes were toned down by Garnett himself. The libraries after all took the novel, after an initial scare that they would not; but it was by no means Lawrence's last problem with them.[4]

III

The novel was published on 29 May 1913, but by then Lawrence had already received half his advance. He had had to ask for it at the beginning of March, in spite of at last getting, via Garnett, £10 in bank-notes – always more useful than a cheque in Italy before the war – out of the cheque of £12 (the equivalent of $60) for his story in *The Forum*. But the £50 advance on his advance for *Sons and Lovers* 'must take me on five months or so, and then if there's any more due, I can draw, and if there isn't, I must wait' (*Letters*, I, p. 527). The attitude was typical: he would live according to his income, and try not to exceed it:

> I have always been determined *never* to come to my last shilling –
> if I have to reduce my spending almost to nothingness. I have
> always been determined to keep a few pounds between me and
> the world.[5]

He was himself entirely responsible for the money affairs of the household; Frieda had never dealt with money matters, either as a young woman or as a respectable professor's wife, and Lawrence knew that 'I have to watch it, because Frieda doesn't care' (*Letters*, II, p. 46). He therefore had to budget and plan, and write accordingly.

But, during 1913, we can observe how his attitude began to relax a little towards his self-imposed obligation always to write fiction that he felt would sell. He had spent his time since finishing *Sons and Lovers*, first, in attempting to write books that wouldn't get started (two false starts survive, of the so-called 'Burns Novel' and of 'Elsa Culverwell', neither of them longer than 19 pages). He had then spent three months between January and March 1913 trying to write a 'fearfully exciting' new novel, 'The Insurrection of Miss Houghton', which 'lies next my heart, for the present'. He could only write, he told Garnett, 'what I feel pretty strongly about: and that, at present, is the relations between men and women' (*Letters*, I, p. 546). And this novel was 'all crude as yet', but 'I think it's great – so new, so really a stratum deeper than I think anybody has ever gone, in a novel' (ibid., p. 526). However, having spent the time since November 1912 trying to write serious novels that were almost certainly uncommercial, he felt he had for the moment to give up in favour of 'another, shorter, absolutely impeccable – as far as morals go – novel . . . or else what am I going to live on, and keep Frieda on withal' (ibid., p. 526). The money from *Sons and Lovers* – with the expenses of a visit to England planned for the summer – would only take them a few months forward, unless the novel turned out to be a resounding success. Lawrence, planning carefully ahead, did the sensible thing and abandoned the serious novel around p. 200. He then began his pot-boiler.

But, characteristically (as it would turn out), within its first 110 pages the 'pot-boiler . . . has developed into an earnest and painful work' (ibid., p. 536); and, this time, at the start of April 1913, Lawrence did not resist his own desire to write what he wanted to. That was another step forward, though it was also a step into the unknown. But he had, at the worst, five months ahead of him paid for by *Sons and Lovers*; and if the worst came to the worst, as he told Garnett in June 1913, 'I shall get some work when I am in England – teaching I suppose' (*Letters*, II, p. 21). He did the first draft of 'The Sisters' between the end of March and the start of June, knowing that it *was* only a first draft and not trying to write it immediately as a publishable novel. That again was something new.

By June he was back in Bavaria with Frieda, living in yet another house borrowed from her family. The exciting novel draft behind him, he did exactly what he had done in the summer of 1912, and wrote three more short stories; but this time he knew he would shortly be coming back to England, when (with Garnett's advice) he could attempt to place them in magazines. He had also done some travel sketches which he could sell. Three went to the *English Review*: Harrison must have relented.[6] In the middle of June 1913, Lawrence and Frieda came back to England after an absence of thirteen months; naturally enough, they stayed at The Cearne with Garnett. For more than a year, with a little help from Frieda's family, they had managed to survive on the proceeds of Lawrence's work; they had been poor, but they had survived.

3
Success and Catastrophe: 1913–15

When Lawrence returned to England in June 1913, he was known in literary circles primarily as the author of two novels with a small but good reputation, and as the author of some interesting stories and poems in the *English Review*. From the summer of 1913 onwards, however, he would be 'the author of *Sons and Lovers*': his reviewers (and publishers' readers) thereafter would frequently compare his subsequent works with *Sons and Lovers*, and often lament the falling-off they found. And the novel remained his most widely read work until *Lady Chatterley's Lover* was published in 1928.

This makes it the stranger that *Sons and Lovers* was not much of a success when it was first published. It had some very good reviews, but it did not sell. We do not know for certain how many copies Duckworth printed of it (all Duckworth's records were lost in the Second World War); but as the calculation of royalties was done on the basis of 15% for the first 2500 copies, and $17\frac{1}{2}$% after that, the first edition was almost certainly of 2500 copies. That would have showed Duckworth's confidence in Lawrence and in the book: a first edition of a not particularly commercial novel would often only run to 1500 copies. The relatively large print-run for *Sons and Lovers* meant that the novel did not have to be reprinted in England for three years. Lawrence had been paid the second half of his promised £100 advance on royalties shortly after the book's publication,[1] the advance of £100 being offered in expectation of the whole edition selling out; but it did not do so, in spite of its good reviews and the sales to libraries which Duckworth's and Garnett's judicious cuts had safeguarded.

It is impossible to say, at this distance of time, why the book did not sell better. In May 1913, before publication, Lawrence had remarked that 'Duckworth will have to wait till my name is made, for his money. I can understand he is a bit diffident about putting me forward' (*Letters*, I, p. 546); and Duckworth may have failed to capitalise on the good reviews, though Lawrence – very unusually for an author – later defended the advertising the book received (*Letters*, II, p. 117). However, Lawrence himself suspected that the book's relative failure was due to his 'erotic' reputation, and the book's supposed immorality. Quite a number of reviews had drawn attention to this: the *Daily News* referred to its 'hot-houses of amorous writing' and its 'exaggerated sense of the physical side of love': the *TLS* criticised its lack of 'reticence': the *Academy* noted that 'there is no delicacy nor reticence about his work', and that it had no warmth 'but the warmth of lust', while the *Nation* commented on its 'startling verbal frankness'.[2] Lawrence wrote angrily on 22 July 1913 that – although the book had been 'well received, hasn't it?' – yet:

> I don't know whether it has sold so well. The damned prigs in the libraries and bookshops daren't handle me because they pretend they are delicate skinned and I am hot. May they fry in Hell. (*Letters*, II, p. 47)

The libraries had at one stage apparently agreed to take the book, yet this suggests that there continued to be problems. (There was a good deal of controversy currently about the libraries' attitudes to supposedly immoral books; a best-seller by the immensely successful novelist Hall Caine was rejected by the libraries in August 1913, for example.) A month later, on 4 September 1913, we find Lawrence sadly responding to the news from Garnett that '*Sons and Lovers* has gone down so – God grant it may pick up – though that is not what things usually do' (*Letters*, II, p. 67).[3] In January 1914 he agreed with the literary agent J. B. Pinker that '*Sons and Lovers* does not seem to have done wonders'; later in the month he was again depressed by Garnett's news that 'The sales of *Sons and Lovers* are rather disappointing' (ibid., p. 135). However, he was starting to hear from literary agents like Pinker, who were interested in acquiring him as a client, that 'that fine novel hasn't had the success it deserved' (ibid., p. 135): the publishers Methuen had approached Pinker as early as July 1913, wondering if they could interest him in taking Lawrence on. Duckworth's statement of accounts in April 1914 showed that the publisher had not only

failed to make a success of the book during its first year; they had
not yet succeeded in breaking even.[4] Lawrence had remarked in
February 1914 that 'I hate feeling that people might publish me at a
loss' (ibid., p. 144); he was now feeling that:

> It was horrid ... to see that Duckworth has lost a number of
> pounds on the book – fifteen or so, was it. [That would have
> meant a sale of 1425 copies.] That is very unpleasant. Because I
> only had a hundred pounds even then ... If a publisher is to lose
> by me, I would rather it were a rich commercial man such as
> Heinemann. (*Letters*, II, p. 165)

Lawrence was deceived by the statement of accounts; even a
moderately successful novel might easily lose a few pounds in its
first year (a loss of £15 meant that the sale of only 75 more copies
would allow the publisher to break even). A book with 1000 sets of
sheets left over might – as *Sons and Lovers* did – go on selling, and
eventually make its publisher a decent profit. Either way, a
publisher's profit would only come towards the end of the period
of sale. Lawrence did not know enough about the publishing
business to realise that Duckworth's position was not really a bad
one. But what mattered to Lawrence, as an author living by his
pen, was the fact that Duckworth – handling an exceptionally
well-reviewed novel which later proved highly successful – had
not only failed to make a profit for themselves: they had failed to
make their author any money over and above his initial £100
advance. That *was* serious.

Since the spring of 1912, Lawrence had lived primarily from the
profits of his novel sales: he had remarked in January 1913 that 'I
can make, I should reckon £100 a year by novels' (*Letters*, I, p. 506).
But he was able to survive the winter of 1913–14 because of the
sales of his other writings, and because he was once more living in
Italy, where Frieda and he had returned in September 1913. He
found himself able to live on about 130 lire (£5) a month, everything included: a four-room cottage in Fiascherino, on the gulf of
Spezia, costing less than £4 a month complete with servant. He and
Frieda could afford to hire a piano and even to buy in a quantity of
wine; and he could, astonishingly, afford not to do any writing
work at all during October 1913. If we list what we know he earned
during the six months between August 1913 and the end of
January 1914 – and some items are probably missing – we can
include:

£4 from the *New Statesman* for the story 'The Fly in the Ointment'. (*Letters*, II, p. 82)

£25 from the *English Review* for three Italian sketches. (ibid., p. 66)

£10 from the American magazine *Smart Set* for a 'very short story', 'The Shadow in the Rose Garden', (ibid., p. 127)

£3 and £4 for reprints of the poem 'Snapdragon' in the first two editions of the *Georgian Poetry* volume. (ibid., pp. 39, 140)

£20 for poems in the January 1914 issue of the American magazine *Poetry*. (ibid., p. 138)

£35 from Mitchell Kennerley, the American publisher of *Sons and Lovers*. (ibid., p. 165)[5]

There was a further £15 promised by the *English Review* for each of the two short stories they bought in the autumn of 1913: the money may not, however, have been paid until the summer of 1914 (the *English Review* was consistently slow in paying Lawrence for his work). The money from *Georgian Poetry* is a reminder of Lawrence's debt to his friend Edward Marsh, who both now and later did what he could for Lawrence's finances.

Lawrence's attitude towards his earnings in the autumn of 1913 may be summed up by his cheerful response to the appearance of his poem 'Service of all the Dead' in the *New Statesman* in November 1913: 'Some people loved it – as for me – I got a guinea for it' (*Letters*, II, p. 118). He also remarked to Ezra Pound that, if the new magazine *The Egoist* wanted his slightly risqué story 'Once – !', 'then I don't see why they shouldn't have it, for as much as they can afford' (*Letters*, II, p. 132). Although at one stage he had hoped to make £150 during the winter – from the items listed above, plus as much as £60 from the *English Review* for four stories (but they only printed two), another £25 promised by Kennerley from *Sons and Lovers* (which, however, he never got), and an advance on his play *The Widowing of Mrs Holroyd* also published in America by Kennerley – yet in spite of disappointments his income in these months must still have been rather over £100. And he did not really start work on 'The Sisters' until December. He had noted back in January 1913 that 'I can't live under £200 a year – not as things are' (*Letters*, I, p. 506); but he was now managing to earn a little more than that. It is striking, however, how much of his income was starting to come from American sales. Ezra Pound had been his contact with the *Smart Set* (*Letters*, II, p. 26) and had probably introduced him to its editor Wright in the summer of 1913; Pound may well also have pointed him in the direction of Harriet Monroe and her magazine *Poetry*. At the end of January 1914, Lawrence still had £50 in his Italian bank (ibid., p. 143), and further money left in Garnett's bank in England; this, in spite of paying for a typist for his stories in the summer of 1913 (for only the second time in his writing life: 9d per 1000 words, 1/- with carbons), and in spite of having no income from England for his novels. 'But somehow, the money seems to turn up, from odd ends of the earth, just enough to get along with' (ibid., p. 144). At the end of January 1914, he was sure that his £50 in the Spezia bank would 'last into May – before May I shall not need money from anybody' (ibid., p. 143). And in the spring of 1914 he got a further £16 from the *Smart Set* for 'The White Stocking'.[6]

However, the disappointment over Duckworth's *Sons and Lovers* meant that he was also seriously considering whether another publisher would not be able to sell more copies of his novels, and therefore be able to give him a greater royalty percentage and larger advance. A firm of literary agents who wrote to him in the winter of 1913–14 (they may well have been Curtis Brown) offered him 'a "considerable advance on a 20% royalty" – for America' (ibid., p. 98); and in January 1914 they offered him '£200 down for my next' (ibid., p. 135), which was twice as much as Duckworth had been able to pay him. Such offers were very tempting.

Just to make matters worse, Edward Garnett began responding extremely critically in the early spring of 1914 to Lawrence's at last recommenced novel, 'The Sisters'. He saw its first half, and did not like it at all. It was the first time the two men had really disagreed; and this, coupled with the offers from the agents, prompted Lawrence to ask whether Garnett really wanted the book for Duckworth.

> You told me in your last letter that I was at liberty to go to any other firm with this novel. Do you mean you would perhaps be relieved if I went to another firm? (*Letters*, II, p. 165)

Lawrence owed a huge debt of gratitude to Duckworth and to Garnett; he had told the literary agent J. B. Pinker – who had also made an approach in December 1913, on behalf of Methuen – that he really could not 'in decency' part with them. And yet it was becoming a very real question, whether – after the failure of *Sons and Lovers* to make him more than his initial £100, and now with Garnett's severe criticisms of the new book – it was sensible for him to stick to Duckworth. He wrote to Garnett again:

> If Duckworth is not really *keen* on this novel, we will give it to Pinker ... I don't think I want to sign an agreement with Duckworth for another novel after this. I did not like to see he had lost on *Sons and Lovers*. And I *must* have money for my novels, to live ... And *nobody* can do any good with my novels, commercially, unless they believe in them commercially – which you dont very much. (*Letters*, II, p. 166)

Quite apart from his disagreements with Garnett, his worries about Duckworth, and the tempting offers from Pinker and others, Lawrence must have been wondering whether he didn't also need an agent to help him keep track of his increasing number of publications. In January 1914, after the publication of a batch of his poems in *Poetry*, he had remarked that 'My things are getting more and more beyond my control. I have no idea what these people have put in their paper – of mine' (*Letters*, II, p. 139). Up to now, with the initial help of Hueffer, and latterly of Garnett, Lawrence – like many writers of the period – had managed without an agent to place his work, and to collect his payments and royalties. But he was starting to wonder whether an agent would not be able to look after his income better than he himself could, particularly while he was living in Italy. An agent might also place his work with more success than he himself, with advice from Garnett, had managed to.

And, of course, with at least the possibility of a break with Duckworth looming, his relationship with Garnett was likely to change too; even if they remained friends – which was starting to look unlikely – he obviously could not expect the same kind of help from Garnett if he were no longer one of Duckworth's authors. The fate of the American royalties for *Sons and Lovers* may finally have convinced him that he needed an agent. Lawrence had played no part in Duckworth's arrangement with Kennerley for the book's publication: he later confessed that 'I haven't kept proper accounts with him, because Duckworths made the agreement and all that. I will write to them' (ibid., p. 243). He had had an initial £35 from Kennerley, but had been promised a further £25: eventually, in

May 1914, a cheque for £10 came to Italy. But the local bank in
Spezia and a bank in London both refused to cash it; and although
Lawrence sent it back, Kennerley never made it good. As a result,
£35 was all Lawrence got for American royalties on his most
popular novel: and £135 in total was all he received, from both
England and America, during the first three years of *Sons and
Lovers'* publication.

II

He had promised Garnett (and Duckworth) that at any rate he
would not make any change in his publishing arrangements for his
new novel (now called *The Rainbow*) until he returned to London in
the summer of 1914, and was able to talk to them in person, as well
as to the agent J. B. Pinker. The latest offer from Pinker, however,
had been for a £300 advance from Methuen, together with a
contract for two more novels. Methuen, as a large publisher, could
afford to give their authors a 25% royalty, and their advance could
be correspondingly large: £300 was more than Lawrence had
earned for his first three novels together. It was, he told Garnett
sadly:

> a pretty figure that my heart aches after. It is wearying to be
> always poor, when there is also Frieda. I suppose Duckworth
> can't afford big risks. (*Letters*, II, p. 174)

Garnett, realising that Lawrence was in great danger of slipping
away from Duckworth, made sure that Lawrence was sent another
£10 in Duckworth royalties at the end of May 1914. This may have
been for the edition of *The Widowing of Mrs Holroyd* which Duckworth were about to issue; though as Duckworth were this time
buying sheets from Kennerley, the £10 may well have been an act
of thoughtful generosity rather than an actual payment. The
money tided Lawrence over at an awkard moment; without the
money still owed him by Kennerley for *Sons and Lovers*, he was
worried about having enough cash to travel back to England.

But the useful £10 could not make up for Duckworth's failure to
make a success of *Sons and Lovers*, nor for Lawrence's desire to earn
more in future; and even before he went to Duckworth's office on
Saturday 27 June 1914 he had decided to 'get my new novel away

from Duckworth for Methuen' (*Letters*, II, p. 186), and to supply Duckworth with a volume of short stories instead. When he actually saw Duckworth, matters were very quickly settled.

> 'Well?' he said when I came in.
> 'Pinker offers me the £300 from Methuen,' I said.
> 'He does?'
> 'Yes.'
> 'Then,' he said, as if nettled, 'I'm afraid you'll have to accept it.' Which rather made me shut my teeth, because the tone was peremptory. (*Letters*, II, p. 189)

Lawrence then tried to see Garnett before keeping his appointment with Pinker on Tuesday 30 June, but Garnett was unfortunately not in his office.

> I called to see you ... Then you weren't in. And I hung a few moments on the pavement outside, saying 'Shall I go to Pinker?' And there was very little time, because we had to lunch with Lady St. Helier. And Frieda was so disappointed that she couldn't have any money. And most of all, I remembered Mr Duckworth on Saturday ... So I went to Pinker, and signed his agreement, and took his cheque, and opened an acc. with the London County and Westminster Bank – et me voilà.
>   I am sorry. (*Letters*, II, p. 189)

The agreement with Methuen turned out to be one of the great mistakes of Lawrence's professional life. A publisher had decided that he was a commercial proposition, and he was prepared to go along with their estimation of him, although he must have known that he was going to give them a thoroughly uncommercial novel. However, for the moment he was more firmly than ever before a professional author: exactly like Joseph Conrad, he had one of Methuen's famous three-novel contracts and J. B. Pinker as an agent; and he had a bank account containing – after Pinker's 10% – £90: Methuen's £300 being divided into £100 on signing the contract and £200 on publication. As part of the celebrations, Lawrence and Frieda (her divorce at last finalised) got married in London on 13 July 1914, and Lawrence went on a walking tour of the Lake District at the end of the month. They must have spent with great freedom (and probably repaid some debts): by the end of July, Lawrence had to ask Pinker for another advance out of the expected cheque from Methuen, and Pinker provided him with a further £50 (*Letters*, II, pp. 201–2) – probably out of his own pocket: he regularly funded his authors.[7]

Lawrence also felt that he could fulfil his obligations to Duckworth by giving them the volume of short stories which he had been planning, on and off, since Martin Secker's enquiry in June 1911, but which was now a sensible proposition since many of his stories had received magazine publication. Accordingly, he spent a busy fortnight at the start of July gathering and revising the stories, so that he was able to submit almost the complete book to Garnett on 14 July: only one story out of the twelve had not previously been published ('Daughters of the Vicar'), but that had proved too long for the magazines to which it had been submitted, and it made sense to include it too. The volume, however, marked the end of Lawrence's close association with Garnett; the latter took it upon himself, in October, to call the first story 'The Prussian Officer' (in place of Lawrence's title 'Honour and Arms'), and to name the whole volume after it. Lawrence was extremely annoyed: 'Garnett was a devil to call my book of stories *The Prussian Officer* – what Prussian Officer?' (*Letters*, II, p. 241). Garnett was presumably trying to give a topical and commercial title to a volume of stories being published in wartime (the war had begun in August and the book came out in November): had not Lawrence always been critical of Duckworth's abilities to sell his books? And Lawrence had also failed to provide a suitable title himself. At all events, although in 1916 Duckworth published two more of Lawrence's books, Garnett was by then away on war-service; his association with Lawrence effectively ended with *The Prussian Officer*.

III

It was the war, in fact, which made the first dent in Lawrence's new status as a successful author. Methuen had paid over their first £100 to Pinker; but on the outbreak of war at the start of August they returned (for a period of six months) unpublished manuscripts to their less-well-known authors. At the same time, they also made some critical comments on the outspokenness of the book they had received from their new author. Lawrence, far from being at last financially successful, was back where he had started: he had spent his £90 advance from Methuen, was well into Pinker's personal advance of £50: and now he had little prospect of getting his final £130 – after Pinker's commission – for at least another nine months.

With the help of some friends, Lawrence applied (successfully) for a grant from the Royal Literary Fund, laconically giving 'The War' as his 'Cause of Distress'. He received £50, so that at the end of October 1914 he had 'about £70 in the world now', with debts of £20: and, hanging over him, a bill of £144 from Ernest Weekley's solicitors for the costs of the divorce action against Frieda – though he was also determined that 'This I am never going to pay' (*Letters*, II, p. 226). He was also unable to go back to Italy, as he had planned; the cheap living of Italy was denied him. Like a number of London friends, he rented a cheap cottage outside London, in Buckinghamshire, and settled down there to write 'a tiny book on Thomas Hardy' which had been commissioned from him; a book which turned out to be 'about anything else in the world but that' (ibid., p. 220), and although most important for developing the thinking which dominated the yet-to-be-written final version of *The Rainbow*, was itself unpublishable. It would, however, only have made Lawrence £15 (ibid., p. 193).

Besides the grant, and two lump sums of £10 charitably sent by two literary friends, Alfred Sutro and Edward Marsh, only a trickle of money was now coming in from Lawrence's literary earnings, compared with what he had earned the previous autumn. He earned £25 for the publication of 'Honour and Arms' in America (ibid., p. 222) – and now probably received the £15 for its appearance in the *English Review*; he had perhaps £2 for a piece of journalism in the *Manchester Guardian*, and *Poetry* sent another £8 for six poems in November (ibid., p. 232). 'Pinker, however, promises me some money somehow' (ibid., p. 213), Lawrence remarked in September: he had 'a little money – not much – enough' (ibid., p. 222). His American friend the poet Amy Lowell, one of the promoters of Imagism, casting around for a way of helping Lawrence, sent him a typewriter to help him offset typist's bills. He was not a good typist; he typed seven pages of his revision of *The Rainbow* on it, that winter, before giving up, though he would use it to type a good deal of *Women in Love* the following summer. She also (perhaps more practically) tried to get Mitchell Kennerley to pay Lawrence what he owed him – 'exactly £10.7.6. – by his own computation. It isn't much but it would be worth having' (ibid., p. 256). But she had no success.

Lawrence and Frieda survived the early winter of 1914 in Buckinghamshire, where at the end of November – unable to re-submit his novel, anyway, until the end of January – Lawrence started to re-write *The Rainbow*. At Christmas he felt like 'kicking everything to the devil and enjoying myself willy-nilly: a mild drunk and a great and rowdy spree' (ibid., p. 245): the sum of 25/- was earmarked for the celebration (ibid., p. 243). In January, the Lawrences moved to Sussex, to live even more cheaply in a cottage loaned by Viola Meynell (who would also save Lawrence money by organising the typing of *The Rainbow*); another £5 turned up from the publication of 'Honour and Arms' in America (ibid., p. 256), but Lawrence knew in mid-February that he would 'soon be penniless' (ibid., p. 279). At the end of the month he appealed to Pinker: 'Do be getting me some money, will you? I heard the wolf scratch the door today' (ibid., p. 293). Although *The Rainbow* had still not gone to Viola Meynell for typing, he felt he needed to impress Pinker with the fact that it would soon be ready, and rather artlessly apologised that 'Miss Meynell is somewhat behind with the typing' (ibid., p. 293). Pinker provided a little more cash, probably £25 out of his own pocket (ibid., p. 327); and in March Lawrence finished the novel. There only remained the typing of it (together with some final revision) to be done, and this was complete by the end of May.

But before then Lawrence had had to appeal twice more to Pinker, remarking the second time, 'Do get me some money, will you: I am at the end' (ibid., p. 331). He got a further £25, presumably advanced in expectation of earnings from magazines. One wonders what he would have done if he had not had a literary agent as supportive as Pinker. But by the end of May Lawrence's financial situation was further complicated by the problem of the money he owed Weekley's divorce solicitors.

> I am afraid, if I hand in the MS., the Goldbergs – Goldberg, Newall, Braun and Co, solicitors in the city – will serve a summons on me and on Methuen, ordering Methuen to pay to them the £50 [probably an error for £150] due to me . . . You see I can't pay this £144, or I shall starve for ever. This money for the *Rainbow* is all I have to look forward to at all – and Mrs Lawrence can't get any money from Germany now. So it is a hole. (*Letters*, II, pp. 348–9)

It is unclear what finally happened to the money Lawrence owed the solicitors; he may have arranged to pay it gradually, over a period of years (*Letters*, II, p. 354); the sum may have been reduced; it is most likely that Weekley eventually instructed his solicitors not to bother any further. At all events, Pinker was generous enough to pay over another £90 to Lawrence in June, in advance of the £130 Lawrence would get on publication of *The Rainbow*, and Lawrence felt sufficiently in the clear to come back to live in London in the summer of 1915: a house in Hampstead cost 'only £36 a year' (ibid., p. 354). He was planning a series of lectures with Bertrand Russell, and early in the autumn would start a magazine and organise a series of public meetings – all of them concerned to explain his feelings about the war, and how English society needed to be changed. For these he obviously felt he needed to be back in London.

However, with the onset of war, a certain heightened concern with national morality had begun to be in evidence, in newspapers, reviews and magazines. The reviews of *Sons and Lovers*, back in the golden days of 1913, had been worried about the book's lack of reticence: there had, even then, been problems about library sales. One or two reviews of *The Prussian Officer* in November 1914 had been very severe about what was seen as the perverse sexuality of parts of it, and there had even been a rumour in February 1915 – untrue, as it turned out – that the book might be withdrawn from circulation 'by order of the police. God save us – what is the country coming to' (ibid., p. 280). Mitchell Kennerley had been worried about the sexuality of the 1914 version of *The Rainbow* (ibid., p. 246), as had Methuen; now, at the proof stage of the novel, Methuen started to be seriously anxious about the propriety of parts of the book: initially, in respect of a loss of library sales. They supplied Lawrence with a list of phrases they objected to, and they queried some passages and paragraphs. Lawrence made some changes, but was far more reluctant than he had been with *Sons and Lovers* to agree to blanket alterations: he was now banking on his status as an established author, and he also believed deeply in the book.

The passages and paragraphs marked I cannot alter. There is nothing offensive in them, beyond the very substance they contain, and that is no more offensive than that of all the rest of the novel. The libraries won't object to the book any less, or approve of it any more, if these passages are cut out. And I cant cut them out, because they are living parts of an organic whole. Those who object, will object to the book altogether. These bits won't affect them particularly.

Tell Methuen, he need not be afraid. If the novel doesn't pay him back this year, it will before very long. Does he expect me to be popular? I shan't be that. But I am a safe speculation for a publisher. (*Letters*, II, p. 370)

As Methuen did not press the point about the passages in question, it seems likely that they decided to run the risk of a library boycott; anything worse happening was not foreseen by them, and, at the end of July, Pinker felt able to give Lawrence an 'assurance' about Methuen (*Letters*, II, p. 372). At the start of August, Lawrence and Frieda moved to Hampstead; the idea of the lectures with Russell had been abandoned, but together with Middleton Murry and Katherine Mansfield, Lawrence was going to launch a little magazine called *The Signature*; for this, he had rewritten his 'Hardy' essay as a philosophical speculation called 'The Crown'. That kind of publication now mattered to him as much as that of *The Rainbow*.

The Rainbow was published on 30 September 1915 (with what Lawrence rightly considered 'a vile cover wrapper'), and for a fortnight there was very little critical comment; Lawrence was busy with *The Signature*, and with revision of his old Italian sketches for a book for Duckworth. The most important and annoying event connected with the novel was the arrival of Methuen's final payment of £50 – reduced not only by Pinker's 10% but by a further £9 3s 9d to cover a printer's bill for Lawrence's excessive proof changes. 'I think he is rather stingy about the correction of proofs' (ibid., p. 406) commented Lawrence.

But soon, critical reviews started to appear; the earliest of all took it for granted that the book was 'indecent', 'a monotonous wilderness of phallicism', but hoped that Lawrence's reputation would not suffer from it.[8] The next, in the *Sphere*, was damning, and specifically set out to try and provoke police action against the book:

There is no form of viciousness, of suggestiveness, which is not reflected in these pages. I can only suppose that Mr Methuen and his two partners for some reason failed to read this book in manuscript ... Let them turn to the chapter entitled 'Shame', and unless they hold the view that Lesbianism is a fit subject for family fiction I imagine that they will regret this venture. The whole book is an orgie of sexiness. I write thus strongly because I consider that the publishers should protect the public . . .[9]

What is more, the review specifically rejected the idea that the artistic truth of the book should be a protection against prosecution; it insisted that 'In this novel, *The Rainbow*, Mr Lawrence has ceased to be an artist' and that there could be 'no justification whatever for the perpetration of such a book'.[10] A good review by Lawrence's friend Catherine Jackson (later Carswell) in the *Glasgow Herald* did little to stem the tide against the book (though it cost her her job as a reviewer); and a review in *The Star* on 22 October 1915 probably sealed its fate, by linking its objectionableness with the problems of a country at war. Not only was the reviewer clear 'that a book of this kind has no right to exist' and that 'There is no novel in English so lacking in sexual reticence', but that:

The wind of war is sweeping over our life, and it is demolishing many of the noisome pestilences of peace. A thing like 'The Rainbow' has no right to exist in the wind of war. It is a greater menace to our public health than any of the epidemic diseases ... The young men who are dying for liberty are moral beings. They are the living repudiation of such impious denials of life as 'The Rainbow'. The life they lay down is a lofty thing. It is not the thing that creeps and crawls in this novel.[11]

From whatever angle they looked at it, Methuen knew they had made a mistake. On 18 October they wrote to Pinker pointing out:

what a disastrous fiasco we have had with D. H. Lawrence's new book. Not one of the big libraries would touch it nor will Smith or Wymans put it on their stalls. The result is that our sales have been up to the present 706 at 6s., 440 colonial, and the book has earned in royalties roughly £60, against an advance of £300.[12]

It actually sold a little under 1500 copies in its first month, compared with the 11 months it had taken Duckworth to sell 1500 copies of *Sons and Lovers*; but Methuen were in a different league from Duckworth – and stood to lose far more money. And, besides, threats of something worse than a mere bookstall and library boycott were starting to circulate. Methuen withdrew the book from their advertising around 28 October; but it was too late. The police called at their offices on 2 November, and again the following day, to remove all available copies of the book. Methuen co-operated fully with the police and did their best to recall copies from bookshops and distributors; altogether, they managed to recover some 1011 copies, either bound or in the form of unbound sheets, which they handed over to the police, who also commandeered the plates from which it had been printed.[13]

Lawrence knew nothing of any of this until an acquaintance in London, Walter George, noticing the book's absence from the shops, rang up Methuen and discovered what was happening. Lawrence had been aware that a potential American publisher, Doran – Pinker had managed to sidestep Kennerley – had rejected the book on the grounds that 'Am legally advised distribution would be forbidden' (*Letters*, II, p. 419 n. 2), so he knew a little of the danger the book was facing. On 29 October he made a joking reference to Pinker about 'a set of more cheerful and not at all improper stories' which he was now starting to write (ibid., p. 419), while on 3 November – perhaps with the reviews of *The Rainbow* in mind – he promised Pinker stories 'even more suitable for the family' (ibid., p. 426). But the blow when it came was a heavy one, though Lawrence – a day later – splendidly declared himself:

> not very much moved: am beyond that by now. I only curse them all, body and soul, root, branch and leaf, to eternal damnation. (*Letters*, II, p. 429)

The suppression had come at a critical moment in his life; deeply disillusioned by the war, feeling that he could himself no longer bear to remain in England or in Europe – something to which the reviews of the book during October must have contributed – he had already, in mid-October, decided to leave the country.

> I think I shall go away, to America if they will let me. In this war, in the whole spirit which we now maintain, I do *not* believe, I believe it is *wrong*, so awfully wrong, that it is like a great consuming fire that draws up all our souls in its draught ... If thine eye offend thee, pluck it out. And I am English, and my Englishness is my very vision. But now I must go away, if my

soul is sightless for ever. Let it then be blind, rather than commit the vast wickedness of acquiescence.

... I feel like a blind man who would put his eyes out rather than stand witness to a colossal and deliberate horror. (*Letters*, II, pp. 414–15)

We may guess how the suppression of *The Rainbow* confirmed such feelings. He told Pinker on 6 November that 'It is the end of my writing for England. I will try to change my public' (*Letters*, II, p. 429).

And yet another side to Lawrence, equally strong, was almost at once determined to do something about the suppression; to stay and fight it, so far as he could. Later on 6 November, he wrote to Pinker again: 'On second thoughts, I want to see you at once . . . we must do something about this suppression business. I must move a body of people, we must get it reversed' (ibid., p. 430). He wrote to friends asking for advice and support: 'Do you know what we can do? What about Bernard Shaw?' (ibid., p. 430); and he asked Cynthia Asquith whether she and her husband (son of the Prime Minister) could help: 'I think it is possible to have the decision reversed. If it is possible, and you and Herbert Asquith can help, would you do so?' (ibid., p. 431). He joined the Authors' Society in the hope that they would be able to exert pressure; he tried to organise a letter to the newspapers, signed by prominent writers; an MP friend, Philip Morrell, arranged to ask a question in Parliament about the suppression.

The processes of law had meanwhile taken their natural course. At Bow Street Magistrates' Court on Saturday 13 November 1915 the case was heard why the book should not be suppressed. The solicitor of the Commissioners of Police, Herbert Muskett – whose 'painful duty' it had been to read the book – declared it:

a mass of obscenity of thought, idea and action throughout, wrapped up in language which he supposed would be regarded in some quarters as an artistic and intellectual effort. He was at a loss to understand how the firm had come to lend their name to such a bawdry [presumably bawdy] work.[14]

Lawrence himself was not a party to the prosecution, and was not (so far as we know) in court; Methuen (as the defendants) were the only party entitled to speak for the book, and their solicitor described how they had more than once protested against the book and had appealed for changes from Lawrence; and how, in the end,

> the author refused to do anything more. No doubt the firm were unwise in not scrutinising the book more carefully and they regretted that they had published it.[15]

Lawrence's own summary of events, written ten years later, conveys his lasting opinion of Methuen's behaviour:

> Methuen ... almost wept before the magistrate, when he was summoned for bringing out a piece of indecent literature. He said he did not know the dirty thing he had been handling, he had not read the work, his reader had misadvised him – and Peccavi! Peccavi! wept the now be-knighted gentleman ...
>
> There is no more indecency or impropriety in *The Rainbow* than there is in this autumn morning – I, who say so, ought to know.[16]

Methuen's capitulation was a sign that they thought their good name might be rescued from the debacle; that was all they were after. The magistrate, Sir John Dickinson, declared their reputation soiled, while confirming that it had previously been very good, and he rapped them over the knuckles for their behaviour – but he did not fine them; and they were not prosecuted (as they might well have been) for publishing an obscene book. The magistrate simply ordered the book's destruction:

> how it ever could have passed through Messrs. Methuen's hands he failed to understand. It was greatly to be regretted that a firm of old standing and the highest repute, whose name on the title-page of a book justified anyone in taking it into their home, should have allowed their reputation to be soiled, as it undoubtedly had been ... He was very glad to hear that the libraries refused to circulate it, and it seemed to him that when the defendants read the reviews referred to by Mr Muskett, as they must have done, they should have done everything in their power to recall the book. They did not do so. He made an order for all copies of the book in the possession of the police to be destroyed, and the payment of £10.10s. costs.[17]

The power of the press as public watchdog was thus explicitly confirmed.

Lawrence's own efforts came too late to have any effect; and after the court proceedings, there was no chance of any reversal of the decision (the defence had, after all, agreed with the steps taken by the prosecution). Philip Morrell's questions in Parliament on 17 November and 1 December about the rights of an author, though well-meaning, were answered by the fact that the author was not legally involved: only the publisher was actually concerned in such a case. The single (though extremely dim) ray of hope lay in the Home Secretary's statement on 1 December:

> I imagine it will be possible, if the author thinks he has been wrongly treated, for another copy to be seized by arrangement, in order that he might defend the book.[18]

But such a proceeding would obviously be very expensive, and its result (given the consensus of police, magistrate, press and publisher on 13 November) all too certain. Besides which, by 1 December Lawrence was more interested in his original plan of leaving England, and in schemes to publish the book elsewhere: in America, perhaps in Paris (*Letters*, II, pp. 453, 458–9), perhaps in England by subscription (ibid., p. 456). The idea of another law-case depressed him: he wrote on 3 December how:

> my spirit will not rise to it – I can't come so near to them as to fight them. I have done with them. I am not going to pay any more out of my soul, even for the sake of beating them. (*Letters*, II, p. 462)

There was actually no chance at all of 'beating them'. At the bottom of the problem was the fact that the people he had hoped would help him defend the book did not actually like it (which probably put paid to the idea of the letter from fellow authors protesting about the prosecution). They were concerned by the general point about an author's rights, but not by the fate of *The Rainbow*. Middleton Murry and Katherine Mansfield were Lawrence and Frieda's closest friends of the time; but Murry later confessed how 'neither of us liked *The Rainbow* and Katherine quite definitely hated parts of it ... I disliked it on instinct'; he also remarked 'neither could I understand his surprise and dismay that the critics were out for his blood. As far as mere feeling went, I felt with them'.[19] With friends like that, who needed enemies? And with Lawrence veering between moods of fighting inspiration and vituperative resignation, it was clear that no further action would either be sustained or productive.

But we must not, for that reason, underestimate the damage that had been done to Lawrence as a writer. The fate of *The Rainbow* had made him aware for the first time of a gap between what he wanted to write, knowing that he should write it, and what England was prepared to accept. Whereas a novel like *Sons and Lovers* had been written 'because I want folk – English folk – to alter, and have more sense' (*Letters*, I, p. 544), and he had believed it could also be a genuine commercial success – 'People *should* begin to take me seriously now' (ibid., p. 544) – *The Rainbow*, accepted by Methuen as a commercial proposition, proved that his best and most exploratory work was, after all, not acceptable. England in wartime seemed to Lawrence an increasingly alien country which had taken a great plunge into communal madness; and with the prosecution of *The Rainbow* it also started to become a country in which he could no longer believe, as he had once believed in it.

It was also clear that he himself no longer had a voice that might be listened to. During the spring, summer and early autumn of 1915 it had seemed to him that his country needed approaches like lectures and meetings and little magazines – not just novels – if it were to be affected profoundly. But *The Signature* had inevitably not been a success; a wildly impractical gesture from the start, it had never achieved the subscriptions it needed to survive. It died early in November after only the first three of the first six planned issues had come out. There were only two meetings in London; and then the rent for the room in Fisher Street was given up. And now his novel had not only failed to sell many copies, but had actually been banned.

The other kind of consequence of the war – upon Lawrence's capacity to live by his writing – was slower to show itself, but inexorable. By the end of 1915, he was living more and more upon what generous people – like Edward Marsh, who sent another £20 in November (*Letters*, II, p. 432) – were prepared to provide. Only in America could he continue to earn decent sums of money: but still nothing like what he had been earning in the heady days of the autumn of 1913. Publication in England during the war was going to become increasingly hard; to a shortage of staff at publishers and printers would be added a growing shortage of paper and a dramatic increase in its price. Printing costs rose to two or three times what they had been before the war. In such a situation publishers had no choice but to concentrate upon what would, in a world of shortages, make secure profits. Fewer books were published and, in particular, fewer works of fiction. The consequences for all writers of fiction and poetry were dismal; for a banned author like Lawrence, disastrous. Only the continuing loyalty of a few friends and magazines – and the sales of his books and shorter pieces on the American market, which was never affected in the same way by war and did not see him as a 'banned author' – allowed him to survive as a writer.

4
War: 1915–16

At the start of the winter of 1915, Lawrence's financial position had not been particularly good, but at least he had had the final lump of money from Methuen for *The Rainbow* (albeit reduced to £33), and he had had a story in the October *English Review* which would probably have brought him in £10 or £12. He was also hoping for sales of his now revised Italian sketches in American magazines; if two were probably too long, two others, he told Pinker, 'are just right for magazine publication as they stand ... But the whole set would look nice as a serial. But I suppose nobody will want to do that. Yet it would go well, I'm sure' (*Letters*, II, p. 398). Pinker was either unconvinced or unsuccessful: none of the sketches appeared in American magazines.

Lawrence could not, however, have expected that his *English Review* story, 'England, My England', would be his last periodical publication of any kind in England or America for more than a year, apart from his essays from 'The Crown' in *The Signature* during October and November 1915 which almost certainly lost him money rather than earned it. Such a change was a dreadful set-back for a man who, for once, had no new novel on hand: the second half of the material excised from *The Rainbow* in January 1915 was in a fragmentary state and not publishable without complete re-drafting. On 16 November 1915, shortly after the *Rainbow* prosecution, Lawrence announced that 'We are horribly poor', but with £20 or £30 in hand (ibid., p. 437), that was nothing compared with what would follow in the next few years. Practically the only financial prospect Lawrence had late in 1915 was the book publication of his Italian sketches by Duckworth as *Twilight in Italy*, a volume which – published in June 1916 in an edition of only 1500 copies retailing at 6s and therefore bringing in a maximum of £300 to Duckworth – would not have given Lawrence an advance of more than £50 at most, and probably less; minus, of course,

Pinker's 10%. And, in an ironical reversal of roles, on 9 December 1915 Methuen actually asked for their £300 advance on *The Rainbow* back. Their attitude was that since Lawrence had effectively failed to deliver a work they could sell – which was true – 'there has been a complete failure of the consideration for which we paid our money. Mr Lawrence should now repay this sum' (ibid., p. 457 n. 2). We do not know Lawrence's response to this claim: he certainly never repaid the money. If he had been able to do so, given that £30 would have stayed with Pinker and the printers' charges for proof corrections would not have been refunded, he would actually have made a loss of £40 on the book.

During October 1915, perhaps in anticipation of more difficult times ahead, Lawrence had been promising Pinker to try and write saleable short stories, of the kind suitable for the *Strand* magazine – that is, wholly and very profitably commercial; but he actually only produced two stories – 'The Overtone', which was not published in his lifetime,[1] and 'The Thimble', which did not see print for more than a year, and then in America, and never appeared in England in periodical form. It seems probable that, following the disaster of *The Rainbow* – which occurred only a week after he had sent Pinker 'The Thimble' – Lawrence consciously or unconsciously stopped writing fiction; and that Pinker agreed that, for the moment, there was no point in his producing it. We only know of a 'mid-winter story of oblivion' (*Letters*, II, p. 493) which Lawrence was planning to write at the end of December 1915, but it is likely that he never wrote it.[2] Magazines were not going to accept fiction from him, and novels were for the moment out of the question. It would be a year and a half before another piece of his fiction appeared in print, either in England or America; and then, only in the magazine which had been publishing him since 1909: Harrison's *English Review*, with Harrison almost certainly once more playing the role of 'personal benefactor' which he had enjoyed back in 1912.

What, then, could Lawrence write or publish? His 'philosophy' was certainly not a commercial prospect: it had effectively taken over his 'Hardy' book back in the autumn of 1914, and though he had laced his revised Italian essays with it, in August 1915, *Twilight in Italy* would sell in spite of it rather than because of it. But he had written to Fiascherino for his old poetry notebooks, which he had left there in the summer of 1914; they contained poems dating back to 1905, as well as the long sequence about marriage he had been writing since 1912. And accordingly, early in 1916, hopeful that

'My poetry will sell sooner than my prose, if it is properly marketed' (ibid., p. 513), and having received back the notebooks, Lawrence began to collect and revise some of the old poems for a new volume, which became *Amores*. He also encouraged Pinker to try various publishers, to see where he could place the poems best. Reviewers, after all, had continually told him that he was really a poet, and he was far better known now than he had been early in 1913, when Duckworth had produced *Love Poems*. An editor in a position 'to know how Lawrence has sold in the past' remarked to Pinker that 'I am afraid he has never been a paying proposition as a poet, but his name has some weight.'[3]

However, after rejections of *Amores* in February 1916 from Constable and Co. and from Sidgwick and Jackson Ltd, the latter sending Lawrence 'an unasked and very impertinent criticism of the MS., together with instructions as how to write poetry' (ibid., p. 558), in the end it turned out that only Duckworth was prepared to accept the poems: another indication of Lawrence's altered reputation. Duckworth had reprinted *Love Poems* in February 1914, thus proving some market for Lawrence's poetry: so 'I suppose we shall go trickling slowly on with dear old Duckworth, till the end of the story'. Though unexcited, Lawrence was also grateful: 'But I must say, I *like* Duckworth for sticking to me' (ibid., p. 576). Such support came increasingly rarely. In July 1916 *Amores* appeared, but – in an edition of 900 copies, retailing at only 5s – it could not have produced an advance for Lawrence of more than £20; and, of course, there was always Pinker's 10% to be deducted.

As far as can be seen, apart from some money back for his transfer of the lease of his Hampstead flat in December 1915, and lump sums of £20 and £30 given by his friends Eddie Marsh and Ottoline Morrell, the advances that Lawrence earned for *Twilight in Italy* and for *Amores* were his only actual income from his writing in England between November 1915 and the end of 1916: something rather under £70, less than a third of what he had earned for his writing in 1913 or 1914. And this, after the period in the spring of 1914 when publishers had been so keen on signing him up for contracts, and when his short stories had commanded relatively high prices and many markets. During 1916 he would have had a few pounds in royalties from America: but with no further money coming in from Kennerley for *Sons and Lovers*, and probably nothing either for Kennerley's American editions of *Love Poems* and *The Widowing of Mrs Holroyd*, he only had his new American publisher Benjamin Huebsch to rely upon. The latter had taken on the production of a (slightly expurgated) American edition of *The Rainbow*, late in 1915; but that was not yet publicly on sale (it sold privately in ones and twos for the next five years). Huebsch's editions of *The Prussian Officer*, *Amores* and *Twilight in Italy* were the only items that could have produced royalties from American book production – and such royalties must have been small.

Following the ban on *The Rainbow* in November 1915, the Lawrences immediately cut back on their expenditure, giving up (for example) their Hampstead flat: Lawrence's plans for lectures and magazines were all at an end, and London now seemed 'mouldering in a dank fog. I am glad we have let this flat' (*Letters*, II, p. 461). He had other reasons for wanting to go away from London, however; his idea of emigrating to America, first formulated in October 1915, had been developed into a plan of going with a few friends to form a small colony; the most likely venue being in Florida. The intended membership of the colony changed regularly, but Lawrence's hopes for it did not: 'We shall have our little colony yet – which is what I have always wanted' (ibid., p. 462). The idea of the American colony was also, however, connected with his sense of his market for his writing:

We are all ready to go to America. I cannot live here any more: and I am sure I cannot do any more work for this country. I know America is bad, but I think it has a future. I think there is no future for England: only a decline and fall. That is the dreadful and unbearable part of it: to have been born into a decadent era, a decline of life, a collapsing civilisation. (*Letters*, II, p. 441)

Various boats were chosen – the most likely being the hopefully named *Crown de Leon*, in December; but it turned out that, to leave the country, Lawrence needed to attest for military service – that is, declare himself ready to serve. He queued for two hours on 11 December, then gave it up: 'such an utter travesty of action on my part, waiting even to be attested that I might be rejected . . .' (*Letters*, II, p. 474). He was also ill, and money – in spite of the generosity of Marsh and Ottoline Morrell – was still short; he had too little to start a new and utterly different career in an unknown country. The plan for Florida had reluctantly to be abandoned, though the idea of the 'Community' was not: it 'is what I want; a new life, a life *together*, in a new spirit' (ibid., p. 485).

But, without Florida, the Lawrences had an immediate problem of where to live: for the moment even renting property was difficult, and they had to rely upon what they could borrow. They considered Berkshire (where a friend – Dollie Radford – had a cottage she later regularly lent them) and Oxfordshire, in accommodation provided by the Morrells: 'What a wandering state we are in' (ibid., p. 476), Lawrence remarked. However, a friend of the Murrys, the novelist J. D. Beresford, offered his Cornish house for three months. Cornwall even felt like the first stage of a journey out of England towards Florida, and Lawrence – packing up to leave London – enjoyed the sense he had first had in 1912, of being 'Vogelfrei, thank God – nothing but the trunks to bother us – no house nor possessions – thank heaven again' (ibid., p. 487). He and Frieda travelled to Cornwall on the penultimate day of the old year.

He had already been often ill that winter, and was so again in Cornwall; he passed a good deal of January in bed, during the second half of the month selecting and revising the old poems for *Amores*, and starting yet another rewriting of the 'philosophy' first written as the 'Hardy' essay and then rewritten as 'The Crown'. He was also, when ill and low in spirits, coming to feel 'pushed to the brink of existence', although he enjoyed Cornwall:

> I feel absolutely run to earth, like a fox they have chased till it can't go any further, and doesn't know what to do. I don't know what to do nor how to go on: like a man pushing an empty barrow up an endless slope. (*Letters*, II, p. 500)

The banning of *The Rainbow* had endangered his very existence as a professional writer; his capacity to earn, and his desire and need to speak out to his contemporaries through his writing, were both threatened. The excitement of the attempts to fight the ban, and then the plans for communities, for boats and for Florida – which had kept him going at the end of 1915 – had now given way to a deep sense of depression. 'I don't know what to do any more' (*Letters*, II, p. 500) referred to his writing as well as to his general sense of hopelessness in the England of 1916. Early in February 1916 he tried to formulate plans with his friend Philip Heseltine – currently staying with the Lawrences in Cornwall – to get round the problem of conventional publishers altogether. They planned:

> to start a private publishing concern, by subscription, to publish

any real thing that comes, for the truth's sake, and because a real book is a most holy thing. We could begin with the *Rainbow*, which is likely to give a start, publish at 7/6. Then we can go on with the next as we like. (*Letters*, II, p. 532)

The plan for 'The Rainbow Books and Music', like Lawrence's other publishing plans at this date, was thoroughly impractical. *The Rainbow*, given its public reputation, would certainly have been seized again, even if issued privately, and the scheme had no machinery for distribution; even the selling price of 7/6 ('post free') would have been unlikely to have brought in enough capital to start production. The name of the banned *Rainbow* also probably succeeded in putting off, rather than attracting, potential subscribers – hard enough to find, anyway, among the depleted incomes of artistic sympathisers in England during the war. Eight hundred leaflets about the scheme were distributed; not surprisingly, only a handful of potential subscribers showed any interest; and that was that. Lawrence had to return to using – or not using – the normal machinery of the publishing world. It was not the last occasion during the war when he became interested in such plans; but it was not until 1928 that he successfully carried out a scheme of private publication for a book via subscribers. *Lady Chatterley's Lover*, printed in and distributed from Florence, stood a much greater chance of getting distribution before seizure; book production in Italy was relatively cheap; and in 1928 Lawrence was working with Pino Orioli, a bookseller who had published books privately before. The 'Rainbow Books and Music' scheme stood no chance at all.

On 10 February Lawrence wrote to the painter Mark Gertler – another man suffering the problems of being an artist in wartime – how

we shall stay in Cornwall till our money is gone – which will take three or four months – then I think we may as well all go and drown ourselves. For I see no prospect of the war's ever ending, and not a ghost of a hope that people will ever want sincere work from any artist . . . It is a damned life. I curse my age, and all the people in it. I hate my fellow men most thoroughly. (*Letters*, II, pp. 530–1)

And yet Lawrence did not drown himself, when his money ran

out: he continued to write, for the world of men he said he hated so much. Frieda once referred to his 'exasperated angry love' for his fellow men:[4] it does not do to take his fulminations too literally. Even in such an extremity, he also felt how important it was, still, to be 'an open door, or at least an unlatched door, for the new era to come in by. That is all' (*Letters*, II, p. 502). It was that kind of faith which, in spite of all his pessimism, would lead to his continuing to write in 1916. Although he could no longer in any sense – even the literal one – 'write for England', yet he could still explore in his writing the possibilities of feeling, of experience, which excited him; and the act of writing, unlike the act of thought, always supposed a reader. The 'philosophy' might not be publishable, yet for him it was still an exploration: it was 'real, again a sort of bursting into new seas' (ibid., p. 556); writing it gave him the confidence to say 'We will have a new world to live in' (ibid., p. 557).

He was going to do everything he could to live by his pen, too; in spite of his situation. 'Poetry', he optimistically told Pinker in January 1916, 'is rather popular now – and particularly in America, where I have some poetic repute' (ibid., p. 513); but that was before it turned out that publishers in England no longer much wanted a volume with 'D. H. Lawrence' on the title page. And Pinker's agency was also suffering from the obstacles which the book trade was now labouring under; the magazine market was also contracting. Pinker proved, however, less good at placing work in America than – before the *Rainbow* disaster – he had been at placing it in England. Even if Lawrence had some reputation in America, Pinker was unable to capitalise on it. Pinker's contacts in America were primarily with the American publisher Doran, and Doran (unfortunately) did not want Lawrence; they farmed him out to Benjamin Huebsch who, with immense caution, was leaking copies of *The Rainbow* on to the market, but who was unable to provide Lawrence with much of an income. Pinker's lack of contacts with American publishers later had severe consequences for Lawrence's publication of *Women in Love*; but that was still four years away. For the moment, Lawrence's American publications remained not particularly profitable.

But he had to live, no matter how many skies had fallen; and after fantasies of a house at £1 a week near Zennor, even further west in Cornwall, the Lawrences found a three-room half cottage at Zennor which cost only the positively Italian sum of £5 a year to rent, unfurnished. 'We shall only have to spend about £5, furnishing ... then we can live very cheaply. I feel I am going to be penniless. We shall do our own work' (ibid., p. 580). As that last sentence shows, the Lawrences had been accustomed – in rented accommodation in Italy or in England – to employ a servant to help with the washing and cleaning. They had not done so in Gargnano, but in Fiascherino they had been served by the loyal Felice Fiori and her daughter Elide: poverty, there, would have meant 'not being able to pay Felice her wages, and she is my first servant, and I feel frightfully responsible for her' (ibid., pp. 80–1). But Lawrence (unlike most authors) was perfectly capable of doing the work himself, just as he had had to do at first in Fiascherino, where Elide 'had never seen a scrubbing brush used' (ibid., p. 88). Frieda was also now capable of washing sheets and doing work which middle-class housewives would not have deigned (or been able) to do. The Lawrences took the Zennor cottage as if they were preparing for a siege, and March passed in a whirl of unpacking, furnishing and painting. They had been joined by Katherine Mansfield and Middleton Murry, who had taken the cottage next door, and all four worked together on both houses. On 15 March, Lawrence told a friend, 'I am not writing at all just now, but I shall begin soon' (ibid., p. 581). He was a writer: and write he would, in spite of his circumstances.

II

The fiction he finally turned to, significantly, was not the continuation of the material left over from the division of *The Rainbow* – the thought of continuing work on that novel may still have been too painful, and any suggestion of the old characters might have doomed the project – but the old, abandoned novel from 1913, whose manuscript had remained in Bavaria with Else. There were 200 pages of good material there, Lawrence remembered, though he seems to have forgotten that he had abandoned it because it was 'too improper'; something unpromising for the author of *The Rainbow*, whose every word in future would be scrutinised for impropriety. Lawrence was under no illusions about how impractical it was to work on another novel in the spring of 1916:

What I write now I write for the gods. I am useless to this

mankind, and this mankind is useless to me. It is no good pretending any more that there is a relation between it and me. If only it will let me alone, and not try to destroy my own inner world, which is real, I don't mind. But my life is not any more of this world, this world of this humanity, and I won't pretend it is. (*Letters*, II, p. 580)

As I suggested above, it is too easy to criticise Lawrence for nihilism and hatred of mankind in these years. For one thing, his habit – in some ways a class habit – was to shout and complain very loud, when he was angry: it was a way of defusing and getting rid of his anger, and it doesn't do to take it too literally. For another thing, his behaviour shows that he was determined for almost the whole of the period of the war to go on writing for the very 'mankind' he professed to be so detached from. He may have comforted himself – and his friends – with talk of his 'own inner world' which could be a conscious retreat; and doubtless it frequently was such a retreat. But it was a creative world into which he retreated, if he retreated, not into solipsism. And, as a professional writer, he was also determined – so far as he could – to make sure that what he created did what it could to earn him a living.

However, it proved impossible to get the manuscript of the old 'Insurrection of Miss Houghton' out of Bavaria in wartime, even via the Swiss correspondent the Lawrences normally went through to communicate with Frieda's family in wartime. And sometime around 20 April Lawrence began to write a continuation of *The Rainbow*. At the bottom of the manuscript of the latter, he had put 'End of Volume I';[5] now he would at last finish the novel he had began as that 'pot-boiler', so long ago, in the astonishingly different life of 1913.

The novel went wonderfully fast, once started, and 'really occupies me. The world crackles and busts, but that is another matter, external, in chaos. One has a certain order inviolable in one's soul. There one sits, as in a crow's nest, out of it all' (*Letters*, II, p. 601). Quite early in the writing of the novel, Lawrence remarked that 'it is beyond all hope of ever being published, because of the things it says' (ibid., p. 602). This was almost certainly a reference to the original first chapter's description of Birkin's feelings of love for Gerald. After the prosecution's and magistrate's attacks on the chapter 'Shame' in *The Rainbow*, the one thing bound to get a Lawrence novel refused by every publisher, library and bookshop in the country would be any suggestion of homosexual or lesbian experience; and to start the novel in such a way was Lawrence's demonstration of his determination, this time, to write simply about what mattered to him, absolutely without reference to prevailing standards. However, some time before July he cut that chapter out: we don't know why, but he would have known that such a beginning made the novel quite impossible for publication – and when he had finished it, he was very proud of it, and tried to get it published. He was thus caught – not for the first time, or the last – between his desire to write about what mattered to him, and what he could (and needed to) publish. He could write bravely about his novel in a letter how 'it is beyond all possibility even to offer it to a world, a putrescent mankind like ours' – and yet he could also very much want to publish it, insisting magnificently that 'a work of art is an act of faith, as Michael Angelo says, and one goes on writing, to the unseen witnesses' (ibid., p. 602). In that last respect, history has proved him right; the number of Lawrence's readers, his unseen witnesses, continues to grow.

Yet he also needed 'seen witnesses', actual readers; above all, because that was the kind of writer he was; partly because his writing was not simply a satisfying private game – and partly because of his simple need to earn by his pen. His idealism about not offering his novel to the world only went so far – and, after that, he had to rewrite, or to publish. Unlike his friend Philip Heseltine, with his £150 a year private income – or his hero Birkin, at first given £200 a year, altered in 1920 to £400 – Lawrence's only source of income, apart from charity, was what he could manage himself to earn. He expressed a wish at the end of June 1916 that 'I had two hundred a year, and could send everybody to the devil' (ibid., p. 620). But the fact that he hadn't got it ensured that he continued to write *for* people, never simply against them, for all his frequently expressed anger with all the world.

By the end of June 1916, after only about seven weeks writing, the novel was finished, and Lawrence wrote immediately to Pinker:

I have finished 'The Sisters', in effect. I thought of writing to Duckworth and saying to him, the novel is done in substance, and I could send him the typed MS. in about six weeks' time,

and would he give me some money. Duckworth is so decent, I
think it is best for him to publish all my books. And I think
probably he would give me enough money to get along with. I
can manage on about £150 a year, here. (*Letters*, II, p. 619)

Twilight in Italy was published, and *Amores* on the verge of
publication; an advance on a novel added to those two would
perhaps have brought Lawrence's earnings for the year up to £100.
And Lawrence suggested 'some sort of business contract' with
Duckworth: 'I give him my writings if he give me enough to live
on' (*Letters*, II, p. 620). It sounded sensible, but Lawrence was
forgetting a number of things: that the contract he had signed with
Methuen in the summer of 1914 obliged him to offer them his next
two novels; that he was not an attractive commercial prospect for
any publisher; that the war was having an extremely depressive
effect upon every publisher; and that Duckworth's current attitude
to his novels might not be what it had been in 1914. Lawrence was
also growing very short of cash again: a fortnight later he had 'only
six pounds in the world' (ibid., p. 630), which suggests that the
advance for *Amores* – tiny though it doubtless was – had not yet
been paid.

Pinker, at any rate, reminded him of his obligations to Methuen,
and offered to supply an advance on royalties himself; he also
reassured Lawrence about his earning capacity. Lawrence replied:

I am glad you take a hopeful view of the financial life of me.
Methuen, for certain, won't want to keep me. What a snake in
his boiled-shirt bosom! . . . Thank you very much for keeping me
going. (*Letters*, II, p. 630)

Lawrence later complained bitterly about Pinker; but at this stage it
was Pinker's financial help which kept Lawrence alive. For his
part, Lawrence demonstrated his intention of saving money by
determining to type out his new novel himself. That would also
allow him to revise the work as he went along. Amy Lowell had
sent him the typewriter in the autumn of 1914, as a helpful gesture
to a man about to suffer poverty on the outbreak of war; but
Lawrence had hardly ever used it. Now he would; and immediately encountered the characteristic problem of the owner of an oldish
and alien typewriter; how to get a new ribbon for it. Typewriter
ribbons were unavailable in Zennor; it took four letters to his friend

Koteliansky in London, and two wrong ribbons, before Lawrence was (at the end of July) finally set up as an author with a properly working typewriter.

Typing the ribbon and one carbon copy turned out to take 'a tremendous time: and the novel itself is one of the labours of Hercules' (*Letters*, II, p. 665). He was not an experienced typist, and on at least six occasions forgot to insert his carbon paper (or inserted it backwards), and had to retype the page. But the typewriter, he told Amy Lowell, eventually became 'a true confrère. I take so unkindly to any sort of machinery. But now I and the type writer have sworn a Blutbruderschaft' (ibid., p. 645). However, he was again ill a good deal in September 1916, and finally resolved to give up the typing about three-fifths of his way through the book. He finished this version of the novel by writing out its continuation in notebooks, and by joining those on to the original ending of the April–June version, also in notebooks, but extensively revised. The notebooks were typed for him in London – for nothing, thanks to Pinker – and he could add that portion of typescript on to what he had himself typed. Thus, at the start of November 1916, he at last had two complete typescripts of the novel; one for his English publishers, and one for America.

His attitude towards the book's publication was characteristically mixed, during the later stages of its composition. The very typing of it demonstrates his determination to have it published. And yet he felt so close to the book that 'It only seems to me horrible to have to publish it' (ibid., p. 659): it was 'another world, in which I can live apart from this foul world which I will not accept or acknowledge or even enter. The world of my novel is big and fearless – yes, I love it, and love it passionately' (ibid., p. 659). This was very often Lawrence's feeling about his work: in 1925 he remarked 'about writing a novel' that:

one can live so intensely with one's characters and the experience, one creates or records, it is a life in itself, far better than the vulgar thing people *call* life, jazzing and motoring and so on. (*Letters*, V, p. 293)

Yet, in *Women in Love* itself, the character Ursula remarks that 'The world of art is only the truth about the real world, that's all';[6] she launches a deliberate attack upon the artist who defends his productions as simply works of art, as belonging to 'the world of art'. Lawrence's feeling that his fiction was some kind of an alternative to the life of 'this foul world' would not, for that reason, be contradicted; he would probably not have agreed that England at war in 1916 was, in any sense, 'the real world'. And yet he also knew that his writing needed to be 'the truth about the real world' – and it could only be that by taking its place in the world.

So even while in the final stages of *Women in Love*, he was also planning ahead; when it was finished, he told Pinker, 'I will *really* get off some stories, and send them you' (*Letters*, II, p. 653). He was as good as his word: he revised one old story, 'The Mortal Coil', simultaneously with finishing the handwritten part of the novel at the end of October, and then during the next week wrote a new story, 'Samson and Delilah', in one of the notebooks originally used for *Women in Love*. Neither would probably be suitable for the *Strand* magazine – whose title Lawrence regularly invoked as his idea of a really popular magazine: 'I really grieve when I send you still another unmarketable wretch of fiction', he remarked to Pinker about the former. But he thought that both perhaps might suit the *English Review*, and felt that the second was '*sure* to be accepted by *some* magazine' (*Letters*, III, p. 22). He knew his market: 'Samson and Delilah' did indeed suit the *English Review*, and it appeared there in March 1917, while 'The Mortal Coil' only ever appeared in America. Lawrence also asked Pinker for some old story manuscripts which, like that of 'The Mortal Coil', had not yet been published: he listed at least four, on 17 November, which he could now revise. Magazines had been keen enough on them back in 1913; they might still be acceptable. As it turned out, Pinker had none of the manuscripts in his possession, but Lawrence – undeterred – went on planning and writing, simultaneously with finishing the revision of the typescripts of *Women in Love*:

> The novel I will send on in a week's time: not longer. Then I will send a batch of poems, for the American magazines. Then I have another short story on hand, which I shall finish when I've sent off the novel. (*Letters*, III, pp. 28–9)

He obviously wanted to give Pinker the impression of being a busy, productive and hopeful author, the letter inevitably going on to say 'Oh, and do send me a little more money. I am at the end of all I have'. Pinker forwarded another £50 – perhaps on the strength of Lawrence's Duckworth publications, perhaps simply as a loan;

almost simultaneously, Amy Lowell suddenly sent a gift of £60 from America. The Lawrences could face the winter – 'I feel so wretched as the winter comes on' – with some assurance.

But only three of the poems appeared in American magazines; the story was not accepted for publication until 1922; the novel was refused everywhere. In 1916, Lawrence had published two books, and finished a major novel. In 1917, the only book he published was a collection of poems; and the year was marked by an even greater reluctance by publishers and editors to handle his work than in the aftermath of the *Rainbow* prosecution. Pinker had sent one of the typescripts of *Women in Love* to Methuen at the end of November 1916, and by 20 December, 'Methuen, having had the MS., agrees to cancel the agreement. I am glad not to be thrown any more under the snout of *that* particular swine'. But Lawrence was also well aware of what Methuen's refusal meant: 'it shows what the market value of the book is likely to be at the moment: the moment being from now onwards, indefinitely' (*Letters*, III, p. 58). He professed not to mind; was, indeed, stoical:

> whether . . . it will find a publisher, I don't know, and don't very much care. It is a very good piece of work: in fact, a masterpiece. So it will keep. What is the good of its coming out into the orgy of baseness which is today. (*Letters*, III, p. 61)

That was something he needed at times to feel, or life would have been even more depressing than it was. A man like Lawrence found humiliation very hard to bear: in Chapter 1 we saw his response to rejection. His skin was by now much thicker than it had been in 1908, but he still needed to feel 'I banish *you*'.

> I don't wonder at it, if no one will publish the novel. When I read the newspapers, I see it would be vain. It does not matter very much – later will be better. It is a book that will laugh last. (*Letters*, III, p. 73)

The typescript passed through the hands of a succession of publishers: Catherine Carswell remarked that 'it must have lain on the table at one time or another of every leading publisher in London'.[7] It was certainly seen (and rejected) by Methuen, by Constable, by Chatto, even by that everlasting last hope 'the faithful Duckworth'. (*Letters*, III, p. 74)

However, early in January, still another reason for publishers to reject it surfaced. A typescript of the novel had been circulating among literary groups in London, and the Lawrence's old friend and hostess Ottoline Morrell at last saw a typescript, following her urgent requests back in late November – 'she hears she is the villainess of the new book' (*Letters*, III, p. 41). In February 1917 she wrote to Pinker to say the character of Hermione was a portrait of her, and that if the book were published she would sue for libel; her husband Philip invited Pinker down to their house in Oxfordshire, Garsington Manor, to compare the house with Lawrence's descriptions of 'Breadalby' in the novel. Lawrence rejected the charge out-of-hand:

> Hermione is not much more like Ottoline Morrell than Queen Victoria, the house they claim as theirs is a Georgian house in Derbyshire I know very well [i.e. Kedleston Hall] – etc. Ottoline flatters herself. – There *is* a hint of her in the character of Hermione: but so there is a hint of a million women, if it comes to that.
>
> Anyway, they could make libel cases for ever, they haven't half a leg to stand on. (*Letters*, III, p. 95)

But he must also have recognised that the threatened libel suit was yet another obstacle to publication, and in the same letter gave up any idea of the book appearing in the foreseeable future: it 'can lie by till there is an end of the war and a change of feeling over the world' (*Letters*, III, p. 95). It took courage to say that; Lawrence was perforce giving up the novels and novel-writing which had so far sustained his literary career.

5
Poverty: 1917–19

At the start of 1917, Lawrence was feeling exactly as he had done a year earlier: 'like a fox that is cornered by a pack of hounds and boors who don't perhaps know he's there, but are closing in unconsciously' (*Letters*, III, p. 86). In 1916, at least, he had been able to go on and write *Women in Love*; but there was no longer any point in such a venture. His idea of going to America returned. In the summer of 1916 he had been rejected on health grounds for military service, so that the previous objection to his emigration no longer applied; he asked to have his and Frieda's passports renewed. And, simultaneously, he 'gathered and shaped' the poems he had been writing into a book: a final book.

> It is a sort of conclusion of the old life in me – 'And now farewell' is really the motto. I don't much want to submit the MS. for publication. It is very intimate and vital to me. (*Letters*, III, p. 87)

It was the book of poems that, consciously or unconsciously, he must have been withholding from completion for the past four years. Whereas the volume *Amores* had been 'a sort of inner history of my life, from 20 to 26' (*Letters*, II, p. 521), this was the continuation: the poems of the start of his relationship with Frieda, many of them first written in 1912 and 1913. They were still very close to him, and very important; so that although he had shaped them into a book, he also decided that 'I shall not send them yet to Pinker. I couldn't bear them to be published yet' (*Letters*, III, p. 93).

But, after all, the volume turned out to be only in one sense 'a conclusion of the old life in me'. The Passport Office, 'in the Interests of National Service', turned down the application for a renewal of the Lawrences' passports. This was 'a bitter blow' (ibid., p. 92): he and Frieda were condemned to remain in England for the remainder of the war, however long that would be. He showed his collection of poems to a few friends; but, specifically for publication, and in response to what he saw as the overwhelming need of the moment, he also began to write a series of 'peace articles – called "The Reality of Peace"' (ibid., p. 102). We can observe the usual contradiction between his insistence that 'For me, the skies have fallen, here in England . . . something is broken. There *is not* any England' (ibid., p. 91), and his determination, early in 1917, to write for it. The articles were 'very beautiful, and I think, important. Something *must* be done with them. They are a new beginning' (ibid., p. 100). He still believed that such a beginning was possible; he still believed in England, and in his role as writer for it. He sent the articles to Pinker in March 1917, and was eager to hear whether they had been accepted: as much because he believed in them as because he needed the money they would earn from magazine publication. The combination of his enthusiasm, and of a visit he paid to Austin Harrison at the *English Review* in April, led to the latter agreeing to accept four of them. Harrison wrote to Pinker that Lawrence was:

> very anxious to have these published and quite realised that it was hardly a commercial proposition, he told me it was not a question of money at all, and on that condition I consented . . . I propose to pay him twenty guineas for the four.[1]

Harrison was getting good work from a major contemporary writer at a knock-down price; he eventually printed what was probably the complete set of seven essays, two at a time and the final one by itself. They appeared in the May–August 1917 issues of the *English Review*: 'I am rather surprised and very pleased, that he is printing the thing untouched' (ibid., p. 113) Lawrence told Pinker.

It was almost his only piece of good news. His pleasure must have helped make up for the fact that Harrison had rejected the story 'The Mortal Coil' in March; the *Fortnightly Review* also rejected it in April.[2] With many misgivings, Lawrence had also at last sent Pinker *Look! We Have Come Through!*, his planned volume of the poems about Frieda and himself: 'This is the best of my poetry, and I feel very unwilling to let it go . . . I feel there is no haste to get this MS. published' (ibid., p. 111). Such an attitude unfortunately inhibited prior publication of the individual poems in magazines; in mid-April, Harrison actually asked Pinker if he could have some of Lawrence's poems for publication, but Lawrence felt protective about the poems when Pinker passed on the request: 'On the whole, I would rather he *didn't* have the MS, but only a selection of the more impersonal poems' (ibid., p. 115). Lawrence suggested six such poems, and Harrison accepted three of the six suggestions. In all, only eighteen of the volume's sixty-one poems received prior magazine publication; and most of those had been much earlier, in 1913 and 1914.

That was certainly unfortunate, commercially, when Lawrence could earn perhaps a pound per poem; but worse was to follow. The volume was first turned down by the publishers William Collins; Pinker then sent it to Duckworth (who had published Lawrence's two previous volumes of poetry), but they did not take it either. Duckworth had had no success with *Amores* the previous year (the book was eventually remaindered) and they were now abandoning Lawrence as an author. It was not until the end of July 1917 that Pinker was able to tell Lawrence that the 'nice old-flavoured people' (ibid., p. 144) at Chatto and Windus were interested in the volume; but there was a catch. Chatto also insisted on some alterations if they were to take the book: 'we consider that some justifiable exception might be taken to certain passages appearing in the MS. as it stands' (ibid., p. 145 n. 1). Yet another volume with alterations demanded! Chatto wanted two whole poems omitted ('Song of a Man who is Loved' and 'Meeting Among the Mountains'), and six lines in three other poems either rewritten or cut completely; 'In addition we venture to question the good taste of the titles 'Candlemas' and 'Eve's Mass' as applied to poems of an amorous character' (ibid., p. 145 n. 1). 'Truly', as Lawrence wrote to Pinker, 'the ways and the taste of publishers is mysterious and beyond finding out'; he pointed out that 'Meeting Among the Mountains' had already been published, first in the *English Review*, and then in the utterly respectable volume *Georgian Poetry 1913–1915*. It was perhaps the narrator's identification with Christ that offended Chatto: it is hard to see what else could have done. 'Song of a Man who is Loved' was more obviously a candidate for censorship, in spite of Lawrence's insistence that it was 'beautiful, necessary, and innocuous as a sprig of mignonette' (ibid., p. 146): its first line runs 'Between her breasts is my home, between her breasts'. That was probably too much for Chatto.

Lawrence was, however, prepared to make the verbal alterations asked for, and he agreed to change the objectionable titles; he didn't even much mind the *Georgian Poetry* poem being omitted, though, as he pointed out, it might have been good for the volume to contain something readers would find familiar. But he did feel strongly about 'Song of a Man who is Loved', and pleaded for its retention. Chatto, however, were quite determined, and wrote to Pinker that:

> the list of poems to be omitted ... by no means represents the total of those which appeared to us and to our Readers to be questionable. But it has never been our intention to emasculate the volume of all such poems. Only, in view of past history, it has seemed desirable from the firm's standpoint, that the continuously sexual tone of the volume should be modified. The list as first presented ... represents the minimum of omissions which we believe could safely insure this result, and to that list we are afraid that we must stand. (*Letters*, III, p. 148 n. 1)

The phrase 'in view of past history' shows what Chatto had in mind: as the author of *The Rainbow* Lawrence was in no position to bargain or insist. Pinker sent Lawrence the publishers' letter, and he replied: 'I have taken out the two poems. Publishers are fools, one wants to spit on them. – But it is not worth while making a real breach' (*Letters*, III, p. 148). Chatto would not be paying very much: a royalty of 15%, and an advance of £20. Lawrence, hopeful as ever, would have liked '20% after the first 1000 or 2000 ... I always have hopes of the future' (ibid., p. 155). But Chatto would only print a first edition of 1000 copies (selling half of them as sheets to Huebsch for American publication); they never ran to a second edition.

But even if it only brought in £20 (less 10%), the book was still the 'one bright beam in my publishing sky' (ibid., p. 156). Apart from their refusal to print the two poems, Chatto proved themselves to be the 'nice old-flavoured people' Lawrence thought them: they provided him with an extra six copies of the book, over and above his six official author's copies, and they even gave him his £20 advance when he signed the contract in September 1917, rather than on the November publication day stipulated in the contract. But in spite of Chatto's genuine niceness, the episode provided yet another demonstration of the terrible weakness in 1917 of Lawrence's position as an author.

He had had to ask Pinker for more money in June, though 'I

don't like asking you for advances, when prospects are no brighter than mine at the moment' (ibid., p. 135). The money he was earning was dreadfully little; there was a steady (if tiny) trickle from the *English Review*, for the articles and the poems they had taken during the year: £13 10s came to hand in September (ibid., p. 161), for example. There were continuing royalties from Lawrence's poems in *Georgian Poetry* (£7 15s in June): and the Duckworth books (including *The White Peacock*, which they had taken over from Heinemann in 1915) provided another trickle. But Lawrence's income must have been about half again what it had been in 1916; only the fact that he had saved from the previous year, and was living in Cornwall and hardly ever left it, allowed him to survive.

Through the summer of 1917 he had been occupying himself with yet another version of his 'philosophy', and this version (called *At the Gates* but not surviving) he was even prepared to try and publish in book form; he went as far as to remark that 'Bits of it that might be very unpopular, I might leave out' (ibid., p. 155). But, all the same, no publisher would take it: Chatto, for example, though 'much interested' by it, turned it down in October.[3] Lawrence also tried to plan an edition of *Women in Love* with the publisher Cecil Palmer, which (however) again came to nothing. But, with no market for his philosophy, knowing he could not publish fiction, and with poetry paying so little, he resourcefully tried yet another genre: literary criticism. As he put it, 'in the hopes of making money, for money is a shy bird', he began the essays later published as *Studies in Classic American Literature*. He thought that these at least might help 'relieving my ominous financial prospects' by being published in America, and – he told Pinker – 'We might get the essays into a periodical here in England – seems my only hope – I won't and can't write *Strand* stories' (ibid., p. 155). But he was also pessimistic about their chances (ibid., p. 163).

Apart from regular revisions to the typescript of *Women in Love* which he himself held, Lawrence wrote no fiction between January 1917 and the end of the year; certainly not 'Strand' stories. In May 1917 he explained that this was because he found:

> people ultimately boring: and you can't have fiction without people. So fiction does not, at the bottom, interest me any more. I am weary of humanity and human things. One is happy in the thoughts only that transcend humanity. (*Letters*, III, p. 127)

Before believing in the literal truth of this – because the reviser of *Women in Love* clearly did not find people 'ultimately boring', and he was also keeping up an extensive correspondence with many different people – we should remember that Lawrence was writing to Middleton Murry, who tended to profess a deep faith in humanity. Lawrence was declaring his opposition to Murry, as well as to the psychological novel which for many people represented the finest achievement of fiction: Lawrence found it a dead end. And we should remember that he also had on his hands an enormously long and complex novel: 'I hate having it lie by', he remarked in February 1918 (*Letters*, III, p. 206). Why write fiction? There was clearly no market for it, and little enough interest in it. So Lawrence would for a time banish humanity, and refuse to write of it, or (he would insist) for it; would live apart and pursue his own life, in Cornwall.

Until, that is, in a flurry of opposition to the small colony of artists and intellectuals gathering in West Cornwall, the police authorities took the Lawrences' friend Cecil Gray to court in the autumn of 1917 for having a light momentarily showing from an upstairs window – he was fined £20[4] – and, on 17 October, after a brief search of their house, the military declared that Lawrence and Frieda would themselves have to leave such a sensitive area. Frieda was German, their house overlooked the Atlantic shipping lanes, and German submarines were taking a heavy toll of allied convoys. They were given three days to leave.

Quite apart from the violent and emotional disruption of their lives which this meant, it was also a dreadful blow financially. The cottage was cheap, and the rent paid; and it turned out that their landlord was unco-operative when they tried to bring their term of occupancy to an end: he very much wanted another year's rent from them (ibid., p. 225). Lawrence had also been growing his own vegetables, and helping at the farm down the road. Now the Lawrences were homeless, and for the first time utterly dependent upon the charity of others. Friends in London took them in; rooms were lent, flats briefly borrowed; they went for a while down to Berkshire, to the cottage owned by Dollie Radford where they had nearly gone two years earlier (it was 'not an ideal – cold, a little comfortless' – (ibid., p. 195). Just after Christmas 1917 they travelled up to the Midlands, to stay with Lawrence's sister Ada and to look for a cottage in that region; Ada was very keen on having her brother back in the Midlands near her, and was prepared to pay his rent for him, though Lawrence himself was much less happy about going back to live so close to his married sisters. Ada in particular always had a tendency to mother him, with all that that implied. Rather as they hoped, perhaps, Lawrence and Frieda found nothing; they went back to Berkshire for a month. It was a restless, in some ways helpless existence, but they could manage nothing else: 'I am up a very high tree of poverty just now' (ibid., p. 202), Lawrence remarked: 'We are rather in a tight corner just now, what with money and houselessness' (ibid., p. 208). Lawrence was particularly anxious about the safety of the corrected typescript of *Women in Love*, his sole real hope of substantial reward in the future. He must have been carrying it around with him, but 'While it remains in manuscript, and myself always in such a state of jeopardy, I feel it may get lost' (ibid., p. 212). Sometime in the winter of 1917–18, he even wrote a little of the novel which, years later, became *Aaron's Rod*; he probably wrote some version of the satirical scenes in London which appear in its first half. But he wrote very little else, and was (as often in winter) frequently ill: 'I sit in bed and look at the trees and learn songs from a book and wait for the Judgement Day – there is not much more to be said for me' (ibid., p. 198).

By mid-February 1918, their money was 'coming to a dead end' (ibid., p. 210), and a letter to Pinker of 2 February 1918 sets out Lawrence's sense of his prospects as an author.

> I am sorry to tell you that I am coming to the last end of all my resources, as far as money goes. Do you think that Arnold Bennett or somebody like that, who is quite rich out of literature, would give me something to get along with. It is no use my trying to delude myself that I can make money in this world that is. – But there is coming a big smash-up, after which my day will begin. And as the smash up is not far off, so I am not very far off from a walk-in ... Do try and tempt a little money out of some rich good-natured author for me, will you – or I don't know what I shall do. And really, you know, one can't begin taking one's hat off to money, at this late hour of the day. I'd rather play a tin whistle in the street. (*Letters*, III, pp. 205–6)

Pinker sent the letter to Bennett, who offered to subscribe something – 'say £1 a week for at least a year' – if others would do the same. But no others were forthcoming; and though Bennett sent a loan of £25 anonymously through Pinker,[5] Lawrence began to feel abandoned. He was also growing angry with Pinker for not taking his distress seriously, and at least gathering in the money he was owed:

> Two weeks ago I wrote to you that my affairs are very low, and asked for help, if you could give it. But you have not answered at all.
>   I am afraid in another fortnight I shall not have a penny to buy bread and margarine. Would you be so good as to ask Austin Harrison to let me have something. He owes me, I suppose, for the last two essays . . . I suppose I am a fair amount in your debt. How much? (*Letters*, III, p. 211)

Lawrence always hated being in debt to anyone – hence the akward tone of this letter. Pinker acknowledged that Lawrence was in debt to him, to the tune of about £15, but he was happy to let that state of affairs continue. All Pinker could do however, apart from continuing to act as banker, was to collect the money from the *English Review*, discreetly pass on Bennett's money, and suggest that Lawrence might try to get a grant from some official body like the Royal Literary Society. Lawrence accordingly pursued that idea through Cynthia Asquith and her friends.

Lawrence's annoyance with Pinker would grow steadily over the next 12 months; he hated being under an obligation, and unfairly commented that his agent – a cheerful and self-confident man – would 'dangle a prospective fish on the end of a line, with grinning patronage, and just jerk it away every letter' (*Letters*, III, p. 216). But it did not pay Pinker to keep Lawrence poor; he was doubtless trying to suggest any possible sources of income. Harrison had at least printed two more of Lawrence's essays in January and February 1918, relatively popular ones called 'Love' and 'Life', and they produced another trickle of money: 9 guineas this time (ibid., p. 217), presumably from what was now Lawrence's standard *English Review* rate of 5 guineas per piece, less Pinker's fee. Individual friends helped, too: Cynthia Asquith dug into the pockets of her friends and got Lawrence £5 to be going along with, as well as doing what she could to persuade Charles Whibley to influence the Royal Literary Fund on Lawrence's behalf; and Montague Shearman (a friend of Koteliansky and others) sent £10.

It is interesting that, in such a situation, Lawrence made no attempt to find other employment. His attitude seems to have been, quite consciously, that he was a writer and that he intended to remain one. He had worked hard and well, for relatively little reward; he had up to now made his living as a writer; and he intended to go on doing so. For the present he would have to accept charity, though for years afterwards he conscientiously went on repaying his debts to his friends and his family, and to individuals like Bennett. So be it. He thanked Shearman for his money, and remarked:

> I have never been so tight put – for money and everything else – damnable. But I don't mind taking from you: no, I am glad to have the money from your hand. But I hate depriving you of it. One's man's gain is another man's loss. But I can't help it. (*Letters*, III, p. 216)

He finally repaid Shearman in 1928.

But Lawrence had fewer and fewer literary projects on hand. The American essays were finished, and Koteliansky had typed them for him; a batch of poems called 'All of Us', written in 1916, might be recovered from Pinker (who had failed to place them) and sold to the printer and publisher Cecil Beaumont: though such a sale would only bring in '£8. or £9. for them – think it is too little – not worth having them published for so little' (*Letters*, III, p. 221). And, anyway, Beaumont 'shied' at them – 'he found them too doubtful little pills – it's a shy world' (ibid., p. 234). There was also an idea that Beaumont might publish *Women in Love*, selling it 'at a guinea a copy, by subscription – says it could be made to pay. I am bored' (ibid., p. 219). It turned out to be an impossibly costly project; Lawrence was quoted a figure of around £370 just for printing the novel, which seems absurdly high: a commercial publisher, even in wartime, would not have had to pay more than about £150.

Apart from that, and apart from going on with the American literature essays, Lawrence could only think of once more going through his old manuscripts and getting out 'a few old things that might possibly meet a publisher in these days of leanness' (ibid., p. 230). His only book in the last year and a half had been of poetry; he knew that, as a poet, he was less dangerous and frightening to publishers than as a writer of fiction (or philosophy). In fact, he constructed two new books of poetry during April 1918, including

an 'impeccable' new one for Beaumont called *Bay*, which made
slightly more money than the old one – though Lawrence was still
doubtful whether it was 'worth while to give you these poems
outright, for £10 – in my present state of hopeless poverty' (ibid.,
p. 233). However, there was little else he could do; and at least
Beaumont's encouragement suggested that there might be a market for such tiny books. 'I shall make other little books of poems
like these', he told Pinker: 'It strikes me as the best thing to do'
(ibid., p. 238). In mid-June, he sent Pinker a second book; but he
also showed how far his position had changed since Chatto's
objections to *Look! We Have Come Through!*: 'I think there is nothing
in it to offend anybody – tell me if you think there is: or if you think
there is anything that would be better left out' (ibid., p. 255). Pinker
naturally sent the volume first to Chatto, but they refused it: *Look!
We Have Come Through!* had not been profitable for them either.
However, a suggestion from Lawrence to his agent that Martin
Secker might take the new volume (ibid., p. 262) resulted in Secker
offering to publish the misleadingly titled volume *New Poems*;
while his terms were 'better than nothing – a trifle better than
nothing' (ibid., p. 274). We don't know exactly what those terms
were; but Secker's edition of 500 copies, retailing at only 2/6 each,
could not have provided Lawrence with an advance of more than
£10 at the very most, and it may well have been less. Secker also
asked Lawrence to remove the poem 'Late in Life', and Lawrence –
in his new mood of not offending – told Pinker 'I don't care if
Secker leaves out the poem – but I don't want to hear his literary
criticisms' (ibid., p. 278). The poem was dropped. The fact, however, that Secker issued a 'New Edition reset' of *New Poems* in August
1919 (ibid., p. 379 n. 1) suggests that he had managed to sell out the
tiny 1918 edition; and following this first, miniature success, Secker
continued as Lawrence's main English publisher through the
1920s. To that extent *New Poems* was extraordinarily significant.

During the summer of 1918, fewer remarks about his financial
situation appear in Lawrence's correspondence than in previous
years. This should not, however, lead us into thinking that he was
doing better; it was in part because, having abandoned his desire
not to live too close to his family, he was now living in Middleton-
by-Wirksworth in Derbyshire, in a house paid for by his sister Ada;
partly because he was becoming used to getting by in a situation of
extreme poverty; partly because he was by now reconciled to the
fact that he could not live by his writing, and that what he could

earn – he calculated it as 'considerably less than £100' between August 1917 and June 1918 (ibid., p. 249) – was practically a supplement to the charity which otherwise supplied his necessities; and partly because that charity – for example, $200 from Amy Lowell in March 1918, and £50 from the Royal Literary Society in July – meant that he was just able to keep his head above water. On being told that Huebsch was accepting *Look! We Have Come Through!* for American publication, his reaction was pleasure, but not only pleasure: 'One day – God knows how late a day however – the Americans will read me. But be damned to them – it is the same to me, so long as I can go on by myself: which isn't so easy, after all' (ibid., p. 255). Going on 'by myself' was all that really mattered to him; and, for the moment, his writing by itself did not allow him to do that. Huebsch's *Look! We Have Come Through!* made him $37.05 in its first year: almost exactly £10.[6]

His only other project on hand, his essays on American literature – which as late as June 1918 he had told Pinker he didn't 'dare offer to publishers in the present state of opinion and tyranny' (ibid., p. 255) – he began sending his agent at the start of August 1918, while expressing a new kind of optimism that may have been specially contrived for the encouragement of Pinker. And yet his optimism was also extraordinary and magnificent: he knew how good his work really was:

> we may really sell these essays, both in America and in England – and really make something with them. I have a feeling that they will make all the difference. Will you send Harrison this first essay at once? He might do it quickly . . .
> Really, I place my hopes of the world on these essays, so you will help me with them as much as possible. I know it has been a thankless job so far. But it won't always be so. (*Letters*, III, p. 270)

Harrison, at the *English Review*, was indeed persuaded by Pinker to take the first – and shortly afterwards the seven subsequent – essays, which appeared at monthly intervals in the magazine between November 1918 and June 1919. The *English Review* had continued to be the only magazine in England to print pieces by Lawrence regularly, during the war; three more poems, from the *Bay* collection, had appeared there in June 1918, and another six of the *Bay* poems had appeared in the American magazine *Poetry*, which had also stuck by Lawrence in difficult times: *Poetry* paid

him 7 guineas for the poems. However, magazine payments too
had gone down, in wartime: Harrison offered only the usual 5
guineas for the first American essay, and apparently paid the same
for the subsequent ones. The eight American essays together
cannot have made more than about 40 guineas – only 36 guineas to
Lawrence. And although Lawrence felt that 'they would make a
decent little book – about 70,000 words' (*Letters*, III, p. 287), no one
at this stage was going to offer to publish a book of literary criticism
by Lawrence.

It was at this stage that, in some despair, he took up the writing
of the 'history book for schools' which Vere Collins, a sympathetic
friend in Oxford University Press who had been impressed by
Lawrence's grasp of history, had some time earlier suggested
Lawrence might do. Back in July 1918 he had first considered the
idea, and written a draft of three chapters with some pleasure and
speed; but when the book was actually commissioned from him, it
turned out to be something he hated doing. 'I am struggling with a
European History for Schools – and cursing myself black in the
face' (ibid., pp. 304), he noted in December 1918: 'I hate it like
poison', he remarked later in the month (ibid., p. 309). He went on
with it simply because the publisher 'will give me £50 when I give
them the MS., so that will solve my financial difficulties for the
moment' (ibid., pp. 321–2): but a major imaginative writer was
being condemned to wretched piggling work'.

II

With the completion of his essays on American literature –
Lawrence finished revising them at the end of September 1918 – he
was practically at an end of his literary projects, as well as at the
end of his patience. He felt in a 'sort of cocoon'. In the words of
some biographical notes he made for a friend going on an
American lecture tour, he had 'always lived with no money –
always shall – very sick of the world, like to die with the nausea of
it' (ibid., p. 282). All he and Frieda could do was to stay in
Derbyshire, 'trying to be patient'; all he had to work on was the
novel he had begun at the end of 1917, which he was again 'slowly
working at':

though I feel it's not much use. No publisher will risk my last, and none will risk this, I expect. I can't do anything in the world today – am just choked. – I don't know how on earth we shall get through another winter – how we shall ever find a future. Humanity as it stands, and myself as I stand, we just seem mutually impossible to one another. The ground dwindles under one's feet – what next, heaven knows. (*Letters*, III, p. 280)

The answer to the question 'what next' was not slow in coming; on 26 September 1918, Lawrence was again medically examined for military service, and this time conscripted as a 'C2' man: 'Fit for non-military service'. It was unlikely that he would actually have to serve; but the decision provoked him, for the first time since his anxiety for the success of *Sons and Lovers* in the summer of 1913, to talk about trying to get 'a bit of a job, to prevent them calling me up for some of their dirty work' (*Letters*, III, p. 289). He had, after all, trained as a schoolmaster: 'I want a job under the Ministry of Education: not where I shall be kicked about like an old can: I've had enough of that' (ibid., p. 287).

It is striking that it had taken so long for Lawrence to try to get a job. Only with *Movements in European History* had he ever taken on writing work that was unsympathetic to him; and even now, he was considering a job not only 'because it is hopeless to go on any longer, with no money and no hope' (ibid., p. 289), but to prevent himself being called up for menial, non-military duties. With the shortage of manpower in England during the war, getting a job might have been possible earlier – though, as he told the Royal Literary Society when they were assessing him for his grant in June 1918, 'I have not tried to obtain work in any Government department, because my health does not allow me to undertake any regular employment' (ibid., p. 253). But that had been at best a half-truth. Lawrence certainly was frequently ill, but the point was that he really did not want to waste his time doing anything except the work he had singled himself out to do, and which he felt he did exceptionally well. Now, however, under the pressure of an even stronger necessity than poverty, he went to London and saw G. S. Freeman, the editor of the *TLS* and deputy editor of *The Times*: 'he will give me some work . . . I must keep the accursed military at bay till the war ends' (ibid., p. 291). Lawrence tried to write what Freeman wanted: 'tried so hard'. But 'it wouldn't work in me – no go' (ibid., p. 297); and though he eventually managed to produce 'four nice little essays' on education, they were never printed.

However, within a few days of going to London he became convinced that it would be 'peace soon. So be damned to all jobs and jobbers' (ibid., p. 292). He gave up London and the *TLS* and he and Frieda went back to Berkshire. They gathered chestnuts and bilberries, and wood-flakes for fuel, 'in the late, wistful autumn';[7] and Lawrence started the first piece of fictional writing he had done for almost a year. It was as if the ending of the war released him to recreate his world imaginatively again. Within a few days he had finished the play *Touch and Go* – 'very nice – which *might* be acted'. He felt that, if it were, he would have to 'remain anonymous – my name is like red pepper in people's noses':

> But no, truly, I am ashamed in daylight to confess it, I have written a play out of my deep and earnest self, fired up my last sparks of hope in the world, as it were, and cried out like a Balaams ass. I believe the world yet might get a turn for the better, if it but had a little shove that way. And this is my attempt – I believe the last I am capable of – or the first, perhaps – at a shove. (*Letters*, III, p. 293)

The play was based on a topical situation, and drew upon some of the characters from the unpublished *Women in Love*. The theatre tended to infect most authors of the period with the belief that they might make a breakthrough into sudden success and spectacular prosperity; but as Lawrence's remarks suggest, it was less because he thought it would make his fortune than because he wanted to provide a 'shove' to his world that he wrote his play. It was one of his self-conceived roles as a writer, and he was – in spite of himself, in spite of the last three years – taking it up again.

Within a month, too, by the end of November 1918, he had 'written three short stories', and felt they 'ought to sell . . . I hope we shall sell them, for I can't live' ((*Letters*, III, p. 299). One of them was, at last, the *Strand* story he had been joking about for three years, and which Pinker continued to hope Lawrence could write: 'Tickets Please' appeared in the *Strand* magazine in April 1919. But it was his only story ever to appear there.

Lawrence's financial and personal situation was never going to be as desperate again as it had been during 1916, 1917 and 1918, but he was not out of the wood yet. In December 1918 he had received £10 from J. D. Beresford and another, anonymous person, and wrote to thank Beresford:

What a lot of trouble you are taking for me. I wish I were a more satisfactory person. – But now I have got £10. money ceases to trouble me, I go gaily on, since the morrow, at any rate, is all right . . . Don't you bother any more: the skies may open. (*Letters*, III, p. 310)

In February 1919 he had exactly £20 in the world – the payment had come in for yet another of the American essays in the *English Review*, and £15 had come from – at last – 'selling up in Cornwall'. But he rejected yet another attempt by his friend Koteliansky to lend him £10: 'If I thought I had thirty pounds to lash out with, heaven knows what I might do' (*Letters*, III, p. 327). The worst thing to happen in February 1919 was that he went down with the influenza that was sweeping the country; this not only meant that he was wretchedly ill (he nearly died), but that he was delayed in revising the schools history book and therefore in receiving his advance. He could only finish it at the start of May and at last get his £50: 'There is a sum for you!' (ibid., p. 347). It was, ironically, the most he had earned for any book since *The Rainbow*.

III

The spring of 1919, after his illness, Lawrence felt marked 'a new phase' (*Letters*, III, p. 332), though he wasn't able to go outdoors until the end of March, and was not out of the doctor's hands until the middle of April. Now that the war was over, he and Frieda at last would be able to go abroad again (Frieda was most anxious to see her family in Germany); it seemed important that he should start to write again, and to earn what he could before going. But he felt, all the same, that 'I don't want to write – still less do I want to publish anything.' It still felt 'like throwing one's treasures in a bog' (ibid., p. 348); and 1919, in spite of the *Strand* story and the school history book, showed very little change from the previous years. The excitement, early in 1919, that Middleton Murry's editorship of the magazine the *Athenæum* might lead to a good deal of Lawrence's work being published there turned out to be a huge disappointment. Murry only accepted one brief essay, 'Whistling of Birds', and rejected Lawrence's other contributions, the essay 'Clouds' and the splendid sketches of early family life in the Lawrence household, 'Adolf' and 'Rex' – in spite of their being deliberately made 'pleasant and a bit old-fashioned' (ibid., p. 332), as a professional writer could indeed make them. Some more poems appeared in the American magazine *Poetry*, and a couple of essays got into print in America towards the end of the year; but that was all. Only one of the short stories he had written at the end of 1918 had found a publisher, and the play *Touch and Go* was neither performed nor printed (though plans emerged for both). Lawrence's only book to be published during 1919 was the tiny, long delayed and already-paid-for *Bay*. Not a year since 1910 had gone by when so little of his work appeared in book form. For an energetic and prolific writer, it was a dismal situation; even with the war ended, it took a long time both for the publishing business to get back on to something like a pre-war footing, and for Lawrence to be rehabilitated as a writer. The school history book appeared under the name '*Laurence H. Davison*, because they were afraid of my own name' (*Letters*, V, p. 117); and even 'Whistling of Birds' in the *Athenæum* acquired the pseudonym 'Grantorto', 'Great Wrong'.

So – what was he to write, and for whom? To start with, he had no idea. The school history done at the end of April,

> I have nothing on hand at all, can turn tramp or bolshevist or government official, any of those occupations one takes up in one's leisure . . . I am afraid of becoming bored at last. (*Letters*, III, pp. 350–1)

He again promised Pinker, however, that 'for the next six weeks' he would write 'nothing but short stories, if the short stories will come. It's as good a promise as I can make' (*Letters*, III, p. 355). Pinker had, after all, managed to sell a Lawrence story to the *Strand* magazine, and apparently still believed that Lawrence's way back to success as a writer was through unexceptionable short stories. It was certainly true that Lawrence could earn far more from them than from his 5 guinea essays: £20 or £30 could be earned by a single story; the *Strand* story paid over £20, and 'The Fox', which sold in June 1919, made £30, although it was not unfortunately published – or paid for – for another year.

Lawrence accordingly announced to Pinker that he would write six stories; he was a professional writer, and if his job was to write stories – then stories he would write. He actually wrote three: 'Fanny and Annie', 'Monkey Nuts' and 'You Touched Me'. It so happened, too, that small lump sums of money continued to come his way; following the money for the history (together with another instalment of the now regularly expected money from the *English Review*), he received an unexpected £20 out of a fund run by Edward Marsh out of royalties received from his memoir of Rupert Brooke; and Lawrence was actually able to send Catherine Carswell £1 for her train journey to Hermitage in mid-May, just as she had sent him money for his journey to Gloucestershire the previous August. It was the first act of financial charity he had been capable of for years. And there was another £29 from Pinker in June – probably the *Strand* money for 'Tickets Please' together with the final *English Review* instalments.

However, in spite of this – very modest – run of luck and success, Lawrence's thoughts were again turning towards America as a place where he might live, or earn most of his living: 'I'm sure I can make enough to live on in America, fairly easily' (*Letters*, III, p. 367). What sold there continued to pay well, but not enough sold. 'The Fox', for example, accepted in England, was turned down in America as 'rather too unpleasant in theme and conception ... its appeal would have a rather limited audience'; while Lawrence's royalties from Huebsch between April 1919 and April 1920 came to only $59.10, equivalent to 16 guineas.[8] There were, however, tentative plans from Huebsch for him to embark on a lecture tour in America, as a number of British writers were currently doing. That plan did not work out, and by August 1919 Lawrence had decided not to try to go to America yet; but the idea stayed in his mind and would come to fruition a couple of years later.

For the moment, in the late summer of 1919, he collaborated on a translation of the Russian writer Shestov with his friend S. S. Koteliansky – who had stood loyally by him all through the war, with free (if rather dreadful) typing, offers of money which he could ill afford, and temporary accommodation in London whenever Lawrence and Frieda needed it. The Shestov translation was perhaps Lawrence's first way of being able to repay some of that debt, just as the money to Catherine Carswell had been a repayment for *her* kindness and money when Lawrence needed it. As well as revising the translation, he also wrote Koteliansky a foreword for the book, while characteristically insisting that Koteliansky take two-thirds of any profits.

He also insisted to Koteliansky that 'I don't want my name

printed as a translator', giving the reason that 'It won't do for me to
appear to dabble in too many things' (*Letters*, III, p. 381). According
to Koteliansky many years later, Lawrence felt that his reputation
as a creative writer might be damaged if he were seen having to
work as a translator:[9] another sign of his care for his reputation,
even in a climate as arid as 1919. But it seems rather more likely
that he wanted Koteliansky to appear responsible for the book
because he did not want to have to pay Pinker 10% on it (or to lose
Koteliansky any bit of his advance), as he would have to do if he
appeared as co-author or co-translator. Accordingly, 'no Pinker'
(ibid., p. 398). This was the first sign of another significant development. In spite of Pinker's support during the war, Lawrence now
wanted to take responsibility for his own work.

It is easy to be misled into thinking that Lawrence did not very
much bother about his 'literary property' by remarks such as 'it is
hard to imagine the pitch to which I don't care. I'm always having
to kick myself into making an effort for my own rights' (ibid.,
p. 403): or – to Koteliansky, about Shestov – 'You keep the
Agreement – I am so careless' (ibid., p. 405). In fact he cared a great
deal; especially at a time like 1919, when he was trying to
re-establish himself as a writer; and he was also an habitually tidy
and organised person. But it was also true that he did not *deeply*
care about business matters: he mostly wanted simply to safeguard
his capacity to earn his living, and then get on with what really
interested him – the writing, the travelling and the living.

We can observe a characteristic care for his 'literary property' in
his action over the American edition of *New Poems*. Upon being
advised by Huebsch that the book – appearing in America 20
months after the English edition – had no copyright in America,
and that the best way of assuring copyright would be to alter the
book in some way, he immediately wrote a short preface for it –
while expressing his irritation, yet again, over the way Pinker had
failed to arrange things for him. His irritation was yet another sign
of his alienation from Pinker. He had asked his agent in November
1918 whether he would like to end their agreement, and Pinker had
then said that he did not wish to. Although his business with
Lawrence had made him very little money during the last four
years, with the end of the war there was a chance that Lawrence's
publications would re-establish themselves: and thus at last re-pay
Pinker for his support. It was not surprising that Pinker now
preferred to stick with Lawrence. But here was Huebsch on the

point of bringing out a book, and Pinker declaring that he knew nothing of Huebsch's intentions. Lawrence wrote angrily and perhaps justifiably to Huebsch:

> This is what one has an agent for. – I wish you would tell me personally what the sales are, and what becomes due in royalties: the business part: also make the arrangements with me – and if Pinker has to come in, he can come in after. (*Letters*, III, p. 388)

Lawrence's anger was perhaps a little contrived: he was looking for a way out of his obligation to his agent, and finding Pinker at fault was an obvious way. The whole basis of the relationship between literary agent and client, of course, is that the client should agree 'not to send anything to any publisher direct – only to act through you' (*Letters*, III, p. 705), as Lawrence formulated it to the agency Curtis Brown when he took his business there in 1921. The affair of Huebsch's *New Poems* was the first time that Lawrence deliberately went behind Pinker's back. He had previously committed only minor infringements of their professional relationship, such as when he apparently tried to get a payment from Harrison and the *English Review* direct and not via Pinker (ibid., p. 310), in 1918: and even then he was not trying to defraud Pinker of his percentage, but only trying to get the money more quickly.

But this declaration to Huebsch in August 1919 came at the turning point. The arrangements for the Shestov translation (without Pinker) had been designed mainly to benefit his friend Koteliansky; but Lawrence was also starting to feel that he could manage 'the business part' of his work better and more profitably than his agent was doing. He had begun to make arrangements in July and August 1919 for his play *Touch and Go* to be published through Douglas Goldring, telling the latter that 'I should like you to do *Touch and Go*' (ibid., p. 372) and 'You may announce it in your series of plays' (ibid., p. 374). All he told Pinker was 'I wish you would let me go ahead and do as I like with this play – on my own' (ibid., p. 374). Pinker naturally refused to accept that, and Lawrence at first reassured him that 'I will tell Douglas Goldring to arrange with you in a little while'. In fact he was encouraging Goldring to go ahead on his own; and then – when it was too late – disingenuously told Pinker that 'I'm sorry, Douglas Goldring and Walter Peacock were arranging it before I really knew' (ibid.,

p. 385). Pinker naturally protested, but Lawrence insisted that 'I explained to you that owing to circumstances I had to settle *Touch and Go* with the People's Theatre agent, Walter Peacock, – so that he'll have to go through with it' (ibid., p. 396). Pinker probably saw through the explanation, and asked himself how long it would be before he would be giving up Lawrence as a client altogether.[10]

But Lawrence's taking responsibility for the play was only a start. He was also beginning to feel that, with the war over, *Women in Love* should find a publisher; but there was no sign that Pinker was doing anything about it. So Lawrence himself started negotiations. Martin Secker, having done a new edition of *New Poems*, had also accepted the Shestov translation; he had always admired Lawrence's work. He had, at some stage, also expressed interest in the novel (he must have seen one of the typescript copies Pinker had of it), and in the autumn of 1919 was considering publication in the spring of 1920. Almost simultaneously, however, came a cable from the new American publisher Thomas Seltzer asking to see the novel. Lawrence immediately began to act as his own agent, rather than passing on the correspondence to Pinker. He told Seltzer that Secker would be publishing the book next spring; while simultaneously telling Secker that printed sheets would probably be available from Seltzer. He was obviously trying to make both publishers think that the other was going ahead, so as to commit them both into making firm plans for publication. But he also told Secker: 'don't speak yet to Pinker, wait a bit till I let you hear about America' (ibid., p. 391).

His behaviour caused almost immediate problems. He had written to his American publisher Huebsch about various publishing matters – remarking, incidentally, that 'I think I shan't let Pinker make any more agreements' – and had mentioned in passing that he was sending *Women in Love* to 'some other New York people who asked to see it – presumed you were not keen on it – you must have seen the MS – Pinker has had it for two years' (ibid., p. 400). It was the natural assumption to make: Pinker had reassured him that every possible publisher had been tried. And although, as Huebsch confessed, *The Rainbow* was currently out of print (ibid., p. 399 n. 1), he remained Lawrence's major American publisher: he had taken on *The Rainbow* when no one else would, had brought out *Twilight in Italy*, *Amores* and *The Prussian Officer* in 1916, and *Look! We Have Come Through!* in 1918; he was going to publish *New Poems*. Lawrence was also sending him the manuscript of *Studies in Classic American Literature* (again, without reference to Pinker). But, astonishingly, Huebsch had never seen *Women in Love*. When he heard about it, he was extremely angry that it was now in danger of passing him by: a successful novel would earn him far more than the Lawrence books he had so far published. He cabled Lawrence immediately: 'Certainly I want novel. Pinker never submitted' (ibid., p. 409 n. 1).

That was a staggering piece of news; but the cable arrived almost simultaneously with Lawrence setting off for Italy; Frieda had already left in mid-October 1919 to see her family in Germany. Lawrence, taking on his own shoulders a good deal of publishing responsibility, was now going away without even a direct forwarding address; he was having to use Koteliansky's London address. To be fair to him, he immediately tried to get the novel back from Seltzer – though without at this stage mentioning Huebsch's claim on it: he didn't want to make Seltzer think he had an American rival, and only told him that Martin Secker, in England, wanted the typescript to print from. Nor did he tell Huebsch how far he was committed to Seltzer; he implied that he was simply having the typescript returned so that he could send it straight to Huebsch. A literary agent is exactly the person one employs to resolve such problems: Lawrence was in a mess almost at once.

But it turned out that Seltzer was extremely pleased at having been given a chance (by the author himself) of publishing the novel; and in spite of Lawrence's demands that he send Secker the TS, he hung on to it. But he did more; he despatched a 'pledge to print it', and sent an advance of £50 on royalties (ibid., p. 429). All Lawrence could do – apart from being very pleased that at last someone was going to publish the novel and pay for it – was apologise profusely to Huebsch, and blame Pinker; and, not surprisingly, he took the chance of using the affair to break off his agreement with Pinker. Rather coldly, he wrote to his agent that 'What bit of work I have to place, I like to place myself. I am sure it isn't worth much to you' (ibid., p. 439).

Pinker must have written back asking whether Lawrence didn't think he was being a little ungrateful for all that had been done for him during the hard times of the war. Lawrence replied:

Yes, I am grateful to you for all you have done for me in the past. But I am an unsatisfactory person, I know. And therefore it would be best for me to act just on my own responsibility . . . I feel I have been an unpleasant handful for you, and am sorry. (*Letters*, III, p. 453)

But the fault was not only on Lawrence's side; as he himself wrote to the angry Huebsch:

Simply, it never occurred to me that Pinker could have had that MS. for almost two years, all the while assuring me that he was doing everything possible, without ever even mentioning it to you. It just didn't occur to me. I thought you'd seen it and turned it down months and months before ... If I'd thought Pinker hadn't shown you the MS. – he had 3 copies – wouldn't I have sent it you a year ago? (*Letters*, III, p. 466)

The fact that Pinker apparently never sent the novel to the man who was actually publishing Lawrence's work in America only provides evidence of Pinker's narrow approach to the American market (he preferred to deal with Doran), and his lack of faith in *Women in Love*. And while it is by no means certain that Huebsch would have accepted the novel during the war, at least he might have agreed to publish it as soon as the war was over.

The episode left Lawrence with an angry feeling about how he had been treated in the literary world, though his anger was also probably a cover for his bad conscience over Pinker:

Pinker, publishers, everybody ... treated me with such vagueness and evasiveness, as if I were an aimiable imbecile, and left me to contrive to live on sixpence – no, basta! Abbastanza ['No, that's enough']. One could eat ones old shoes, while Pinkers and publishers were complaisant and vague. That's why I've done with Pinker: whatever mess I make in the future, I'll make myself, not through an agent. (*Letters*, III, p. 466)

There is probably no way of judging the ultimate rights and wrongs of Lawrence's attitude. An agent's job, after all, is not to trouble his client with details, but to make sure he produces the right kind of material, to place his work as rewardingly as possible, and to keep him informed about his financial situation. And Pinker had done a great deal to support Lawrence during the war; had advanced him money, had got extra loans from friends like Arnold Bennett, had allowed Lawrence to get into debt with him, had tried to suggest what Lawrence had best produce. But Lawrence had never liked Pinker, any more than he liked most of the London literary world – he once referred to Pinker as 'that little parvenu snob of a procurer of books' (*Letters*, III, p. 136) – and he never felt that Pinker believed in his work. He believed that Pinker expected him to write commercially successful fiction; and Lawrence knew that he was not going to do that very often. It does, however, also seem clear that Pinker had not pursued the publication of Lawrence's work in America very efficiently; and, increasingly, that was where Lawrence's market appeared to be.

Anyway, Lawrence was now determined to make his own 'mess'. On 1 February 1920 he started to keep a diary of his correspondence, his dealings with publishers and of his financial situation. Although he was careful to record important details in the diary, problems were caused by the fact that – particularly during the hot summer in Sicily, where he was now based – he was often away from home. Correspondence also took a long time to get to Sicily, and as he wrote his letters by hand he retained no copies of his own side of the correspondence. He managed to survive without any agent in England for over a year, until April 1921, when with some misgivings he asked the literary agency Curtis Brown to take up his affairs for him. But he recognised from the start that, above everything else, he needed an agent to deal with his American publications; as soon as the break with Pinker was complete he took one on. However, instead of going to an established literary agency, he wrote to an old American friend, the journalist Robert Mountsier, to ask if Mountsier would like to handle his business affairs in the USA. He preferred to deal with a friend than with an agency; but it was not a very sensible move.

6

Struggling Through: 1919–21

The period of his writing starting in late 1919 was in every sense a new beginning for Lawrence, as he lived and worked abroad again, without an English agent, and with a whole career to rebuild. He had left England in November 1919, after scraping together all the money he could; for example, 'selling my books in Reading' (*Letters*, III, p. 407) at the end of October. He was also lucky, just before leaving in November, to get a cheque via his American publisher Huebsch for £20, for the magazine printing of his Introduction to Huebsch's edition of his *New Poems*. He was going, via friends of friends in Turin, to Florence, where he had asked Norman Douglas to get him a cheap room, and where he was to meet Frieda; he set off (he remembered) with 'nine pounds in my pocket and about twelve pounds lying in the bank in London'.[1] He and Frieda were on their way to yet more free accommodation: this time, a farmhouse in the Abruzzi mountains, south of Rome, which an English friend wished to consider as possible accommodation for herself and her children; the Lawrences would form an exploratory expedition.

The Abruzzi farmhouse, however, was quite impossible as winter quarters. Even Lawrence and Frieda, hardened travellers, could not take more than eight days of it: 'It is a bit staggeringly primitive' (ibid., p. 431). They fled to Capri, to accommodation which Compton Mackenzie quickly arranged for them. The friendship with Mackenzie on Capri, and Lawrence's subsequent correspondence with him, was particularly important for Lawrence; Mackenzie was a popular author with a great deal of knowledge about publishing and making money out of books. After his success with novels such as *The Passionate Elopement* and

Sinister Street before the war, with Secker, he had recently become a partner in Secker's publishing firm. Successful, knowledgeable, business-like, he was just the kind of person from whom the agent-less Lawrence could get advice.

Italy was not what Lawrence and Frieda had remembered from before the war – for one thing, it was 'frightfully expensive, particularly travelling', so that 'One lives on the financial verge as ever – but so be it' (ibid., p. 441). And a certain amount of money came in, as when Pinker settled his accounts and sent on Lawrence's accumulated American royalties in January 1920 – a rather splendid cheque for £105. This was yet another sign, together with the extra £20 for the *New Poems* introduction, that America was at last starting to pay better than England did for Lawrence's work. Amy Lowell also remained very helpful, and sent Lawrence a gift of $100 in lire in February. It was, however, 'a blow' when the Italian bank would not honour her cheque – not until June 1920 did Lawrence get the money. He still felt very poor; and in Italy, of course, he no longer had his family or friends to fall back on in an emergency. He wished he didn't have to take the money from Amy Lowell: 'it irks me a bit. Why can't I earn enough, I've done the work' (ibid., p. 475). What, interestingly, made things worse for him was the defence of him in the American press by the novelist Gilbert Cannan, whom he had known in Buckinghamshire in 1914. Cannan was now lecturing in America, and had promised to collect Lawrence some money while there. But Cannan made Lawrence feel 'I am a sort of charity-boy of literature, apparently. One is denied one's just rights, and then insulted with charity'. Accepting charity, as he had had to do so often during the war, was never easy for Lawrence; and when the charity was proffered by so smooth and accomplished a literary figure as Cannan, then it was doubly objectionable. Lawrence would have preferred simply to earn from what he had written ('I've done the work'), and leave it at that.

Between leaving England and finally settling in Sicily in March 1920 – Capri, in spite of Mackenzie's friendship, was too much of 'a nice cats cradle of semi-literary and pleni-literary pussies' (ibid., p. 471) – Lawrence wrote very little, though his journeys gave him a good deal to store up and use later: his arrival in Turin found its way into *Aaron's Rod*; the stay in Florence with Douglas (and his trip to Montecassino in January) were recreated in his Introduction to Maurice Magnus's *Memoirs of the Foreign Legion*; while the primitive life in the Abruzzi gave him the clue for the ending of *The Lost Girl*.

This was particularly appropriate, as he planned to start work as soon as he could on another novel. The log-jam was broken, his novels could once again be published, and he could once again earn the substantial lump sums which novels could generate. However, the 1917 novel *Aaron's Rod* still refused to get itself written; Lawrence turned again to the 1913 manuscript of 'The Insurrection of Miss Houghton', which it had been impossible to get back from Bavaria in 1916. He told his publisher Martin Secker – still on the verge of accepting *Women in Love* and even considering republishing *The Rainbow* – that this other novel, when rewritten, 'would be quite *unexceptional*, as far as the censor is concerned' (ibid., p. 459). He also told his American publisher Huebsch that – after *Women in Love* was out – then this other novel, 'a more possibly popular one' (ibid., p. 426), would be available. Lawrence was deliberately presenting his as yet unwritten novel as a genuine commercial possibility, one with which he would reward the publisher brave enough to risk the large, difficult and probably uncommercial novels, *The Rainbow* and *Women in Love*. And he finally rewrote the old 'Insurrection' as *The Lost Girl* between March and May 1920.

However, Secker's terms for publishing Lawrence's novels at first turned out most disagreeable. He wanted Lawrence to sell the copyright of *The Rainbow* outright to him for £200 (ibid., p. 468), and Lawrence had sufficient confidence in the selling potential of even that book to refuse any such suggestion. We can compare his anxiety, later in 1920, for his friend Catherine Carswell and her prize-winning novel *Open the Door!*: 'My hat, I hope you're not sold outright to that Melrose. What you do want is money, so you must get it' (ibid., p. 537). Feeling that Secker's terms were impossible, Lawrence turned instead to negotiations with Duckworth for both *The Rainbow* and for *Women in Love*.

His negotiations for the two novels turned out to be long and complicated. Having finally agreed (greatly to Huebsch's annoyance) that Seltzer would publish *Women in Love* in America, it then took Lawrence four months to persuade Seltzer to send the typescript (or a copy of it) back to England for potential English publishers to see. Seltzer had a reason for his delay; to try and elude the 'smut-hounds', he would be producing *Women in Love* as a privately published, expensive, $15 book. At the current exchange rate of $3.73 to £1 sterling, that meant a novel costing the equivalent of £4, whereas the normal publishing price for a novel would be (post-war) 9/- in England and $2.00 in America. It was vital that no English copies of the novel got into America and undersold Seltzer's edition; so he stalled over sending the typescript to an English publisher. Seltzer had at first thought of selling his edition at $25, but even Lawrence thought that that

> seems much for a price. But I suppose I must depend on a succés d'estime at the best, and at the worst, a succés de scandale. If so, let them pay for their scandal. Pah! – and for their esteem. How it wearies me. (*Letters*, III, p. 485)

But if matters were relatively uncomplex – if protracted – in America, because Lawrence had in Seltzer a publisher who liked the novel and who very much wanted to print it, in England new difficulties emerged. Duckworth refused to take *The Rainbow* unless a particular chapter ('Shame', for certain) were cut; and Lawrence was also trying very hard to link the re-issue of the earlier novel with the first publication of *Women in Love* in England. He felt there was nothing he could do except go back to Secker; and was further encouraged to settle with him because Secker had privately taken advice from Compton Mackenzie, and was (he told the latter) 'prepared to take risks fortified by what I know to be your wishes'.[2] Secker now offered Lawrence a royalty on both *The Rainbow* and *Women in Love*, rather than demanding the outright sale of the books' copyrights.

Lawrence agreed with Secker that he could 'Start with *Women in Love* if you wish', but he also made the condition 'that you publish *The Rainbow* within a reasonable time after the publishing of *Women in Love*' (*Letters*, III, p. 499). The contract, however, stated that Secker's *Rainbow* would bring Lawrence his £100 advance no earlier than three months after publication, and that Secker could deduct from the £100 'all charges of any legal proceedings, if such should occur' (ibid., p. 525); the publication would also only go ahead at the publisher's discretion. And although Secker gave Lawrence to understand in May 1920 that – if all went well – he would be printing the book 'in early autumn' (ibid., p. 521), and he was examining a copy of Huebsch's bowdlerised 1916 edition in July, he did not actually reissue *The Rainbow* for another eight

years. Lawrence continued to press him about it, telling him in
January 1922:

> I hear from Huebsch that he sold out his five-dollar edition of *The
> Rainbow* at once. Why don't you take your courage in your hands
> and do the book this year? You would certainly sell it. (*Letters,*
> IV, p. 173)

Secker pretended to issue the novel in 1926 – the official date of the
reprint; but he did not advertise it, he did not place copies in the
copyright libraries, and no copy is known to exist. Not until 1928
did Secker dare risk putting *The Rainbow* publicly on sale again in
England, in his 3/6 reprint series, and then only in Huebsch's 1916
bowdlerised text. The full text was not printed in England again
until 1949. Lawrence was thus denied almost all royalties in
England during his life-time for the book which eventually became
one of his most famous and best-selling. His attempt in 1920 to link
the publication of the two novels had in theory been a very clever
plan, but in practice a complete failure; he had trusted that Secker
would follow his 'condition', and he had not attempted (as a
literary agent would have done) to tie Secker down to a firm
agreement. The 'discretion' Secker could – and did – exercise was
practically unlimited. But to Lawrence, in the spring of 1920, the
agreement seemed 'good so far. I trust to nothing these days'
(*Letters,* III, p. 500). It was just as well.

For his part, Secker was very worried about the venture of
publishing Lawrence at all; he told his partner Mackenzie that he
felt 'instinctively that anything to do with D.H. is rather
dangerous'.[3] Experience was to prove him right; the pleasure of
handling a Lawrence novel had cost his last publisher around £200,
plus a magistrate's censure, and while Secker never had that
experience, it remained true that Lawrence – out of the country –
risked nothing except the loss of his earning capacity; his publishers stood to lose far more. On the other hand, Secker wanted to
publish Lawrence: the more credit to him. Lawrence, however,
thought Secker 'rather in a funk, fearing the censor. I wish
someone could hold his hand while he gets the thing through'
(ibid., p. 517). Secker asked for cuts in *Women in Love,* too, before he
would publish it; even the title worried him, because he thought it
might suggest a lesbian relationship; and – in a book by the author
of the *Rainbow*'s chapter 'Shame' – that would be the first thing

objectors would look for. Secker was positive that 'it is important from D.H.L.'s point of view to be as unprovocative as possible in order to get the book taken anywhere. To give it that title is to tie a red rag on to it'.[4]

Secker's problems and fears were compounded by the fact that he had still not received from Seltzer the text which he would actually print; he had accepted the book without seeing the heavily revised final typescript, and made a worried joke about it perhaps differing from the version he had seen 'by having all the best bits taken out & a lot of Lesbianism written in'.[5] All spring and summer 1920 Lawrence pleaded with Seltzer to send off the typescript, while promising Secker that he was doing his best to get it; while Secker simply had to wait to see what he had actually contracted to print. Again, it seems probable that a literary agent would have had more success.

In the meanwhile, Lawrence had got on with his new version of the old 'Insurrection' manuscript, and he had gone back to his original idea of promoting the resulting novel – *The Lost Girl* – as a reward for frightened publishers. It was – Lawrence told Secker – 'amusing, and might be quite popular' (ibid., p. 503); and, best of all, it was not at all improper: 'quite fit for Mudies' (ibid., p. 512). The circulating libraries could still have a dramatic effect upon the sales of books which were a commercial success, and upon profits for publishers and novelists alike; we can contrast Lawrence's carelessness about the suitability of *The Rainbow* for libraries in 1915 with his attitude now. Lawrence was hoping that – like Mackenzie – he might manage good sales from the libraries; while in another idea also probably originating with Mackenzie, Lawrence wondered if he might also manage to serialise the novel in England: 'It would also be a safeguard against prosecutions, and it would bring me some money. I think I shall try' (ibid., p. 537). He does not seem to have noticed that his first reason – 'a safeguard against prosecutions' – contradicted his assurances to Secker about the book's propriety. But operating from Sicily, not closely in touch with the London literary world, and without an agent, Lawrence found serialising the book an almost impossible project; and he did not bring it off. Although Robert Mountsier very nearly succeeded in America (a telegram with an offer came too late), the novel was not serialised there either.

In the end, Lawrence actually offered *The Lost Girl* to Secker with some reluctance; he thought (probably rightly) that 'a commercial firm' might do such a novel far more profitably (ibid., p. 503). But Secker gratefully took up the book, probably in the belief that a morally unobjectionable novel by Lawrence was exactly what he needed to pave the way for the potentially dangerous *Women in Love*. If Lawrence's reputation could be rehabilitated, it would be a huge advantage to his publisher. But the very title *The Lost Girl*, when he heard it, once again made Secker anxious. That allows us to gauge how dangerous he thought Lawrence still was; Lawrence rather unkindly suggested that 'There should be a committee for his moral encouragement' (ibid., p. 513). But to placate his publisher, and to show how amenable he could be, Lawrence offered 'Bitter Cherry' as an alternative title, although (as he told Secker) 'Everyone cries out that *The Lost Girl* is so much better title than Bitter Cherry. More selling, I'm sure' (ibid., p. 537). It was a new argument, almost a new language for Lawrence, and not altogether convincing.

And yet Lawrence was perfectly aware of his peculiar status as an author. Works like *The Rainbow*, *Women in Love* and *Studies in Classic American Literature* were, he knew, 'all more or less "dangerous"': and for that reason he was aware that a 'standard' publisher would not handle them:

> Yet they are the works I set my heart on most – myself privately. My chief interest lies in them. I have to go softly and gently to get them properly published and established. If littler men like Huebsch and Seltzer do them, I owe gratitude, up to a point ... I like still less the semi-gentleman, successful, commercial publisher, who is always on the safe side: Duckworth, Methuen, Chatto, all that crowd. They, *bourgeois*, are my real enemy ... Remember I am a *typo speciale*: you can't handle me like any other simple commercial proposition – J. M. Barrie or Hugh Walpole. I am different, and must approach the public rather differently. (*Letters*, III, pp. 546–7)

There is a degree of simple shrewdness in this which should not, after all, surprise us; Lawrence now had more than ten years' experience of publishing, as well as the devastating experience of the war to look back on, when he had painfully learned many lessons about publishers. He had now set his heart on writing the books he really wanted to write, and on publishing them with firms suitable for his kind of writing; while making his living, if necessary, with books like *The Lost Girl*. The latter was the first piece of fiction that he had considered primarily commercial since his idea of 'The Sisters' as a 'pot-boiler' in 1913.

He arranged that Thomas Seltzer would do the American edition of *The Lost Girl* as well as *Women in Love*, but had not fixed terms for either book – another indication of his preferring to do business on a basis of trust, rather than in strictly commercial ways. It was up to Robert Mountsier in America to bother about the details; and while it is clear that Mountsier worked hard for Lawrence, he was inexperienced and awkward with publishers. He also disliked Jews in general, and Thomas Seltzer in particular: Lawrence had to caution him 'Don't be too sniffy of the risky little Jew. He adventures – these other all-right swine, no' (*Letters*, III, p. 547). But Lawrence would rather work, trustingly, with a friend and amateur like Mountsier than with the kind of professional Pinker had shown himself to be; he always hoped for a personal and trusting relationship with agent and publisher alike.

He was, in fact, exceptionally energetic in suggesting what Mountsier should do to forward his business in America: serialising *The Lost Girl*; getting proofs of *Women in Love*; getting a story typed and published in America and perhaps in England; looking into Huebsch's account books; enquiring 'rigorously after *Sons and Lovers* in America' (ibid., p. 576) – Kennerley's failure to pay for it naturally still rankled. All these suggestions were contained in one letter Lawrence sent Mountsier at the end of July 1920: a full-time agent would certainly have resented the level of advice, and Mountsier may also have done so. But Lawrence's letters to Secker and Seltzer were also full of plans and suggestions; he was in no respect neglecting his business. He arranged, for example, to correct proofs both of Seltzer's *Women in Love* and Secker's *Lost Girl* while on his summer travels away from Sicily.

Seltzer had at last sent Secker a copy of his revised typescript of *Women in Love*, and had also forwarded more of Lawrence's advance on the book (another $100 – roughly £25). Gilbert Cannan, too, had collected $300 for Lawrence in America, which Lawrence accepted cheerfully, if satirically, in April (ibid., p. 502); by early May Lawrence found that he had £171 4s 5d in his bank; while in June yet another $100 came from Amy Lowell, to make up for the January cheque which (yet again) a bank had refused to cash. For the rest of 1920, Lawrence found himself able to maintain a balance of around £150 in his account; he was even able to burn a cheque for £50 which Catherine Carswell sent him, for his contribution to her prize-winning novel; and he was also able to offer Koteliansky a loan of £10 at the end of June. By no standards was he well off; but he was at last getting a return on his writing that began to match the work he had put into it. At the end of June 1920, for example, the *Metropolitan* magazine bought his story 'Wintry Peacock' for $250 – over £60. And he was starting to live his life as and where he wanted to; he told Goldring in July 1920 how 'I am creeping on in my own measured way, cook and the captain bold, etc. But even we have a little bit more than usual' (ibid., p. 573).

Therefore, as he went on to say, 'it is going to be busted': he and Frieda left Sicily at the start of August 1920 and did not return until mid-October; Frieda went to Germany to her family, and then came back to Italy, while Lawrence spent his time travelling and visiting friends in north Italy. He wrote only poems, apart from his work on his proofs; but the poems comprised the bulk of the *Birds, Beasts and Flowers* collection. The summer travels of 1920 were the nearest thing to a holiday which either Lawrence or Frieda had had for years, probably since the lazy autumn of 1913 at Fiascherino; but 'holiday' has perhaps the wrong associations. Lawrence's 'work' was not something for which he required the peace of his own house or study; the poems he wrote were, as always, outcrops from his own subterranean experience, and he did not stop being 'a writer' just because he was off on his travels. However, the summer had been paid for by the modest success of his writing: that in itself was a reason for celebration.

II

Back in Sicily in October, Lawrence found Secker's *Lost Girl* on the point of publication, and knew he would shortly be getting proofs of Secker's *Women in Love*; Seltzer's American edition had been proof-corrected back in the summer, and would be coming out in December, safely ahead of the English edition. At last, more than five years since he had last published a novel, Lawrence had two about to appear.

But almost at once there broke the kind of news which publishers dread. The three main circulating libraries in England – Boots, Mudies and Smiths – refused to take *The Lost Girl* if p. 256

(describing the heroine's first sexual encounter with the hero) remained in its current state. 'White, mute, motionless', Alvina Houghton is taken to her room by her lover, Ciccio:

> at the back of her mind all the time she wondered at his deliberate recklessness of her. Recklessly, he had his will of her—but deliberately, and thoroughly, not rushing to the issue, but taking everything he wanted of her, progressively, and fully, leaving her stark, with nothing, nothing of herself—nothing.
>
> When she could lie still she turned away from him, still mute. And he lay with his arms over her, motionless. Noises went on, in the street, overhead in the workroom. But theirs was complete silence.
>
> At last he rose and looked at her.
>
> 'Love is a fine thing, Allaye,' he said.
>
> She lay mute and unmoving. He approached, laid his hand on her breast, and kissed her.
>
> 'Love,' he said, asserting, and laughing.
>
> But still she was completely mute and motionless. He threw bedclothes over her and went downstairs, whistling softly.
>
> ... Luxuriously, she resented having to get up and tackle her heap of broken garments. But she did it. She took other clothes, adjusted her hair, tied on her apron, and went downstairs once more.[6]

The book had been printed, and many copies already bound, but Secker urged Lawrence to rewrite the page; he had printed 4000 copies, a very large print order, and knew he would not sell anything like 4000 without the libraries buying the book. He asked Lawrence

> whether it would not be possible for you to rewrite the passage in question in such a way as to remove their objections. After all these three libraries should account between them for some 2,000 copies, possibly more if the book should have the success I anticipate, and as well as this direct result there is the even greater indirect benefit of your work gaining the widest publicity which only the libraries can afford.[7]

The arguments were persuasive, especially for an author trying to rebuild a career and make his books profitable; and in particular because Lawrence had always viewed *The Lost Girl* as a commercial enterprise.

Lawrence rewrote the offending passage with artful precision so that the new version took up exactly the same amount of space as the old, while simultaneously accommodating the sense of the sentence which described her changing her clothes, and which ran over on to p. 257. The couple in the revised version do not make love, do not go upstairs to a bedroom, and there is (therefore) no reason for Alvina to change her clothes: at the end of the revised passage, she now 'went upstairs and looked in the mirror at herself and at her clothes, adjusted her hair, tied on her apron, and went downstairs once more.'[8] By 9 November, Secker had the rewritten page back in his hands. However, without telling Lawrence, Secker had himself also made a small cut in a passage mentioning 'bedrooms' and 'beds' on p. 268; and, as soon as his printers could produce the necessary pages, he also introduced two further cuts, on pp. 45 and 223: the first in a passage describing how the young doctors during Alvina's training as a nurse 'pinched her haunches and attacked her in unheard-of ways', the second a description of Ciccio's 'shamelessness, his smiling, progressive shamelessness'. Whether these were in response to further suggestions from the libraries, or because Secker himself felt they were dangerous passages, is not clear; but Lawrence was not told about them. There were, inevitably, delays in tipping-in new leaves into already-bound copies, and in printing new leaves to replace those in the sets of unbound sheets; the edition finally came out a month late, on 25 November. Without a literary agent to chase him, however, and with Lawrence out of the country, Secker deliberately delayed sending Seltzer a copy of the book from which he could print; he himself had been held up for months by Seltzer over *Women in Love*. So that although Lawrence very much wanted Seltzer's edition to come out simultaneously with Secker's, and although proofs for the English edition of *The Lost Girl* had been corrected and ready by early October, no text – in spite of Lawrence's urging Secker to make haste – was actually despatched to Seltzer until the end of November. The American edition came out on 28 January 1921.

The problem with the libraries and *The Lost Girl*, however, had one important side-effect: that of making Secker even more cautious about *Women in Love*. Lawrence had finished correcting proofs for the English edition of the latter on 22 November 1920, but three days later – the same day as the emasculated *Lost Girl* came out – Secker wrote to him about *Women in Love*:

> I wonder whether you would mind making the very few verbal alterations in chapter [VII] for England removing the references to the unconventional manner in which occupants of the flat used to sit about in the morning. I do not expect that you attach any particular importance to the scene or think that it is in any way vital to the book. It is just the sort of thing that enemies are likely to concentrate on.[9]

Secker was referring to the fact that Halliday and his friends go about naked in their flat. Lawrence, while believing that 'If enemies want to fasten, they'll fasten anywhere', also 'altered it a bit: enough, I think' (*Letters*, III, p. 628). Eight alterations of wording in this chapter, four of them removing references to casual dress and nakedness, appeared in the English edition.

Up to now, Secker had been planning to make *Women in Love* a 'library book', but his experience with *The Lost Girl* obviously made him think twice. When he got his first month's sales figures for *The Lost Girl*, he grew even more cautious: only 2000 copies of the edition of 4000 had sold in the first five weeks, of which only 1000 – not 2000 – had been taken by the libraries. Secker therefore told Lawrence, on 31 December 1920, as the first stage of a campaign to get *Women in Love* bowdlerised, that a profitable circulation of this second novel would require a further 'two or three excisions or paraphrases in the text'. In its present state it would not be taken by the libraries; and if Secker were to ignore the library market, he said he would have to cut his print order from 2000 to 1500, while reducing Lawrence's advance on the novel from £100 to £50.

That was a sure way to arouse an author's interest, and Lawrence's first reaction was to ask to see the 'excisions or paraphrases' which his publisher had in mind; though he also told Mountsier that 'Secker wants me to cut *W. in Love*. I won't' (*Letters*, III, p. 651). Having prepared the way for Lawrence seriously to consider both cuts in the text and cuts in his royalties, Secker then wrote again to say that, after all, he had decided that the book should be sold only through bookshops: he agreed with his author that it would be impossible to expurgate the text to the 'Mudie-Boots level'. And he would, after all, not reduce Lawrence's royalties to £50, only to £75, this being – he considered – especially generous, as they would be 'the Royalties due if the whole of the first edition were sold'. Lawrence must have been getting a royalty of 12%: better than before the war. However – having tried to impress Lawrence with his generosity – Secker went on to say:

> At the same time, there are three or four passages where I think you might make verbal alterations in order to remove any possible chance of misconstruction. (*Letters*, III, p. 660 n. 1)

He sent references to four passages, and also remarked that a reference to Eleanora Duse was 'I think, actionable'. Lawrence was once again, in spite of his anger, wholly co-operative; he sent revised versions of the four passages, and altered 'Eleanora Duse' to 'the great Rachel'. After all that had happened to the book – and particularly now that a largely uncut text had been published in America – he probably considered these small changes not especially important. Secker incorporated his alteration to the 'great Rachel', and three out of the four rewritings. However, exactly as with *The Lost Girl*, he went ahead and himself cut an extra passage (not asked for) on one of the pages Lawrence revised; and he also cut two whole paragraphs at the end of Chapter XXV in which Birkin and Gerald discuss Birkin's special concern for a 'creative' relationship between two men. Secker never told Lawrence about this; though as the latter remarked 'I don't trust Secker, however: *at all* or *in anything*', he certainly suspected his publisher capable of it.

For the moment, that was the end of the business of cuts and revisions; but there was an interesting side-effect upon Lawrence's writing. During the winter of 1920–21, he had been at work on his novel *Mr Noon* (started back in May 1920); and the requests for cuts in both *The Lost Girl* and in *Women in Love* to fit the sensibilities of publishers, libraries and genteel readers considerably influenced the tone of address to the reader which is such a distinctive feature of *Mr Noon*. The 'reader' of *Mr Noon* is always 'gentle': 'I call you gentle, as a child says "Nice doggie" because it is so scared of the beast'. The references to the 'gentle reader', however, increase markedly in that part of the book written between November 1920 and January 1921 (exactly the period when Lawrence was having his problem with *The Lost Girl* and *Women in Love*); and the references to the 'gentle reader' start being accompanied by those to the 'sterner sex', the critics, who are invited to 'bend your agitated brows away from this page, and suck your dummy of sympathy in peace': 'So darling, don't *look* at the nasty book any more: don't you then: there, there, don't cry, my pretty'.[10] In the end, the gentle reader turns into someone else:

And so, gentle reader—! But why the devil should I always *gentle-reader* you. You've been *gentle reader* for this last two hundred years. Time you too had a change. Time you became rampageous reader, ferocious reader, surly, rabid reader, hell-cat of a reader, a tartar, a termagant, a tanger. —And so, hell-cat of a reader, let me tell you, with a flea in your ear, that all the ring-dove sonata you'll get out of me you've got already . . .[11]

It was a pleasant way of revenging himself upon those readers with whom he had had to be so concerned in the winter of 1920–21; he told Seltzer about the book in January 1921 that 'I get much wicked joy out of it' (*Letters*, III, p. 646).

The novel *Mr Noon* had itself gradually become unpublishable, however, for a combination of reasons: its sexual explicitness, which made it '*most* dangerous: but humorously so' (ibid., p. 653), its recreation of real-life people, its increasingly intimate and personal recreation of the early marriage of Frieda and himself, its awkwardness of tone. Lawrence abandoned it in February, hoping only to publish its first part (which suffered from fewer of those disadvantages). He still had the unfinished *Aaron's Rod* on his hands – incomplete since late 1917, though he was now determined to finish it, and had probably thought of how to do it. Meanwhile he had been writing new poems in Sicily, which he could add to those written in the summer in Florence, and which were starting to appear in magazines before he collected them as his next book of poems, *Birds, Beasts and Flowers*; and early in January he and Frieda had 'made a dash to Sardinia', and he had written 'a little itinerary of the trip' (ibid., p. 660), which became *Sea and Sardinia*.

With this quantity of work flowing out of him, and the publication during 1920 of a number of the short stories he had written before leaving England at the end of 1919, he was managing to make his living reasonably successfully; but he continued to have problems with the actual placing of his work, with his American contracts, and in particular with arrangements with Mountsier. The post between New York and Sicily was often terribly slow, and

Lawrence himself was not filing his correspondence (or keeping up his business diary). He found himself increasingly unwilling to act as his own business man; 'Curse *all* business affairs' (ibid., p. 693). Mountsier was often irritated by what he considered his friend's unreasonable changes of mind and failure to reply to questions. He sent Lawrence numbered lists of questions to be answered; at one point he even sent him a questionnaire with sections to fill in about Huebsch, about Pinker, about keeping manuscripts, about books from Seltzer. Lawrence replied:

> Your letters drive me perfectly frantic. I've written you *dozens* of letters. Oh, if only I could but keep my diary . . . I always answer your letters *the same day I receive them*. I do so because I can't keep count afterwards. (*Letters*, III, p. 674)

He was also having to deal with nearly all his arrangements for English publication by himself, and problems were arising, in particular, over work published around the time of his break with Pinker. The story 'The Blind Man', for example, published in the *English Review* in England in July 1920, had appeared in the magazine *The Living Age* in America the following month. Lawrence knew nothing about its appearance in America for at least four months; when he heard about it from Mountsier, he assumed that the American publication had been arranged by Pinker. Lawrence was annoyed: 'no word to me, and no cheque: sharp letter to him' (*Letters*, III, p. 633). But Pinker had had nothing to do with it, and suggested that the arrangement must have been made by Harrison and the *English Review*. There the matter rested for three months, until March 1921, when Lawrence, forgetting that he had already written his 'sharp letter', wrote to Pinker again with exactly the same query. He never seems, however, to have got any satisfaction either from Harrison or from the American magazine: it was another of the 'literary mix-ups' (*Letters*, V, p. 30) from which he needed an agent to save him.

In the light of such experiences, he had even started to wonder (in February 1921) whether to 'go back to Pinker for *English* agency only?' (*Letters*, III, p. 662). Pinker would perhaps not have taken him back, however. In March, Lawrence asked an old friend in London, Barbara Low, whether she would take on the job for him; he began to treat her as his agent and to send her manuscripts. She had no experience at all as an agent, and even the unprofessional

Mountsier disapproved – 'perhaps she is a bit wobbly', Lawrence agreed (ibid., p. 692). But, feeling desperate, and certain that 'I *must* have a London agent *at once*' (ibid., p. 697), he settled instead with the well-known London agency Curtis Brown to represent him for the next five years; the fixed time being 'so that we needn't be tied to one another' (ibid., p. 700). 'I wish I'd come to you ten years back: you wrote me just too late', Lawrence told Curtis Brown: he had had a letter from the agency during the winter of 1913, just as he was also getting offers from other agents. Instead of closing with Curtis Brown in 1913, Lawrence had gone along with J. B. Pinker's offer of a contract with Methuen: the fatal contract.

III

The English publication of *Women in Love* on 10 June 1921 was the next significant event in Lawrence's publishing career. Seltzer's expensive American private edition had received few reviews, but those which had appeared had been either favourable or non-condemnatory, and the book sold reasonably well (it earned Lawrence almost $200 in its first two months). Seltzer hoped that most of the 1250 copies would be sold by the end of 1921.[12] In England, however, the book was being published in the usual way, and Lawrence had originally suggested to Secker that he should not

> send out review copies *at all*, but just ... publish and leave it at
> that. I do so hate the critics, they are such poisonous worms,
> especially for a book like this. (*Letters*, III, p. 625)

Secker agreed, in principle, and originally sent out only one review copy, to the *Times Literary Supplement*. However, the review there was written by a personal friend of Ottoline Morrell, and was slanted accordingly; it singled out her recreation in the novel, Hermione Roddice, as a character of 'immense dignity', the 'one thing in the whole work which was worth Mr. Lawrence's powers and time or the reader's'; on the whole, however, the book was 'a dull, disappointing piece of work'.[13] But although Lawrence had dreamt of 'huge blue prosecution papers' in June 1921 (and hoped that dreams went by contraries), at least there was no call for the book's suppression. Secker decided to risk sending out a few more

review copies, and gradually other reviews of the book started to
appear, though Secker was cautious about those to whom he sent
copies (he refused one to the *Daily Herald*, for example).

The only thoroughly dangerous review appeared rather late, in
September 1921, in the patriotic and scandal-mongering magazine
John Bull (to which Secker would certainly not have sent a review
copy). This called for the suppression of the book, and knew
exactly what comparison would serve its case best: 'If *The Rainbow*
was an indecent book this later production is an obscene abomina-
tion. The police must act'. According to Lawrence, Secker was
'very sick' over the review, while Curtis Brown also feared 'the
likelihood of police suppression';[14] but while the police never acted
against the novel, quite a different threat emerged from another
quarter; and turned out to be genuinely destructive.

Back in 1917, Pinker had been worried that the book might
provoke a libel action from Ottoline Morrell. There no longer
seemed any danger of that (it seems possible that private assurances had been given); but on 5 September 1921 a letter from
solicitors representing Philip Heseltine arrived at Secker's offices,
alleging that the characters Halliday and the Pussum were libellous
recreations of Heseltine and his wife, and demanding the book's
withdrawal from circulation. In fact, the first printing had been
only of 1500 copies, and by mid-August stocks were (according to
Secker) 'almost exhausted', so that by early September there
cannot have been many copies left. Secker undertook that the
novel 'shall not be further circulated until the matter is settled',[15]
which probably meant that he simply delayed his reprint. After a
meeting between Secker and Heseltine's solicitors on 12 September
1921, marked pages from the novel were sent to Lawrence in Sicily
for him to consider. It seems most probable that Heseltine's
solicitors were demanding that the characters be completely
altered in appearance – that was certainly how Lawrence understood the matter; but Heseltine was also hoping that any changes
Lawrence made would prove that the libel charge was being
admitted, and would allow him to press further claims.

Just as in 1920, the summer of 1921 had seen Lawrence and
Frieda away from home – but this time they had been away since
April, and only got the news about Heseltine on 15 September:
'Heseltine trying to make himself important', was Lawrence's
comment, as he asked for Secker to send on the details to Sicily: 'I
will consider the alterations: – if they are necessary' (*Letters*, IV,

p. 87). Lawrence's diary, restarted in October 1921 after a six-month break, succinctly records his reaction to this 'Snotty little lot of people' (ibid., p. 105):

> Got back a month ago ... Found Secker's letter with John Bull attack on *W. in Love*, and with Heseltine's marked pages, which he will prosecute for libel. – A week after I give Halliday black hair & Pussum yellow, & send pages back. Haven't heard more from Secker.[16]

He also received 'a solicitors information ... that a libel action is impending. – Sweets to the sweet' (*Letters*, IV, p. 90). On 8 October, under protest – because 'I think it all perfect nonsense' – he provided Secker with the required alterations: 'I do it since you wish it this way' (ibid., p. 94). As soon as he received the alterations, Secker communicated them to Heseltine's solicitors, stating that Lawrence was

> prepared to make the verbal changes shown on the marked pages which I send herewith, not ... that he considers the matter important, but in deference to my wish that no reasonable effort should be spared to remove any possible objections which your client may have. If your client agrees to the text as modified in this manner, I will undertake to carry out the alterations and to see that no further copies are issued in the original state. (*Letters*, IV, p. 94 n. 1)

Secker very naturally attempted not to admit that Heseltine had 'been grossly libelled', but Heseltine hoped that

> the submitting of a proof (in Lawrence's handwriting) containing alterations in the personal descriptions, constitutes an admission of the charge of libel on the part of both author and publisher ...[17]

Accordingly, Heseltine felt that he and his solicitors could press on in 'threatening further proceedings'.

Secker's worst fears about Lawrence being 'dangerous' were being realised. Heseltine's attack was apparently motivated by a desire for money and for personal revenge; he had quarrelled with Lawrence in 1916 over what he thought was Lawrence's interference in his private life, and he was now showing what he thought of such interference. Lawrence himself judged that the attack was largely malicious, and warned Secker that 'the most likely thing is that Heseltine is trying to blackmail you . . . money is at the bottom of it' (*Letters*, IV, p. 113). He was right: Heseltine's own letters to his solicitors show that he had instructed them to

> press the claim for damages . . . without involving me in great expense or embarking upon an actual case. I can't afford to fight them, but it will be as well to give Mr. Secker and the author the impression that proceedings will certainly be taken if the matter cannot be settled out of court.[18]

To this end, Heseltine's solicitors reported that their client 'refuses in any way' (ibid., p. 123) to accept the rewriting that Lawrence had done; they succeeded in convincing Secker that a court case was the next step. Given Lawrence's tacit acceptance of the charge – he had, after all, rewritten the offending passages – that was not a case Secker thought he could win. When Secker informed Lawrence of Heseltine's insistence, Lawrence responded 'May rot set in his bones & blood';[19] his reaction to paying off Heseltine was 'I'd see him in several hells first', though he sympathised with Secker: 'I'm sorry you have the annoyance' (ibid., p. 113). Still, 'Heseltine ought to be flushed down a sewer, for he is a simple shit' (ibid., p. 116). Secker, however, felt he had to compromise; and, just as Lawrence had suspected, Heseltine's solicitors turned out to be prepared to accept an out-of-court settlement of their own costs, and a lump sum for their client. When Secker told Lawrence about the money – he paid Heseltine £50 – Lawrence felt 'sick with rage to think that Heseltine got that money out of you. *Really*, one should never give in to such filth' (ibid., p. 129): his diary commented simply 'Hell'.[20] It was easier for Lawrence to feel that way than for Secker: Heseltine had a case.

The episode demonstrated once again how expensive Lawrence could be to his publishers; not only did the settlement cost Secker £50, but he was involved (yet again) in the expense and trouble of printing revised sheets and having them bound up. As in 1920, with *The Lost Girl*, the modifications were introduced in stages, and various partly-modified copies were released before the novel's proper second edition of November 1921: when (Secker told Lawrence) 'it will once more be on sale after a lapse of three months. I hope there will be no further bother'.[21] His worst fears of the spring of 1920 had been realised.

If the *Women in Love* affair in England had been yet another striking example of how vulnerable Lawrence and his publishers still were, in America Seltzer had published *Women in Love*, and had not only so far got away with it: he had made Lawrence around £450 into the bargain; while Secker's first and second editions together sold only 2500 copies in the period up to October 1922, making Lawrence about £150. Secker had had to ask Lawrence for rewrites in the English text of *The Lost Girl*, too; he had held back the novel from Seltzer to prevent any kind of competition, but his English edition had still sold very slowly. To make matters worse, in December 1920 it had turned out that copies of the English edition of *The Lost Girl* were on sale in New York, before Seltzer was able to bring out his own edition. Lawrence declared himself not satisfied with Secker's explanation that the book's appearance in New York, in the stock of an import book seller, was none of his doing: 'I still think it is inexcusable that you send this *Lost Girl* edition to America, and a breach of faith' (*Letters*, III, p. 638). It says a good deal for Secker's belief in Lawrence's work that he went on publishing it in spite of such problems, and such a barrage of criticism. No other English publisher was particularly keen on bringing out Lawrence's work: without Secker, Lawrence would perhaps have lost his English market entirely.

When Seltzer's American edition of *The Lost Girl* finally appeared in January 1921, Seltzer gave Lawrence an advance of $500 on it;[22] it also sold fast and well, and was the occasion for more praise of America and denigration of Secker. Lawrence thought the book 'very nicely done ... much better than shoddy Secker' (ibid., pp. 674–5). Seltzer also published *Psychoanalysis and the Unconscious* in May 1921, while Secker – according to Lawrence – did not want to 'bother' with it (*Letters*, IV, p. 35); it was two years before he brought it out. But Lawrence told Seltzer, when his edition was published, 'I am always so pleased when the books come from you, they *look* so nice. Whereas Secker's are so scrubby!' (*Letters*, III, p. 732). Lawrence was also not happy with Secker as the potential publisher for his travel book *Sea and Sardinia* – he thought it needed a thoroughly commercial publisher – but he was happy for Seltzer to do it. And when he started a novel in Venice in 1921, 'not pretty pretty – but no sex and no problems: no love, particularly' – which makes it sound thoroughly 'popular' ('a proper *story* novel', he called it) – he declared it written solely for his American public: 'It won't go to England at all', he told Seltzer (*Letters*, IV, p. 93). By late 1921, he knew that 'Nowadays I depend almost entirely on America for my living' (ibid., p. 114); his stock of English money was almost gone, and he felt that 'England will provide me no more' (ibid., p. 110). Almost every comparison shows the advantage he gained by publishing in America; while the *Metropolitan* paid £60 for 'Wintry Peacock', Lawrence got only £21 for its English publication. For a long time he had felt that 'in direction I am more than half American. I always write really towards America: my listener is there' (ibid., p. 97).

Robert Mountsier, as early as the spring of 1921, had been in no doubt what this meant: 'Your chief publishing field is here, and the nearer you are to it the better' (*Letters*, III, p. 685 n. 1). Lawrence, for all his belief that Mountsier was probably right, hesitated for a long time about going to live in America, despite feeling (in the spring of 1921) 'absolutely at an end with the civilised world' (ibid., p. 689). He had then told Mountsier that 'I don't think I want to come' (ibid., p. 693). By October 1921, however, he felt 'more than ever come loose from all moorings. I suppose I shall really leave Europe'. But he still felt 'very mistrustful of the States. Wohin?' (*Letters*, IV, p. 97). We can see, however, that from the autumn of 1921 onwards he was consciously clearing things out of the way, preparatory to making a break with Europe and with his previous work. In October 1921 he began to gather up and revise his old short stories, to create the volume *England, My England* – again, preparatory to leaving Europe (though he still did not know where he would go):

> Think I may as well get the MSS together as far as possible. Feel like making my will also. Not that I am going to die. But to give myself a nice sense of finality. – (*Letters*, IV, p. 105)

To make up another 'really interesting book – perhaps even a real seller' (*Letters*, IV, p. 157), he told Seltzer, Lawrence put together his short story 'The Fox' with two other stories of a similar length he had written late in 1921. His attitude was that 'I want to get all straight. I want to feel free to go away from Europe at any minute' (ibid., p. 114). It was as if all his rage during the war was now finally emerging – 'England has made me too angry' (ibid., p. 131) – and that he no longer cared very much about what he published, as long as he managed to gather it all together and to leave.

Yet there was his serious work, too: his desire to walk out on Europe was always coupled with his combative sense of a fight he had to wage, and a continuing sense of his own special role. In October 1921, after letting it lie on one side for a few months, he had revised his second *Unconscious* book. Seltzer had published the first one, and Lawrence insisted to him that this new book was very important: 'For this book one must put up a fight' (ibid., p. 132). He sent it immediately to Seltzer, and also provided 'a nice peppery introduction' (ibid., p. 57):

> *Do* print the introduction to the *Fantasia*. The motto today is fight, fight, and always fight. Let them have it: they well deserve it, and they can't really do one much harm. (*Letters*, IV, p. 131)

He would remark, shortly before leaving Europe, that:

> More and more I feel that meditation and the inner life are not my aim, but some sort of action and strenuousness and pain and frustration and struggling through. (*Letters*, IV, p. 154)

He also had another novel to fight for: *Aaron's Rod*, finally finished in the summer of 1921, was 'the last of my serious English novels – the end of *The Rainbow, Women in Love* line. It had to be written – and had to come to such an end' (*Letters*, IV, pp. 92–3). He felt that 'it won't be popular' (*Letters*, III, p. 728), but it was, nevertheless, 'what I mean, for the moment'; and he rejected the attitude of Mountsier, who 'takes upon himself to lecture me about it. Says it will be unpopular' (*Letters*, IV, p. 57).

This period of Lawrence's writing, just before he left Europe, marks a significant and in many ways final development in his relationship with his publishers and with his reading public. He was now prepared to let publishers and magazine editors divide off his 'serious' work from his more popular work – like the 'slight' but potentially commercial *Sea and Sardinia* about which he told Secker, giving him 'leave to cut it *ad lib*' (ibid., p. 35): it was that kind of a book. Cuts in the 'popular' work were no problem. But he remained resolved that the serious work be published in England and America 'about as it stands', as he told Seltzer (ibid., p. 104); so that although he was fairly sure that Secker, for example, would not like *Aaron's Rod*:

I want you to publish it none the less. That is to say, I don't in the least want you to if you don't wish to. But I will have the book published. It is my last word in one certain direction. (*Letters*, IV, p. 116)

But the novel struck both Secker and Curtis Brown – particularly in the aftermath of the *John Bull* attack on *Women in Love* – as dangerous in the way they most feared. It provoked Curtis Brown to set down Lawrence's weaknesses as a commercial proposition, from his point of view:

I think there can be no question about the advisability and the necessity of eliminating the portions of 'AARON's ROD' that deal in such anatomical detail with sex. We can't get the book published normally here if these are included, and I doubt if its private printing would really help Lawrence's reputation. It seems to me that his future now hangs delicately in the balance. If only he would turn out the great story which everyone expects of him, without any appearance or shadow of sex-obsession, he could have the world at his feet. Otherwise, those who maintain that his readers buy his books not for art, as they pretend, but for pornography, are going to get the upper hand, and a really big man's chance will be lost.[23]

And although Seltzer declared *Aaron's Rod* 'wonderful, overwhelming' (*Letters*, IV, p. 129) – which Lawrence thought might be 'just a publisher's pat' though at least 'better than a smack in the eye, such as one gets from England for everything' (ibid., p. 124) – it turned out that Seltzer also wanted cuts made in the speeches of Argyle and in the Marchesa episode. At first, Lawrence himself promised to look at the latter, while advising Seltzer to cut the former 'at your discretion, by just lifting a word or two' (ibid., p. 131). Seltzer preferred, however, to send Lawrence the typescript to work on; and when Lawrence considered the matter, he replied:

I can modify the bits of Argyle's speech. But the essential scenes of Aaron and the Marchesa it is impossible to me to alter. With all the good-will towards you and the general public that I am capable of, I can no more alter those chapters than if they were cast-iron. (*Letters*, IV, p. 167)

But he was also prepared to leave it to Seltzer to 'do what you like with the book' and 'leave out anything you like for a popular edition – even if you like substitute something of your own for the offensive passages'. A popular edition – by which Lawrence probably meant a commercial printing – could be published in any shape the publisher liked. But he wanted the full text printed, too: 'Print only a limited edition', he advised, as Seltzer had done of *Women in Love*:

> it is useless asking me to do any more. I shall return you the MS. on Monday. Then say no more to me. I am tired of this miserable, paltry, haffling and caffling world – dead sick of it. (*Letters*, IV, p. 167)

If they followed his suggestion of a 'limited edition', his publishers would still be in difficulties: such an edition would have to be published before a commercial edition, or it would not sell; its marketing would be difficult; and it would draw attention to itself as a potentially 'dangerous' book. Seltzer went ahead with only one edition, a commercial one, slightly cut according to his own wishes. Lawrence's work therefore went on being presented to its readers modified by the taste of the market; he was unable to include sexual experience as part of the wholeness of human experience he wished to describe; and there was nothing he could do about it.

But he would nevertheless go on writing his serious work, in spite of the impossibility of getting it published, because it 'will really matter. To me, I mean'. Experiences like *Aaron's Rod* continued to make him feel 'hopeless about the public' (*Letters*, IV, p. 111); still, if there had to be that gap between what he wrote, and the public which read him, then there would have to be a gap. As he went on to say about the general public, 'Not that I care about them. I want to live my life, and say my say, and the public can die its own death in its own way, just as it likes' (ibid., p. 111). He would 'say his say' in his serious work, even if it never got into print.

The fact that 'I want to live my life' is, however, another recurring theme in his letters of the time. For that, he must be published, must (if needs be) compromise, or allow his publishers to compromise. He told Mountsier in January 1922 that 'A publisher can cut anything he thinks absolutely must be cut' (ibid.,

p. 179). Never again would he be able to live and write as he had
done in 1913–14, confident that his most intimate and serious work
had a chance not only of being published but of affecting people in
general: 'folk – English folk'. The commercial market was something that he would have to accept: but as far as he could, he
would ignore 'the public' – 'bloody swine – or bloodless swine' –
completely. That fact alone accounts for a good deal of the oddity
of Lawrence's publications in the 1920s; he almost always felt at
odds with his readers.

He had been saving his American earnings in dollars, while
managing to live off his English royalties; and the arrival of an
invitation from Mabel Sterne to go and live in Taos, in New
Mexico, came at exactly the right moment. 'I think I have enough
dollars in America to get us there' (ibid., p. 111), he told her; and
though he found himself still unwilling to go direct, it was with the
intention of finally going to America that, early in 1922, he decided
to go to join his friends the Brewsters in Ceylon: he would 'go west
via the east' (ibid., p. 175). It must have been a wonderfully ironical
surprise that the single piece of official recognition he ever
received from England should at that moment arrive. He heard on
9 December 1921 that *The Lost Girl* – of all his novels! – had been
awarded the James Tait Black Memorial Prize (worth £100) for the
best English novel of 1920. But although the 'recognition' must
have been nice, if comical, the money was even more welcome; the
journey from Naples to Colombo cost '£140 for the two of us' (ibid.,
p. 203), so that the poor uncommercial English *Lost Girl* finally lent
herself to good use. In 1920, while writing the novel, Lawrence had
remarked 'I feel as if I was victualling my ship, with these damned
books' (*Letters*, III, p. 522): the metaphor became almost the literal
truth.

For all his earlier bravado, leaving Europe was also a trauma:
'My heart quivers now, mostly with pain – the going away from
our home and the people and Sicily' (*Letters*, IV, pp. 198–9). Almost
the last thing he wrote was his Introduction to Magnus's *Memoirs of
the Foreign Legion*, with its anguished farewell to the past. He
recalled sitting with Magnus on the mountain top at Montecassino
in 1920, and feeling 'in the Middle Ages', while down below was
the modern world, with its railway lines and its politics:

> Both worlds were agony to me. But here, on the mountain top
> was worst: the past, the poignancy of the not-quite-dead-past.

'I think one's got to go through with the life down there – get somewhere beyond it. One can't go back,' I said to him.[24]

That was what going away brought home to him: as he put it the following year, 'the sense of doom deepens inside me, at the thought of the old world which I loved – and the new world means nothing to me' (*Letters*, IV, p. 483). But his writing had earned him the chance of going away, even though it had also brought him the pain, the frustration, the alienation and the anger that made him want to go at all. On 26 February 1922, Frieda and he left Europe for Ceylon.

7

Living Blithely: 1922–25

Lawrence's intensive work during his last six months in Europe – and his employment of the Curtis Brown agency in London to 'take everything under your wing' (*Letters*, IV, p. 187), as he put it – had begun to put his English publishing arrangements on a firm footing, even though Curtis Brown 'is a little piqued at having so much work from me, and as he says, *not a penny.* I can't help it' (ibid., p. 201). No one at his stage was getting rich from Lawrence's work. On his journey to Ceylon, and during his six weeks there, Lawrence did (for him) very little writing; he simply completed the translation of Verga's *Mastro-don Gesualdo* which he had started in Sicily, started to translate Verga's *Little Novels of Sicily*, and wrote some poems. Ceylon – in spite of 'a certain melancholy sort of magic' (ibid., p. 232) – turned out to be far hotter than the Lawrences had expected, and Lawrence (who picked up a malarial infection there) had 'never felt so sick' in his life (ibid., p. 239). Following an invitation from some Australians they had met on the boat to Ceylon, they decided to travel on to Australia at the end of April. Letters continued slowly to find their way back to England, and to Mountsier in New York – and it was $1000 cabled by Mountsier to Ceylon out of Lawrence's American earnings that enabled the Lawrences to buy their steamer tickets (£112 for the two of them: about $450) for the next leg of the journey. Lawrence continued to send advice to his agents on what they should do: to Curtis Brown he suggested that some of the Verga short stories might be taken by 'the magazines' (ibid., p. 233); Mountsier was advised that 'you might easily persuade Harpers to do *Gesualdo*' (ibid., p. 219). But there was relatively little business to transact; just forwarding addresses to supply, as the Lawrences moved on from West Australia to Sydney in mid-May 'to see if I want to stop there and write a novel'. He had not quite £50 in his pocket when he arrived in Sydney (ibid., p. 246); he would be relying upon money forwarded by Mountsier from his American earnings to take him any further. Indeed, only the arrival of 700 dollars from America would allow the Lawrences to move on again – the fare to San Francisco would cost the two of them a further '£120 clear' (ibid., p. 257).

And – as a result – the best news he heard from Mountsier was that Thomas Seltzer was pressing ahead with his Lawrence publications. *Women in Love* had been out for 18 months; *Aaron's Rod* had appeared in mid-April 1922; and Seltzer had even taken *Fantasia of the Unconscious*, and would be bringing it out in October. 'I like his courage', Lawrence responded; 'I wonder if he'll do anything with it' (ibid., p. 245). For his part, Seltzer was committed to publishing Lawrence, in whose work he thoroughly believed; he regarded him as perhaps the most important author on his list. And although – as a small publisher – he always had to struggle to make his way in the market, and to make booksellers and magazines pay up, he had reassured Mountsier in June 1921: 'be sure I shall take care of you and Lawrence before anybody or anything'.[1] He paid $200 in royalties up to June 1922, not including those from *Aaron's Rod*, and further sums of $200 on 5 and 16 September. It was money from Seltzer's publications which was currently providing the Lawrences with what they needed – 'about £3. a week to live, lowest estimate' (*Letters*, IV, p. 256) – in a small house about 40 miles from Sydney. Copies of Seltzer's *Aaron's Rod* arrived: 'the book looks so nice – haven't plucked up courage to look out the cut parts yet' (ibid., p. 260), Lawrence told him in June 1922. But – very important – Seltzer 'says its selling' (ibid., p. 261); and it sold 3000 copies in its first five weeks (ibid., p. 278). The English *Aaron's Rod* had had its problems, as Secker explained to Lawrence a little later: 'Smith and Booots will not circulate it though I went to a great deal of trouble to try and overcome their objections' (ibid., p. 262 n. 1). He meant that he too had cut the book without consulting Lawrence; he had told Curtis Brown, back in February 1922, that 'as Mr Lawrence has given Seltzer a free hand to make certain amendments, I gather that this permission applies to me also' (ibid., p. 258 n. 1). This was how he had learned to cope with Lawrence; if the latter supplied him with marvellous books which nevertheless had 'certain paragraphs and passages which are quite unpublishable' (ibid., p. 258 n. 1), he would simply take matters into his own hands, as he had with *The Lost Girl* and *Women in Love*. He removed, in all, about three pages of *Aaron's Rod* in an effort to make it acceptable. Nevertheless, in spite of the libraries refusing to take the book, the English edition sold 1716 (out of a print run of 3000) in its first couple of months: a sign that Lawrence's reputation was slowly on the mend, even if it was only half the number that the book sold in America.

Quite soon after settling in New South Wales, Lawrence began writing fiction again. He had written nothing that would certainly earn him money since putting together his short novel and short story collections before leaving Europe – the translations done on the voyage were purely speculative; but, very fast indeed, he now wrote the book he had been wondering about, *Kangaroo*: 'a rum sort of novel' (ibid., p. 257), 'a weird thing of a novel' (ibid., p. 265), more experimental than any fiction he had ever previously written. It was finished, all but the last chapter, by 15 July; and when it was done, the Lawrences were free to move on again. America still drew Lawrence, as it had done for years; and one of his plans for coping with the 'petty sales' of his books, even there, was to write in and about America itself. He told Seltzer: 'I must come to America and try and do a novel there, that's all' (ibid., p. 278). On 10 August 1922 he and Frieda sailed from Australia, across the Pacific towards San Francisco.

It must have been just as he left that he heard from Mountsier that the story 'The Captain's Doll' had been sold to *Hearst's International* for $1000, around £250. It was – apart from Methuen's £300 for *The Rainbow* – the largest sum Lawrence had ever been paid. Mountsier claimed to have effected the sale, but surviving letters show that Seltzer negotiated it and eventually received the cheque. Seltzer was doing his very best to help publicise and support Lawrence; Mountsier probably resented the fact that Seltzer had managed to effect a sale better than anything he himself had managed. Worse still, he would not have been able to claim his 10% agent's fee if he had not been responsible for the sale. The magazine planned to run the story in a single issue, and would therefore cut it down to two-fifths of its original length; Seltzer thought that Lawrence ought to be consulted about such a massive change, but it was impossible to communicate with him in time. However, Seltzer believed that 'Apart from the money, it will do Lawrence a lot of good to appear with so excellent a story in a magazine with so large a circulation'.[2] The cheque went into Lawrence's New York bank account on 29 June 1922, and (in effect) paid for the Lawrence's journey to America. Ironically, Hearst's never published the story, but, unlike Methuen, they never asked for their money back.

When the Lawrences arrived in San Francisco on 4 September 1922, however, it was with a chronic shortage of cash. Practically Lawrence's first action in America was to send a telegram to Mountsier: 'Arrived penniless telegraph draft' (ibid., p. 287). Money arrived, and they proceeded to Taos, to stay with Mabel Sterne, who had invited them there and provided them with a house. They had arrived in America, however, at a crucial moment for Lawrence's reputation. On 7 July, Seltzer's offices had been raided by the New York Society for the Suppression of Vice, and the remaining stock of the $15 *Women in Love* edition was removed (together with Schnitzler's *Casanova's Homecoming* and *A Young Girl's Diary*, with a preface by Freud). The case was first heard on 31 July, but was dismissed on 12 September, with the Judge remarking, 'I find each is a distinct contribution to the literature of the day'.[3] This was a marvellous piece of publicity for *Women in Love*. By early October, the $15 dollar edition was sold out, and Seltzer was going ahead with a cheaper edition costing $2.00, which came out on 18 October 1922; 3000 copies sold immediately, and by early December 'about 10,000' (ibid., p. 353) had been sold. On 17 December Lawrence told an English friend that it was 'going now into 15,000. Why do they read me? But anyhow, they *do* read me – which is more than England does' (ibid., p. 363).

This was Lawrence's honeymoon period with Seltzer; a stream of books was coming out under the Seltzer imprint. Two in 1920, five in 1921, four in 1922 (including the cheap *Women in Love* edition), six more in 1923. Seltzer paid $2878 in royalties to Lawrence during 1922; together with the $1000 from *Hearst's*, $900 royalties from Huebsch and another $600 from periodical sales, Lawrence's income from American sales during 1922 was over $4100 – over £1000 – even after deducting income tax, and Mountsier's 10% and expenses. In spite of living relatively expensively for the past eight months – spending money on ships, hotels and rail fares – the Lawrences still found themselves better off than for years when they landed in America. Almost immediately, discovering that he still had £500 in the bank, Lawrence paid some old debts (to Edward Marsh, to Ottoline Morrell); he was 'even in a position to lend, instead of borrowing' (ibid., p. 312). What he earned in America was, he felt, the 'kind of money I have to live on', and the comparison with what he was earning in England was distressing. 'England', he told Secker in September 1922, 'makes me about £120 a year' (ibid., p. 299): 'Not enough to pay my steamer fare or even my house rent' (ibid., p. 302).

As a result, he felt he had to put America first. Within a month of arriving in America, for example, he began rewriting his old 'Studies in Classic American Literature' essays: 'Americanising them: much shorter', as he told Mountsier (ibid., p. 338). The abrupt and pithy style he adopted was a direct response to the America in which he now lived and worked: they were his first full-length piece of American writing. The same style appears in a topical piece he wrote in October about the Pueblo Indians, 'Certain Americans and an Englishman'. He took a new attitude towards the English publication of his work: he felt, for example, that he had to prevent Secker bringing out 'The Captain's Doll' in England until the planned (and expensively paid-for) publication in *Hearst's International* had gone through. 'To let Secker publish just as he pleases would simply take the bread out of my mouth' (ibid., p. 302), he told Curtis Brown in London:

> You complain that it doesn't pay you to handle my books. Well, that's not my fault. If you don't want to handle them, then leave them. Non mi fa niente [It doesn't matter to me]. (*Letters*, IV, p. 302)

He wrote to Secker about the matter too, in a way that Secker (who had stood by him for the last two years) must have found irritating:

> America must have the first consideration. On the English crust I could but starve, now as ever ... Since last Christmas Curtis [Brown] has paid less than £100. into my bank for me. Well, if that is all England cares about my books, I don't care if England never sees them.
> Of course I know it's not your fault – and that it is thin rations for you as well as for me. But I can't help it. If America will accept me and England wont, I belong to America. (*Letters*, IV, p. 299)

This was not in fact as absolute a truth as Lawrence here made it; but, for the moment, during Seltzer's boom time and with Lawrence actually living in America, it seemed like the truth. It is worth noticing, however, that Lawrence never felt quite as committed to Seltzer as Seltzer was to him – and not as uncommitted to Secker as these letters (and remarks like 'I don't like him either' – *Letters*, IV, p. 323) suggest. Lawrence was mainly concerned to find publishers who would publish (and make him a living from) what he wrote, who would be loyal to him and to whom he could in return be loyal. He suspected, for example, that Secker would ignore his request not to put 'The Captain's Doll' into print before *Hearst's*: 'I'll *bet* Secker is going ahead with the 3 novelettes because he *likes* them . . . You'll see, he'll bring them out pretending to have had no word to the contrary' (ibid., p. 324). His suspicion was well founded; Secker had the book in proof before permission arrived for him to do it. 'I am getting', Lawrence wrote to Mountsier in September 1922, 'to be a wise and disillusioned bird'. But that did not mean that he would break with Secker; 'I hope really we can go ahead satisfactorily with Secker. I hate futile changes', he told Curtis Brown in 1923 (ibid., p. 380). And in spite of the relatively little money he was currently earning in England, he stayed with Secker. No one else was going to have any more success with his work.

He was likely, however, to reject his agents' advice about publication when it was a question of the integrity of the books themselves. Mountsier disliked the 'Nightmare' chapter – about the war – in *Kangaroo*, for example, and strongly advised that it should be published separately; and apparently Seltzer was not happy about it either. But although Lawrence had originally declared himself ready to fall in with the arrangements of 'you "business" people' (ibid., p. 318) – he had actually agreed that Mountsier should also make his arrangements with Curtis Brown, in England (ibid., p. 343) – he was equally determined to produce (as far as possible) the books he wanted. After revision, he declared *Kangaroo* 'now as I wish it. I want to *keep in* the war-experience piece: and I have made a new last chapter. Now it is as I want it, and it is good' (ibid., p. 322). Mountsier simply had to accept that; and Seltzer brought the book out in September 1923.

The biggest upheaval in his American publishing came, however, within five months of his arrival in America. The Seltzers and (a little later) Mountsier came to Taos to stay with the Lawrences, who had now moved a little further away from Mabel Sterne, and were living on a ranch up in the mountains near Taos. Both visits were decisive. Lawrence found Mountsier personally unsympathetic; and, too, became extremely angry with him over his attitude towards Seltzer. There had often been friction between agent and publisher; Mountsier thoroughly disliked Seltzer, blaming him for the failure of his own book *Our Eleven Billion Dollars*, which had come out under the Seltzer imprint in 1922. When Mountsier left, in late January, Lawrence told him he no longer wanted him as his agent. He had probably been helped in this decision by the fortnight-long visit of Seltzer and his wife Adele a month earlier, when he had decided about Seltzer that 'I think I trust him really' (ibid., p. 364): Adele also believed, now, that 'we need have no more qualms. I think Lawrence means to be absolutely loyal to Thomas'.[4] With the support of Seltzer, Lawrence could face the prospect of once again being agent-less; and if it was a matter of choosing between Seltzer and Mountsier, Lawrence (rightly) judged that he needed Seltzer more than he needed Mountsier.

The break with Mountsier was far more difficult than that with Pinker had been, back in the winter of 1919. Mountsier was losing an income he valued; he did his best to hang on to continuing royalties from contracts he had engineered, and (indeed) to whatever of Lawrence's he could. On Seltzer's advice, Lawrence offered Mountsier 10% of his American earnings in 1923 to make up for what he was losing, 'if he promises to return all papers';[5] and Mountsier accepted. He went on disputing Lawrence's figures about what he was owed, however; and as late as October 1924 Lawrence was still trying to get various manuscripts back.[6] Almost certainly Mountsier insisted on keeping them until Lawrence agreed to his figures about what he was owed. He never returned them, in spite of Lawrence's angry remark 'what name does one give a man who deliberately detains property not his own?' (*Letters*, V, p. 145); they were eventually sold to a collector.[7]

But, apart from negotiating with (and continually offending) Seltzer, Mountsier had made relatively few contacts with magazines and periodicals. Lawrence's contacts with *The Dial* and *Poetry* (which together printed most of his periodical work in America) had both been established well before he knew Mountsier; and the latter had been responsible only for getting a few poems into print. Seltzer was prepared to help with magazines: he had arranged the sale with *Hearst's* in 1922 and it was he, for example, who got Lawrence to write 'The Future of the Novel' for the *Literary Digest International Book Review* at the start of February 1923 (*Letters*, IV, p. 374 and n. 2). He also helped with other publishing matters – keeping copies of Lawrence's published pieces, for example, and fixing a price for the sale of a poem to a little magazine (ibid., pp. 406–7). He advised Lawrence on a new bank, and on how to handle the financial side of his break with Mountsier; and, exactly like an agent, he even arranged to keep track of Lawrence's income 'for the current year' (ibid., p. 394). In February 1923, too, he negotiated with Curtis Brown for Lawrence about 'The Captain's Doll'; and he also took on the lawyer's negotiations – which Mountsier had begun – with Mitchell Kennerley over the publication of *Sons and Lovers* in America, and with Huebsch over *The Rainbow*.

For his part, Lawrence allowed Seltzer to keep some of his unpaid royalties in the Seltzer Corporation, on condition that Seltzer kept him a constant $2000 in credit at his bank; and he was also prepared to be far more flexible and trusting than Mountsier had been, over the matter of 10% and 15% royalties for his Seltzer books. *Sea and Sardinia*, for example, was an expensive book and sold relatively few, and Seltzer wanted to pay only a 10% royalty. Mountsier had resisted strenuously; but, Lawrence wrote to Seltzer, 'I want to be quiet just . . . and you to be the same' (ibid., p. 367): 'as long as you are faithful to me I shall remain with you' (ibid., p. 378). All he insisted on was that Seltzer should tell him 'openly what you are doing and intend doing with my things' (ibid., p. 394). Just as with Edward Garnett before the war, Lawrence was now relying upon this unpaid friend effectively to act as his agent, and he was both grateful to him and worried about the amount of work he was giving him: 'I seem to give you a great deal of trouble', he wrote (ibid., p. 395). In April 1923 he actually asked Seltzer whether he shouldn't put his affairs in the hands of an agent – Curtis Brown had written from London 'urging me to let his American office handle my stuff' (ibid., p. 419). But Seltzer must have advised against it, and Lawrence agreed, with the proviso: 'don't you get too overwhelmed with work. It is what I am afraid of' (ibid., p. 437). The liking and admiration for Lawrence and his work which Seltzer continued to feel were their own reward, and Lawrence was obviously good at arousing such a response; but – just like Garnett protecting Duckworth – Seltzer was also probably worried about literary agents advising Lawrence about how much better he could do with another publisher. Under the current arrangement he at least felt secure of Lawrence's continuing custom.

With Seltzer's help, therefore, Lawrence worked and published during the next six months. His income remained good, though it was *Women in Love* which continued to be its mainstay: 'I should still be poor *sans Women in Love*, shouldn't I?' he mused to Seltzer (ibid., p. 457). But it was 'awfully nice', wrote Frieda, 'that we have so many dollars, Lawrence will feel free and I can help my people' (ibid., p. 385). He could even afford to offer to 'cut down my royalty to a minimum' while Seltzer was fighting to take over the market for *Sons and Lovers* (Kennerley's edition was still available). And when, in August 1923, Amy Lowell wrote with a small cheque for Lawrence's royalties in *Some Imagist Poets*, Lawrence was able to suggest that it was no longer worth sending such a small sum: 'give the money to somebody who is poor' (ibid., p. 488), he told her, doubtless thinking of himself five years earlier. Seltzer's American edition of the three novelettes – *The Captain's Doll*, in America – came out in April 1923, and *Studies* in August: *Kangaroo* and *Birds, Beasts and Flowers* – Lawrence's first book of poems since *Bay* in 1919 – were scheduled for the autumn.

English publishing was naturally also continuing, though Lawrence's books were now tending to appear first in America under Seltzer's imprint: *Women in Love* (1920), *Psychoanalysis and the Unconscious* (1921), *Sea and Sardinia* (1921), *Aaron's Rod* (1922), *Fantasia of the Unconscious* (1922), *Studies in Classic American Literature* (1923) and *Mastro-don Gesualdo* (1923) all appeared significantly earlier in America than in England. Secker had, however, been enthusiastic about the volume of three short novels which he called *The Ladybird*, and also about *Kangaroo*. The only danger for Lawrence was that while publishing these, Secker would ignore the other and perhaps less commercial works, particularly the non-fiction. The two psychoanalysis books, for example, Lawrence found 'hardly sell at all' (*Letters*, V, p. 262); but he still wanted them published. 'I just won't sign contracts for my novels and leave the other books lying unpublished' (*Letters*, IV, p. 391) Lawrence told Curtis Brown: Secker had to 'print all of me' (ibid., p. 394) if he wanted the fiction.

In late March 1923, Lawrence and Frieda went down to Mexico, Lawrence hoping that he could there write the 'American novel' (ibid., p. 385) he had not yet been able to write in Taos; given the continuing success of *Women in Love* in America, an American novel from Lawrence would have been something very special indeed for Seltzer. Lawrence began it beside Lake Chapala, early in May, just a year after he had started *Kangaroo* in Australia. By early June 'my real novel of America' was 'more than half done' (ibid., pp. 454, 457); but Lawrence decided he couldn't finish it that year: 'I must do it when my soul gets calmer'. Early in July, the Lawrences left Mexico and travelled to New York, en route to Europe, giving the Seltzers a chance to return their hospitality in New Mexico; the Lawrences stayed in a cottage the Seltzers specially rented for them in a 'pretty, rural, remote, nice' part of New Jersey (ibid., p. 473). Lawrence could deliver his novel manuscript to Seltzer for typing, discuss plans with his publisher, read proofs for no fewer than three books Seltzer was bringing out, and meet various magazine editors. The Lawrences stayed a month; but in spite of seeing a good deal of the Seltzers (to Adele's continued delight) Lawrence found both people and place 'quenched', 'dim to me' (ibid., pp. 483–4): an ominous sign, perhaps.

The most important decision he took was to refuse after all to go back to Europe. Frieda, anxious to see her mother and her children, sailed by herself on 18 August 1923. It was the most serious break of the Lawrences' lives, but – again – one which Lawrence could these days afford to contemplate financially. Seltzer paid $2000 into Lawrence's account between 15 August and 23 October 1923; and as Lawrence wrote to Frieda in November, when she was living in London,

Don't bother about money – why should you. When I come we'll make a regular arrangement for you to have an income, if you wish. I told you the bank was to transfer another £100 to you. (*Letters*, IV, p. 529)

Living and working in America, he was not touching his English earnings. He spent the autumn working his way down the west coast of America to Mexico in the company of a Danish friend from the ranch days in New Mexico; he wrote a number of essays and rewrote the Australian novel 'The House of Ellis' by Mollie Skinner, renaming it *The Boy in the Bush*. It might, he thought, 'be popular – unless the ending is a bit startling' (*Letters*, IV, p. 517): Jack Grant settles down with two wives. But he was happy for Seltzer to consider publishing it before the Mexican/American novel 'Quetzalcoatl'; although the latter was 'much more important to me', he was equally certain it would *not* be popular (ibid., p. 517). Like *Aaron's Rod*, 'Quetzalcoatl' was a novel he felt he had to write, but was putting off for the moment. It was better for Seltzer to take *The Boy in the Bush* first.

After three months, Lawrence was prepared to listen to Frieda's urging and return to England; the idea, too, of working on Murry's magazine the *Adelphi* – which Murry had started partly as a forum for Lawrence – had a certain appeal for him: 'I think I may put some of myself into it, for 1924, and see if anything results' (ibid., p. 522). He returned in late November 1923, after 14 months in America.

II

Ironically, what he heard in England on arriving made him wonder for the first time if all was well with the Seltzer firm. He wrote to Seltzer on 14 December: 'I hope business is good – there were slightly alarming reports here, from America. But I trust you to keep me informed' (*Letters*, IV, p. 543).

There was, in fact, a fatal flaw in his relation with Seltzer. Lawrence wanted a relationship with his publisher based upon mutual trust and respect; in effect, a personal relationship. And although Lawrence was Seltzer's most published author, Seltzer's other cares and business responsibilities meant that he was not always able to be as frank with Lawrence as the latter wanted. The winter of 1923–24 had turned out to be a desperately difficult time for Seltzer; he was still fighting the litigation started in 1922 over his publication of allegedly indecent books, and he had to make another court appearance in January 1924. But, worst of all, it turned out that during 1923 he had made a loss of about $7000 dollars; and he was unable to pay Lawrence – or his other authors – their royalties. Yet he also felt unable to tell them: and as a result stopped writing to Lawrence, and paid in nothing to Lawrence's American bank account between October 1923 and March 1924.

This was absolutely fatal to a relationship which Lawrence had made a matter of personal trust, and was also very awkward for an author who had come to rely upon his publisher looking after his financial affairs. For several months, while in Europe, Lawrence wrote letter after letter to Seltzer, asking him to arrange for the payment of his income tax, asking whether he had yet paid into the bank what was owing, asking why he was not replying. But only one reply ever came. All Lawrence's fears about yet another publisher keeping him 'in the dark' came back: and this time, with so much of his own money and future income at stake, he felt especially at risk. He did the obvious thing: although continuing to feel grateful to Seltzer for what he had done, and still hoping that 'Things will be just the same between us as before' (ibid., p. 559), he stopped trusting Seltzer to look after things for him, and arranged for an agent to take care of his affairs in America. Very naturally he turned to the New York branch of Curtis Brown.

Things in England had not worked out as he and Murry had hoped, either. Lawrence found that he disliked the *Adelphi* intensely; and though the magazine went on publishing him, he found he had no desire to edit it or to work on it. He gave up. His return to England had been a mistake; he would after all go back to America.

When he and Frieda, on their way back to the New Mexican ranch in March 1924 accompanied by their friend Dorothy Brett, arrived in a blizzard at New York, Seltzer most unexpectedly met them at the harbour. Lawrence had not told him about their arrival, but Seltzer had found out about it from Curtis Brown; he and Adele moved out of their apartment for a week to make space for Frieda and Dorothy Brett. But in spite of his friendliness, Seltzer's business was – as Lawrence had feared – 'in low water' (ibid., p. 600), and he turned out only able to pay the royalties he owed from 1923 in small sums: $500 at last coming in on 17 March 1924. A. W. Barmby, the Englishman in charge of the New York Curtis Brown branch – whom Lawrence was relieved to find 'a very decent sort, no fool' (*Letters*, V, p. 17) – set to work straightening out affairs, and getting Seltzer to pay his debts. Another $200, probably from Seltzer, came in at the start of April. Seltzer nevertheless wrote to Lawrence in May, 'saying business is still very bad, and I am to be careful with my money, not spend much. But the advice would sound better from a different source.—' (ibid., p. 42). Lawrence's main financial need in mid-1924 was money to build up the ruined ranch near Taos which Mabel Sterne had given Frieda, and into which they moved in June; he spent over $450 on it during the summer. After that, he was concerned that while in Mexico during the winter, to rewrite his novel, he should not run out of money. He wrote to Seltzer: 'before I go to Mexico, I should like you to put some more money to my account, as I shall need a fairly large letter of credit to take with me' (ibid., p. 105). By 8 October, 'by being careful' (ibid., p. 148), he had recovered to $2285.21 in his New York account and over £300 in his English account.[8] He and Barmby had been able to get money out of Seltzer to the tune of 'about 3000 dollars altogether, this year. If

I can get it like this, bit by bit, I don't mind at all' (ibid., p. 126).
Even after arriving in Mexico City, he still had over $2000 in his
account.

But like Barmby, Lawrence was growing increasingly suspicious
of the long-term outlook for Seltzer's business. What had happened during 1923 was not perhaps an isolated occurrence: 'My
fear is that he may go bankrupt', Lawrence told his sister Ada in
September (ibid., p. 126), and he also remarked ruefully to Robert
Mountsier that 'We are having the struggle with Seltzer that you
warned me about. You were right and I was wrong about him'
(ibid., p. 127). He had long believed Adele Seltzer 'the bad influence' (ibid., p. 16) on her husband; he believed she was trying to
make Thomas a commercial publisher like the New York firm of
Alfred Knopf. He had himself told Seltzer in July 1924 that 'your
excursions into the popular field are only absurd'; 'You're not born
for success in the Knopf sense, any more than I am' (ibid.,
pp. 78–9). The statement perhaps tells us more about Lawrence
than about Seltzer: the latter was only trying to subsidise his less
commercial projects with more directly commercial books.

However, whereas Seltzer had brought out seven Lawrence
titles in 1923 – hence the huge mass of royalties to be paid – in 1924
he only had *The Boy in the Bush* to offer: and only one book –
another Verga translation – certain after that. In August 1924, in
what looks like a move preparatory to giving him up as a publisher,
Lawrence asked Seltzer to hand over to Barmby all the manuscripts
he had on safe deposit; but Lawrence still wanted advice from
Barmby and Curtis Brown about deciding whether he should stay
with Seltzer or not. Curtis Brown in London, however, had
favoured Lawrence changing his American publisher to Knopf
since late 1923,[9] and Barmby now agreed. *The Boy in the Bush* came
out as planned; but Seltzer's last Lawrence book was his translation of the Verga *Little Novels of Sicily*, which came out early in 1925.
After a telegram from Lawrence to Barmby confirming the break,
Lawrence's major piece of writing from 1924, the short novel *St.
Mawr*, was offered to Alfred Knopf: Knopf, '*rich* and enterprising –
seems very nice' (ibid., p. 245). Lawrence knew Knopf was 'a better
business man' than Seltzer (ibid., p. 269); Knopf took on the
Mexican/American novel when that was finished, too.

Seltzer was distraught, personally and for his business. If his
authors did not stand by him during the bad times, he would never
be able to recover and pay his debts; but authors like Lawrence

were also liable to desert him precisely because he was in difficulties, and looked like continuing to be so. It is easy to criticise Lawrence for letting Seltzer down: yet – like his agents, whose advice he followed – Lawrence needed to be assured an income from his books. He could not afford, in any sense, to stay with a publisher whose business was in difficulties. And Seltzer had also let Lawrence down, in the terms of the special relationship Lawrence had had with him:

> if only he'd have been open and simple with me, I'd have borne with him through anything. But a furtive little flea who hides his hand from me as if I was going to fleece him – whether fleas have hands and fleece or not – why – Basta! (*Letters*, V, p. 194)

Seltzer struggled on as a publisher until 1926; he made a final plea for Lawrence to return to him that year, offering to pay off his remaining arrears if he did. Lawrence resented the threat that Seltzer would not pay the arrears *unless* he came back; he also hated Adele Seltzer's remark that he should come back 'with a best seller under my arm'. 'Why does anybody look to me for a best seller? I'm the wrong bird' (ibid., p. 574). It was just the attitude upon which he had mainly – if wrongly – blamed Seltzer's troubles. But Lawrence and his agents knew his particular, limited appeal, and his market; from 1925 until he died in 1930 Lawrence stayed with Knopf as his major American publisher, benefiting from the latter's commercial success – if not himself much contributing to it.

III

The history of Lawrence's publishing for the rest of his time in America is quickly told. Following his creation of three stories while in Europe in the winter 1923–24, he went on writing short fiction during the spring and summer of 1924; and Curtis Brown were, for example, successful in selling 'The Border-Line' to the *Smart Set* in America (and in getting $175 for it) and to *Hutchinson's Magazine* in England (who paid £40 for it): the American price thus only slightly higher. The advantage of having an active agent again in America had become clear when an article 'Indians and Entertainment', which Lawrence thought would only be taken by 'the more serious magazines' (*Letters*, V, p. 36), was taken by the *New York Times* in October 1924. Lawrence had also at last managed to interest Martin Secker in the Maurice Magnus typescript (then called 'Dregs'; published as *Memoirs of the Foreign Legion*) and in his introduction to it – a piece of publication Mountsier had tried to arrange for more than two years. Lawrence was well aware that there would not be 'a great sale for the book'; but he had written his piece to pay part of Magnus's debts, and would divide his royalties 50/50 with Michael Borg, a Maltese who had loaned Magnus £80 and had never got it back. But, because it was simply important to get the book published, he instructed Curtis Brown: 'Secker can leave out anything he likes from my MS of Magnus, or from Magnus own' (ibid., p. 31). Secker made cuts in the introduction and in Magnus's own part. Seltzer had declined the book, and it actually became the first volume Lawrence published with Knopf, in January 1925.

Interestingly, in June 1924 Lawrence had asked Secker to send him a popular periodical or two:

> the *Strand*, or *Hutchinsons*, or the *Bystander*. I haven't seen one for years, and I think it would be good for me to know *what* popularity is. (*Letters*, V, p. 56)

It was the old temptation and need – at least to know what popularity was, to know whether he was capable of writing for such publications. Secker sent the *Strand* magazine, but Lawrence found it 'terrible piffle. No, the periodical stuff is no go' (*Letters*, V, p. 80). Just as he finished *St. Mawr* ('a corker') a fortnight later, as if to confirm that the leopard had NOT changed his spots, he remarked to Secker: 'It's much better if I'm not *popular*: you'll get much more from me later' (ibid., p. 91); meaning, presumably, that Secker would in the end make more profit. (If Secker had not had, for financial reasons, to sell his rights in Lawrence to the firm of William Heinemann in the middle 1930s, that would certainly have become true.) Hutchinsons, incidentally, offered to publish his 1924 story 'The Woman who Rode Away' in the popular magazine *Woman* if they could cut it; to begin with Lawrence didn't mind a 'small and not significant' cut, but did not 'quite fancy having my stories cut: they aren't like articles . . . why can't they make a bit of a break, and publish the story complete?' As time went by however, and he realised his need of money before going down to Mexico, he changed his mind:

> Hutchinson's can have her and cut her short, if they like ... If the things are coming out whole in book form *soon*, then the magazines can please themselves what they do: the devil take them: they can cut as they please. (*Letters*, V, p. 149)

But the story went to the serious magazine *The Criterion* after all, which did what Lawrence had at first suggested and published the tale in two numbers.

Lawrence was putting off the rewriting of his Mexican novel until going back to Mexico, which he planned to do in the autumn of 1924. He felt he had to do it: 'I've not done a novel this year – nor much small stuff – so not earned much.' But he was not badly off, 'as Seltzer very slowly pays up ... He owes me a good bit yet' (*Letters*, V, p. 114). Still, the novel had to be done: both his English and his American agents looked forward to it, and the great wave of Lawrence publications which had come out during 1921–24 was almost at an end. This time the Lawrences went not to Chapala but much further south, to Oaxaca: 'this isn't touristy at all – quite, quite real, and lovely country around' (ibid., p. 163). On 19 November he started the novel – to be called *The Plumed Serpent*; and he took only a week's break in the composition, just before Christmas, in order to write four little magazine articles about Mexico 'which will probably suit *Vanity Fair*' (ibid., p. 186). They were obviously designed to be popular, for a magazine 'which everybody reads' (ibid., pp. 186–7), and were perhaps designed as some kind of counterbalance to the serious and probably unpopular novel. In fact they appeared in the American magazine *Travel* and in the *Adelphi* in England.

On 31 December 1924, Lawrence started the second notebook containing his novel, and finished it almost exactly a month later. He told Secker: 'It is a long novel. I feel, at the bottom of my heart, I'd rather not have it published at all' (ibid., p. 207). It was so close to him, so important: not for the first time he felt as he had done back in 1912, that 'I give myself away so much, and write what is my most palpitant, sensitive self'. Then, he would have liked *The Trespasser* 'to be issued privately' (*Letters*, I, p. 353). Now, he re-affirmed to Secker that the new novel 'won't be easily popular, but in my opinion it is my most important thing so far' (*Letters*, V,

p. 267). Curtis Brown had suggested that he could be 'a second Anatole France', meaning that he could be both famous *and* successful: but Lawrence replied:

> I shouldn't even be flattered to be the *first* Anatole France – though he was a nice old man. I am afraid, sales or no sales, I prefer the colour of my own flag. (*Letters*, V, p. 207)

The Plumed Serpent nailed that flag to the mast: Lawrence's only compromise would be to allow his publishers to call it *The Plumed Serpent* rather than his preferred title, 'Quetzalcoatl'.

However, the very day he finished the novel, Lawrence collapsed, 'as if shot in the intestines' (*Letters*, V, p. 230). He had a recurrence of his Ceylon malaria; it seems probable that he had typhoid fever (particularly dangerous in Oaxaca); to add to his misery there was also an earthquake. Lawrence thought he would die; and, a month later, when he and Frieda had managed to struggle back to Mexico City, a doctor there told him plainly that he was also suffering from tuberculosis. He had begun to spit blood the previous summer, up at the New Mexican ranch, but had put it down to inflammation of the bronchials. He now knew he was a sick man; the doctor warned Frieda that he might die in the next 18 months. And although he and Frieda had planned to return to England from Mexico – Lawrence feeling 'rather a hankering after England – perhaps because I was ill, then one wants to come home' (ibid., p. 228) – the doctor was against a long sea-voyage, particularly to England. He thought Lawrence's only hope was to stay in a warm climate, or to go back to altitude. The Lawrences gave up their plans for England; they went back to the ranch in New Mexico in April.

Illness meant doctors and expense, meant that he would not always in future be able to work as he needed; meant, too, that his life was certainly shortened, perhaps within sight of its end. In spite of this – or more likely because of it – Lawrence continued to be furiously productive as a writer. Even while ill in Mexico City, he had sketched out some 'Suggestions for Stories' in a notebook – he always tended to think of stories as a way of keeping the wolf from the door when times were hard; and he actually started one of them ('The Flying-Fish'), although he was so ill that he could only manage it by dictating the first nine pages of the manuscript to Frieda. He also began a play, promised to the actress Ida Rauh back in New Mexico in the summer of 1924; though that, too (as *Noah's Flood*) remained a fragment, and it was not until he was back at the ranch that he started (and finished) the play *David* for her. (She never acted in it.) In response to a suggestion from Barmby, when back at the ranch he also wrote a reply to his critics in the essay 'Accumulated Mail', which Knopf published in his yearbook the *Borzoi*. The old, witty, sardonic Lawrence states his feelings about authorship and readership, and proclaims his own freedom:

> Now listen, you, Mr Muir, and my dear readers. You read me for your own sakes, not for mine. You do me no favour by reading me. I am not indebted to you in the least, if you spend two dollars on a book. You do it entirely for your own delectation. Spend the dollars on chewing-gum, it keeps the mouth busy and doesn't fly to the brain. I shall live just as blithely, unbought and unsold.[10]

Almost true: but for the first time in two and a half years, in the spring of 1925 Lawrence was concerned about money. Illness was one thing; but the ranch irrigation was 'rather an expense' (*Letters*, V, p. 244), and Seltzer remained a problem. Lawrence had transferred his business to Knopf – but 'of course I still have to live on what is squeezed out of poor Seltzer' (ibid., p. 269). And the trouble with Seltzer was that he 'just doesn't pay me my money' (ibid., p. 249). In May 1925 Lawrence even had to fall back upon an advance from Knopf for *St. Mawr* – something he had not needed to bother about for years: 'Irritating that one should need an advance, at this late hour!' (ibid., p. 249).

After a quiet and generally inexpensive summer at the ranch, however, with his health apparently improving, things did not seem quite so urgent. Although, for example, Secker offered an advance of £125 on *The Plumed Serpent* (due for publication in England in January 1926), Lawrence felt able to refuse it: he was still hoping that more of his arrears might be extracted from Seltzer (ibid., p. 298). He had spent the summer revising *The Plumed Serpent* and writing and revising essays, but he did not consider such things to be real work: 'We've just sat tight and considered the lily all summer', he remarked at the end of August (ibid., p. 291). For most people, ten essays got into shape in only two months during the intervals of ranch work, while convalescing, would have been work enough. The little volume of essays

Reflections on the Death of a Porcupine, for which he wrote many of them, was his first book since Beaumont's *Bay* in 1919 to be brought out by a publisher away from the public arena; it was produced by the Centaur Press of Philadelphia, who (Lawrence told Secker) 'do rather elegant books, for collectors' (ibid., p. 290); in June they had brought out a *Bibliography of the Writings of D. H. Lawrence* compiled by Edward D. McDonald. The Centaur, he told one of its directors, was 'just the right steed' for his essay collection: 'I am glad to be doing this book, really, *not* through a "public channel". I feel you are half private: which suits me better' (ibid., p. 284). It was the first in a succession of such books which Lawrence was to produce: a sign of his own continuing doubts about the 'public channels', but also of his growing sense of the kind of author he himself was. He would never be popular, but all the same he was very attractive to a small circle of readers. He had tried for years to find the kind of publisher who could live with that kind of author; and the idea of the private press will recur in the story of his career during the last five years of his life.

By the end of August 1925 he had in general recovered, and was feeling 'quite well again, in the mountains with my horses, and the cow Susan' (ibid., p. 291); it was in fact his last time at the ranch, though he planned to come back the following year, after wintering in England and in Italy. In September the Lawrences went to New York for a week before sailing. No staying with the Seltzers this time, of course; the Lawrences lived in a hotel. They saw Barmby, but this time found him 'not nice'; however, they were most impressed by the publisher Knopf and his wife, who had just moved into new offices, and seemed

> set up in great style, in their offices on Fifth Avenue – deep carpets, and sylphs in a shred of black satin and a shred of brilliant undergarment darting by. But the Knopfs seem really sound and reliable: am afraid the Seltzers had too many 'feelings.' (*Letters,* V, p. 306).

Lawrence wrote to Blanche Knopf, just before leaving, that 'I am glad I know you and Knopf – it feels like having something safe behind me – a feeling I've never had before, in America'. He also reassured her about his sales: 'As for the people, they'll buy me again, soon' (*Letters,* V, p. 303). In rather awful contrast with the Knopfs, Thomas and Adele Seltzer were dangling by a single thread, over the verge of bankruptcy, and nobody a bit sorry for them . . . Adele said dramatically to Frieda: 'All I want is to pay OUR debts and DIE'. Death is a debt we all pay: the dollars are another matter (*Letters*, V, pp. 305–6)

The sardonic tone was inevitable, perhaps; it was ironical and painful that a man who had struggled so hard to survive as a writer, and who had at last started to earn decent sums, should have ended up with a publisher unable to pay his royalties.

After buying steamer tickets, and settling up, Lawrence could only leave 'about $30 in the bank: but Seltzer telephoned he was *going* to deposit some more!' (*Letters*, V, p. 307). All the Lawrences could do was rely on such promises – and, as they were going away, leave the matter in the hands of their New York lawyer. On 21 September 1925, the Lawrences sailed for Europe: what Lawrence earned there would have to support them for a while instead. It was the last he ever saw of America; but it was also the end of the high hopes for himself as a writer in America which he had felt back in 1922. During the past three years he had earned more money by his writing than ever before; but the experience, both of business and of the continent itself, had been disturbing, and it was not one which, in the end, he wanted to repeat. And he was coming back to Europe, at the age of 40, with less certainty than ever before that he would be able to go on living by his writing. In fact, it was living itself which would increasingly preoccupy him.

8

Economising: 1925–27

I

Lawrence's writing career had been changing during the first half of the 1920s: from being the man who was, above all else, a writer of novels, and who also lived primarily from the income generated by his novels, he had turned into a writer whose novels played only a relatively small part in his earning power. From 1906 until 1921, he had always had some novel under way, in some stage of completeness: even during the bleak years of the war he had had (first) *Women in Love* to go on correcting, and latterly the draft of *Aaron's Rod*. Then had come *The Lost Girl*; then the abortive though long draft of *Mr Noon*; then renewed work on *Aaron's Rod*. But when Lawrence finally finished the latter, in the summer of 1921 – while simultaneously clear that he would not be going back to *Mr Noon* – it was 10 months before he started his next novel, *Kangaroo*. When that was finished, in July 1922, it was another 10 months before, in April 1923, he started 'Quetzalcoat!', the first draft of his Mexican novel. This remained with him as a draft for a year and a half, until late in 1924, but, in between, he wrote the 590-page manuscript of *The Boy in the Bush*, as if to show that he was still a novelist. But after finishing *The Plumed Serpent* on 1 February 1925, he left the longest gap between novels of his professional career. It was another 20 months before he started on the first draft of *Lady Chatterley's Lover*. This was mostly because of the breakdown of his health as he finished *The Plumed Serpent*: he was most reluctant to lay himself waste again with such a strenuous and exhausting kind of work. Instead, he decided to do 'short things' (*Letters*, V, p. 331): 'just bits, that I have promised' (ibid., p. 346); 'I'm not going to start another novel' (ibid., pp. 340–1). The expenditure of spirit and energy on a novel had to be husbanded.

As a result, it was mostly shorter fiction – and a good deal of non-fictional writing – which occupied him during his last months in America, and during his period in Europe from September 1925

134

until his death in 1930. Seltzer's financial problems in America continued to affect him: 'I wish we were all richer', he remarked in November 1925, 'But it's no good: we've got to go piano-piano' (ibid., p. 345). Financially, he was really back to where he had been five years earlier, though he was not too worried about payment for an old poem in anthology – 'as for collecting a guinea, will you please use your discretion', he told his agent (ibid., p. 387). In November 1925, he felt he had

> to economise, as Seltzer is hardly held together by a safety pin: and he has my five thousand dollars. Barmby writes that Nathalie Crane ... is now suing Thomas for not paying her her royalties, and he is cutting a sorry figure in court. Beastly! (*Letters*, V, p. 342)

Things got worse and worse for the Seltzers; they had 'a very bad winter. Poor Thomas, I'm afraid he's at his last gasp' (*Letters*, V, p. 395). But not only did Seltzer still owe Lawrence a lump sum of $5000 for past royalties; Lawrence's current income in America was also largely at a standstill. In spite of the handful of new books Knopf was publishing, Seltzer was not keeping Lawrence's old books in print, and Lawrence lost the royalties from continuing sales of them. He now had no regular income from America such as had been his mainstay during 1922, 1923 and 1924. He had to survive on what the past royalties of his books with Secker continued to pay him and on what he earned from new work. Secker also began to issue a cheap, 3/6 edition of the books in 1926, 'making what bid he can for a wider public' (ibid., p. 596), something which suggested the kind of established status Lawrence was coming to have. As usual, however, the 'shorter things' promised to pay more easily and more quickly than any novel could do. And there were occasional publications from Secker like *David* in a limited edition of 500 copies (costing 15/- each) in March 1926. On the one hand, Lawrence disapproved of such costly productions: 'I agree with Knopf, these private editions are a bit of a swindle – fifteen bob for that bit of a book' (ibid., p. 415); 'on principle I believe in cheap books' (ibid., p. 626). On the other hand, he dreaded – as always – a book like *The Plumed Serpent* 'going into the tuppenny hands of the tuppenny public', and hankered after private publication. 'Small private editions are really *much* more to my taste. Odio profanum vulgum – though it's not the vulgus, it's literatus literatibus' (ibid., p. 387). His last four years would see his work divided between the two forms.

He was helped in his writing plans by establishing better relations with Secker than he had previously enjoyed. On returning to England, he went to stay with his publisher in the country; and it being increasingly clear that his health needed a place abroad, he and Frieda went to Spotorno on the Italian Riviera, where Secker's wife Rina came from and where her family still lived: 'She . . . writes that it is sunny and warm, and that there is a pleasant house for us to rent' (ibid., p. 334). They took the house from November to April. Secker himself came for a long visit to Spotorno in December–January, and Lawrence found him 'a quiet little man, but very nice' (ibid., p. 378). He continued, though, to be critical of the lack of 'the slightest bit of push' in him. When planning, in the spring of 1926, the potentially popular book which he hoped *Etruscan Places* would be, with 'lots of photographs', Lawrence was certain that 'if Secker has to handle it, it will sell 3,000 and then stop'. Back in 1925 he had feelingly remarked that 'a more popular publisher than Secker would, I believe, handle a little novel like *St. Mawr* much better than Secker' (ibid., p. 214); but, reluctantly, had let Secker take it. 'I feel while I am with him I shall never never get any forrarder, as they say', he told Curtis Brown – 'But I can't quite leave him' (ibid., p. 460). All the same, 'I feel that, even for *his* sake, if I am ever to get a wider public, some other publisher will have to help break down the fence' (ibid., p. 575). But Secker's winter visit to Spotorno was important in ensuring that Lawrence stayed with him as his major English publisher; and Lawrence's breakthrough to that 'wider public', when it came, was not with a book published in England at all.

It was also clear, however, that his health was very much worse than at any time since 1919. In spite of being careful during the winter 1925–26, he caught influenza in February 1926 and spat blood; and although he again recovered a good deal of strength during the summer and autumn of 1926, he consciously took things very quietly. Whole months went by when he wrote almost nothing: March and September 1926, for example. His declarations of being fed up with writing became more vehement than ever:

I feel at present I should love to throw my pen in the sea for ever, and call myself Abinadab Straw, no more D.H.L. walk under the heavens, nor books appear in his name. Ah, if one were rich enough! (*Letters*, V, p. 362)

He was thinking of T. E. Lawrence's metamorphosis into Aircraftsman Shaw. And when Middleton Murry appealed to him for help with a new version of the *Adelphi*, he drew from Lawrence one of his most striking rejections of the role of the serious writer:

> What a man has got to say, is never more than relatively important ... As for your humble, he says his say in bits, and pitches it as far from him as he can ... I don't care a straw who publishes me and who doesn't, nor where nor how, nor when nor why. I'll contrive, if I can, to get enough money to live on ... I'm forty, and I want, in a good sense, to enjoy my life. Saying my say and seeing other people sup it up doesn't amount to a hill o' beans, as far as I go. I want to waste no time over it. That's why I have an agent. I want my own life to live. (*Letters*, V, pp. 367–8)

His rejection of the role of the serious writer is too vehement to be altogether convincing – he was attacking Murry's self-importance – though there is no doubt that Lawrence would have liked to feel like this all the time, and sometimes managed to. On the other hand, he remarked less than a month later that 'I feel it's a betrayal of myself, as a writer of what I mean, to go into the *Adelphi*, so I'd rather stay out' (*Letters*, V, p. 385). He could never really stop himself being 'a writer of what I mean'; was condemned to his own seriousness, his own determination to discover by writing what was true in his experience.

But as a direct result of his bad health, and of his determination not to get himself again into the state to which *The Plumed Serpent* had reduced him, most of his writing between September 1925 and October 1926 consisted of work he could do relatively quickly and easily; in particular his old favourite for easy money, short stories. As he wrote in May 1926:

> There are gods of evil, even Mammon, to be placated. One can't have it all one's own way. – I'm going to try throwing a few sops to Cerberus myself – things like *The Plumed Serpent* have no profit in them, as far as Mammon goes. (*Letters*, V, p. 456)

He was commissioned, for example, by Cynthia Asquith in November 1925 to write a story for an anthology of ghost stories she was editing, and promised her that Curtis Brown would let her have it on 'quite aimiable' terms. She actually paid only £15 for the story she got, 'The Rocking-Horse Winner'; but it sold for £50 in America, to *Harper's Bazaar*. Having started to write fiction again, he actually wrote eight stories in the next 10 months. In December 1925 he wrote 'Glad Ghosts', the ghost story originally planned for Cynthia Asquith – 'not very ghosty' (*Letters*, V, p. 360), as he admitted – 'Smile', accepted by the *Nation* three months later, and 'Sun'. The last would, to Lawrence's annoyance, for a long time stay rejected as 'too "pagan" for anything but a highbrow "review". Fools!' (ibid., p. 389). But although she had no luck with 'Sun', Nancy Pearn, at Curtis Brown's offices in London, could now be relied upon to place Lawrence's periodical work in England: Lawrence told her 'I'll leave all the real arrangements to you, since it's your province' (ibid., p. 360). He found her 'quite golden' (ibid., p. 459). Magazines were by no means his favourite market – 'Damn *all* magazines', he characteristically remarked in January 1926; but they were useful 'for the bit of money they pay', so long as that was more than the '£1. per 1000' words offered him by the magazine *The New Age* (ibid., pp. 374, 483). He was an older writer now, established and with a reputation; and he was more attracted by the '£10. for 1,500 words' offered by *Vogue* (ibid., p. 482). And such work – unlike a novel like *The Plumed Serpent* – he assured Secker, 'I never mind altering . . . a bit' (ibid., p. 382).

While Secker was still in Spotorno in January 1926, Lawrence started his short novel *The Virgin and the Gypsy*, and sent it to him as soon as it was done: Secker had always hoped for another set of short novels like *The Ladybird* of 1923, and Lawrence was obviously trying to please. But Lawrence also cautioned him '*don't count on a book for the autumn, really. I feel at the moment I will never write another word*' (ibid., p. 388): and when, at the start of July, Secker again expressed his desire for another full-length novel, Lawrence remarked:

> I don't feel much like doing a book, of any sort. Why do any more books? There are so many, and such a small demand for what there are. So why add to the burden, and waste one's vitality over it. Because it costs one a lot of blood. – Here we can live very modestly and husband our resources. It is as good as

earning money, to have very small expenses. (*Letters*, V, p. 490)

'He can whistle', Lawrence remarked to his friend Koteliansky – no friend of Secker (*Letters*, V, p. 483). Within three months, however, Lawrence was engaged on another long story which (this time) turned into a full-length novel: his last novel. It was not, this time, a question of money to be earned or of a hefty advance to be secured. So long as he had the strength, he could not resist the imaginative lure of the experimental novel, the making of a new world which writing a novel always was for him.

But for the moment he simply went on with the stories: 'The Rocking-Horse Winner' as a replacement for Cynthia Asquith in February, 'Glad Ghosts' having grown too long; 'Two Blue Birds' in May – 'probably to be another tribulation to you', he told Nancy Pearn (ibid., p. 451); 'The Man Who Loved Islands' in June, and 'In Love?' in October 1926. There were also occasional essays, and six book reviews, the first two for the *New York Herald Tribune*, to whom he had promised them. He found his reviews 'rather nice' (ibid., p. 321): 'It amuses me, this winter, to leave my own books alone, and go for other men's' (ibid., p. 325).

In the spring of 1926, he and Frieda moved from Spotorno to the top floor of an old farm villa near Florence, which cost them only 3000 lire a year (around £25): 'we can sit still and spend little' (ibid., p. 453). Here, he planned a book on the Etruscans, and did a good deal of preliminary reading for it. But he continued not to write very much: 'just go quietly on from day to day: paint the cupboard and window frames, go in to Florence, write a dozen lines of a short story: nothing more thrilling' (ibid., p. 463). His correspondence during the spring and summer is peppered with remarks such as 'I am "off" writing' (ibid., p. 415), 'Why write books for the swine, unless one absolutely must' (ibid., p. 483), and 'I loathe the thought of it all, and wish I could afford never to appear in print again' (ibid., p. 498). Living at the Villa Mirenda, they didn't need to earn much money: '£300. a year would do me', Lawrence remarked in July; 'Let the public read the old novels' (ibid., p. 492). He was not, however, earning quite enough from his past writing to survive.

During 1926, however, came the first hints of a new type of writing, one he would not actually succeed in for another two years: the London evening newspaper, the *Star*, expressed itself willing to consider (and would pay well for) sketches of about 800 words – '800 words should keep one sketchy' (ibid., p. 386), as he told his agent; while *Vogue* would also accept 'little articles' and pay well for them (ibid., p. 482). Lawrence didn't write for the *Star*, just yet; but he did do a couple of little articles – one on 'Fireworks in Florence', one called 'The Nightingale' – to be offered to *Vogue*. He remarked how easy to write they were compared with 'The Man Who Loved Islands', the short story he was currently working on: 'little articles if people like 'em, are much the easiest'. Neither piece was accepted; but the form was one he would come back to, and eventually become expert in. He also agreed to plans for his stories 'Sun' and 'Glad Ghosts' to appear as relatively expensive little books on their own, in editions of 100 and 500 copies respectively: another forerunner of the private press publications to come.

What made the difference to his writing plans (or the lack of them) was the fact that he and Frieda went to England in the summer of 1926. For one thing, he began to feel 'I shall have to do something or other, soon' (ibid., p. 514) because 'I shall get back penniless . . . one wastes every sou in this moving around' (ibid., p. 534). For another, having witnessed the coal strike in England and having revisited the Midlands, he felt compelled to write about it. He actually mentioned the idea of 'an English novel' to Secker in September (ibid., p. 522), though it seemed extremely unlikely that he would write one – especially as magazines were still showing interest in his work. He had sent another little essay, 'Mercury', written in Baden Baden in July, to Nancy Pearn in August, and thought he 'might manage another couple' while in the Midlands, 'if the spirit will move' (ibid., p. 521). He produced just one essay about his time there ('Return to Bestwood'); but, back at the Mirenda in October, he seemed happy 'just to do short stories and smaller things' (ibid., p. 551) such as critical articles on books: 'I'll try some little sketches – I ought to be earning something' (ibid., p. 584). He was also happy for Secker to assemble his Mexican and New Mexican essays into a book, *Mornings in Mexico*. He tried one little essay on the Italian habit of shooting small birds ('Man is a Hunter'), obviously as a potentially popular article; and within five days of returning to the Mirenda had also written the last of the year's short stories, 'In Love?': a story rather similar to the articles on present-day relationships which he would shortly start writing.

Around 22 October, however, he started yet another story, this time set in the heart of the English Midlands, about a gamekeeper and a married woman. And although it began as a long short story, or short novel – the affair between the two of them starts around 14 000 words into the narrative, which could conceivably (like *The Virgin and the Gypsy*) have ended not long afterwards – the piece grew to be a full-length novel: the first *Lady Chatterley's Lover*. The development surprised Lawrence too, who didn't feel 'like a long effort' (ibid., p. 563). He wrote it extremely fast, and almost as soon as he finished it he began to rewrite it. That rewriting was uncharacteristically slow, taking nearly three months; it turned a short novel with risqué elements into a wholly experimental piece of fiction which was 'impossible to print', as Lawrence described it to Secker (ibid., p. 638): *'utterly* unfit for serialising', as he told Nancy Pearn.[1] And in spite of pressure from both his publishers, he did not send it to them; the rewriting and the momentous publication of the novel will be described in the next chapter.

During the latter part of 1926 and during 1927 Lawrence continued to make his living with the old combination of occasional books – now very occasional (*Mornings in Mexico* was the only book he published in 1927), and the regular appearance of short stories and articles in magazines: 'little things' which he went on feeling *'keep me going best'* (ibid., p. 647): 'I could probably live by little things'.[2] America, as usual, continued to pay him better than England – his short essay 'The Nightingale', for example, paid him $75 from the *Forum* publication; *The Spectator* cut it and paid him only £15. He found himself leaving the details of his periodical publication more and more to Curtis Brown and Nancy Pearn; he even told the latter at the end of 1926 to 'make the decision about price in future without bothering to refer to me, when you sell stories or things, – unless it's something very special' (ibid., p. 613). He was, naturally, not particularly well off: 'it's God help us, when it comes to earning money by sincere work. I manage to scramble through, but no more'.[3] But although the lira was falling in value, living at the Mirenda helped a good deal, and in May 1927 the Lawrences took the house for another year. Apart from *Lady Chatterley's Lover*, however, the only book he was now concerned with was his book about the Etruscans, which he told Secker, rather hopefully, 'could be a standard popularish, not scientific' book, 'and might really sell, for the photographs at least are striking and beautiful'. As his only book in hand, he certainly needed it to be 'as popular as I can make it'.[4] Individual essays from the book were published in magazines; but Lawrence's health meaɪt that he never undertook the tour of sites necessary for writing the book's second half, and it remained unfinished at his death. (Secker published it in 1932.)

Like all his friends, however, Secker was increasingly concerned for Lawrence's situation. Following a bronchial haemorrhage at the Mirenda in July 1927, Lawrence thought it best to spend the summer convalescing somewhere cooler, and he and Frieda went to Austria and Bavaria, away from their cheap living in Italy. Secker offered 'money in advance'; Lawrence didn't yet need it, 'thank heaven',[5] but was grateful for the offer. He was translating some more Verga, but again wrote very little of his own between July and October 1927. Matters were made worse by the fact that, in September, he heard about a new tax arrangement for exiles like himself: he would now have to forfeit 20% of his British earnings in tax. With 10% for his agents, that meant he lost £30 of every £100 earned. 'What does one exist for, but to be made use of, by people with money?' he commented.[6] And he felt himself getting rather low financially when he arrived at the Mirenda in October. But – with no prospect of a new Lawrence book for the moment – Secker made two propositions: for a collection of short stories, and for a book made up of Lawrence's scattered poetry. Lawrence was particularly struck by the latter idea: 'I'd like to leave some out, and put some in ... We might make rather a nice vol.'[7] It would be a kind of gathering in of his impassioned utterances of the past twenty years. His American publisher Knopf was also concerned about the lack of a new Lawrence book; Lawrence explained to him, too, that he really did not want to write new books but hoped to 'eke out a living on stories and little articles, that don't cost a tithe of the output a book costs'.[8] But books put together out of old materials would be a different matter. The story volume – to be called *The Woman Who Rode Away* – was quickly assembled; and he started work on the poems when he got back to Italy. It turned out that two volumes would be needed; and Lawrence did a good deal of revising, as he turned his early poems into the poems he felt he ought to have written when young. He also arranged them into a rough chronological sequence: another autobiography, of the kind he had begun to write since 1926; another recognition of completing and of ending.

9

1928

I

Lady Chatterley's Lover was not only Lawrence's last and easily his most notorious novel; it was the largest literary undertaking of the last four years of his life, and earned him more money than any other of his writings. It effectively relieved him from financial cares at just the time when – extremely ill during 1929 and early in 1930 (he died in March) – he needed to be able to rest and not bother about writing; when he would otherwise have been unable, for the first time since 1918, to earn his living.

His financial situation during 1927 had been growing steadily worse, and had – he noted to himself in November – 'got on my nerves lately'. He was no longer writing the amount that once he had – the sheer amount which (for example) had brought in so much from Seltzer during the period 1922–24; he had always been a volume producer. And for all his efforts over the years, he had never produced anything that either sold very well, or brought him in a very large sum of money. 'I'm as poor as a mouse. It's chronic with me: and shameful, really, that I make so little'. He had, 'by living like a road-sweeper', enough to live on;[1] he still helped himself along by writing the occasional short story ('Rawdon's Roof' in November 1927, for example); and magazines took a number of the Etruscan essays from his unfinished book. But, as he wrote to Curtis Brown:

> You know the magnificent sums Secker makes for me – and Knopf. Not their fault, no doubt – nor mine. But without Miss Pearn I might be whistling, simply though we live.[2]

But his problem was that he was actually producing less than at almost any time in his career (and would have known that that was not going to improve), and was more ill than he had ever been, suffering bronchial haemorrhages at the Mirenda in July 1927 from which he took months to recover. As he commented, 'It is not cheap, being ill and doing cures'.[3] He had little energy and little desire to write.

There remained unpublished, however, the unprintable novel *Lady Chatterley's Lover*, started in October 1926 and rewritten early in 1927. Circumstances suddenly combined to show Lawrence what he could do with it. In Florence on 17 November, quite by chance, he met an old acquaintance from 1915, now the extraordinarily successful novelist Michael Arlen, author of the best-seller from 1924, *The Green Hat* (Arlen would contribute greatly to the creation of Michaelis in *Lady Chatterley's Lover*). Arlen accepted an invitation out to the Mirenda for the following day, when the two writers discussed Lawrence's 'poverty' and – obviously – Arlen's success: Arlen would shortly have an income of £10 000 a year, and had made $5650 in one week from *The Green Hat*. Lawrence's reaction to their meeting was characteristic: 'Definitely I hate the whole money-making world, Tom & Dick as well as en gros. But I won't be done by them either.'[4] His talk with Arlen combined with an idea for 'money-making' which he knew other Florentine authors used: the printing and publishing of their books privately. His old friend and enemy Norman Douglas did it: '700 copies at 2 guineas each'.[5] On the day he had met Arlen, Lawrence had also seen Douglas and Orioli – the bookseller who helped organise Douglas's publications, which were printed in Florence and posted to their subscribers.

These things perhaps joined together in Lawrence's mind with the existence of a book he had picked up in Orioli's bookshop a year earlier – *My Life*, the memoirs of Frank Harris, published in Paris. Harris's book was sexually explicit in a way that Lawrence had probably never seen in print before; and Lawrence's unpublished novel was also sexually explicit. It clearly *was* possible to publish such a book, if one went the right way about it. Lawrence determined to do the same himself, but (at this stage) using Douglas's method rather than Harris's; on 22 November he asked Orioli for his help. The usual financing of a book would be turned upside down: Curtis Brown would not be involved; Orioli, as helper, would get 10% of the profits of the Florentine publication (if there were any): Lawrence, as author, organiser and paymaster, would get 90%. And as the book was published outside England, there would be no 20% tax for the British government either.

Orioli agreed to help. Their first plan was the Douglas arrangement of 700 copies costing 2 guineas each, printed by a Florentine printer – and the excitement of the plan overcame Lawrence's extreme reluctance to start working on anything as long as a novel. He had always wondered about revising the book; now he had a plan for its publication which could 'fling it in the face of the world', so that was how he would revise it. The book would become a devastating attack upon his contemporaries, saying exactly what he wanted and what no publisher would ever print: 'a kind of bomb: but a beneficial one, very necessary'.[6] Within a week of enlisting Orioli's help he had started re-writing; and in an extraordinary burst of energy, he took less than six weeks to complete the 728 page manuscript.

By January, with the finished novel beside him, his plans for its publication were almost ready: '1000 copies, 2 gns. each – 500 for England, 500 for America'.[7] The American copies would cost $10 each; in the event the English ones cost £2, not 2 guineas, perhaps to make accounting easier – but Lawrence did not consider himself a gentleman, as Douglas did. At first Lawrence had hoped the book would make him, even after Orioli's 10%, 'a few hundred pounds – even seven or eight – which would be a windfall for me'. By January he was hoping for 'a thousand pounds, which I can do very well with'.[8] He would have to risk his own money in getting the project started, a process he compared to 'throwing some of my few sprats hoping to catch a mackerel in the shape of £1000 for my novel'. 'I hope too I'll get a bit of money by it,' he told an American friend: 'I don't earn my living – it has to earn itself. But if it'll earn me a bit of margin, good luck to it'.[9]

For two good reasons he also decided to try for simultaneous production of an expurgated version of the book by his American and English publishers. He could not be certain that his plan for Florentine publication would work; it might conceivably lose him a good deal of capital and leave him 'looking rather sick'. And he also wanted to try and protect the copyright of a work that (his agents had warned him) would be exposed to piracy in its Florentine form: 'I don't care a straw about a public edition: only the copyright –'.[10] For his English and American publishers he needed typescripts; but getting the book typed turned out to be his first problem with it. His friend Nelly Morrison, who had offered to do the job in Florence, refused to continue after the first five chapters because she thought the book pornographic. In a hurry to get on with publication – Nelly Morrison had actually started

typing before Lawrence had finished writing – he sent the manuscript of the first part of the book to London in mid-January, to
have the rest of it typed (ribbon copy plus two carbons) by his old
friend Catherine Carswell; the second half of the book he retained,
to have it typed by Aldous Huxley's wife Maria in Switzerland,
where he was shortly going with the Huxleys. He hoped to have
the whole book typed and ready for the printer by 20 February.

Maria Huxley made 'a simple chicken-pox of mistakes' in her
part of the typing: 'Dear Maria,' he remembered, 'all those little
mistakes you made, and I followed like Wenceslas's page so
patiently in your footsteps'.[11] But that was not as bad as the fact
that Catherine Carswell was busy, and had to enlist friends to help
her: the London typing, much to Lawrence's irritation, came
slowly and bit by bit, the last chapters not arriving until 1 March.
While the typescript arrived, Lawrence simultaneously revised all
three copies, expurgating two of them for Secker and Knopf,
'blanking out and changing'; he told Martin Secker that 'I think we
ought to manage to make it feasible'.[12] Ensuring the copyright was
his only reason for expurgating the book; he also discussed
publication dates with Secker, to try and safeguard his Florentine
edition by having it appear after a copyright English publication.

But this, of course, was before Secker and Knopf had seen their
typescripts. Secker made up his mind as soon as he saw the book;
it was quite unpublishable in the form in which Lawrence had
presented it, and he knew Lawrence well enough to realise that
their ideas of what was publishable were not compatible. Lawrence
had only cut out a few episodes; he had in general attempted to
modify the effect of the book simply by altering its words. In
Chapter 4, for example, 'penis' became 'tilter', 'jouster' and 'little
Lancelot'; in Chapter 15, 'arse' became 'rear', 'tail', 'bottom' and
'behind'.[13] If that was to be the method of expurgation, Secker
regarded the project as hopeless; when he published his expurgated version in 1932, it was with both verbal omissions and the
excision of 'whole sections' – exactly as Lawrence in 1928 had
demanded he should *not* do it. The Knopfs remained a little more
optimistic for a while, hoping they could 'trim it down';[14] but they
too eventually abandoned the attempt.

Lawrence therefore proceeded with his Florentine edition without the safeguards afforded by copyright publication. On 9 March,
back in Florence to oversee the production of the novel, he and
Orioli at last took his typescript in to the printer. The Tipografia
Giuntina was:

such a nice little printing shop all working away by hand – cosy
and bit by bit, real Florentine manner – and the printer doesn't
know a word of English – nobody on the place knows a word –
where ignorance is bliss![15]

But the Tipografia Giuntina only possessed enough type to set up
half of the book at a time; and although proofs of the first half were
quickly available, printing of the first half could not start until the
special hand-made paper chosen by Lawrence and Orioli was
delivered.

There were however a great many other matters to see to: the
proofs, for example, were desperately in need of correction because of the printers' lack of English. The sheets were almost as
bad as Maria Huxley's typing, Lawrence reported; the printer
produced 'dind't, did'nt, dnid't, dind't, din'dt, didn't like a Bach
fugue'.[16] There were order forms (for '*Lady Chatterley's Lover* or *John
Thomas and Lady Jane*') to be drafted, printed and sent off to
potential buyers; numerous letters to be written by Lawrence
advertising the novel to friends; a binder to choose, and binding
paper to be selected; a block to be made of Lawrence's hand-drawn
Phoenix for the cover: a new bank account to be opened for paying
in subscriptions. Lawrence kept an account book of what he spent
and of what money came in, as the first orders began to arrive at
the end of March; the book was scheduled to appear on 15 May. By
the end of March, it already looked as if 'I'll sell the thing all right';
by mid-April he had '150 orders – eighty-odd paid';[17] by the end of
April, the orders received covered Lawrence's estimate of the costs
of production, which at this stage came to about £250. It was at
least certain that he would not lose on the book. His hope was to
sell as many copies as possible directly to suhscribers and to do
without booksellers so far as he could. Booksellers

take a third commission in America, and a quarter in England –
and then hold the book back and sell it for double the price. I
hate middle-men, and want to eliminate them as far as possible.
If I can carry this thing through, it will be a start for all of us
unpopular authors. Never let it be said I was a Bennett.[18]

That is – he was *not* popular, and never would be. But the money
he was earning would at least go into his own pocket.

The paper was a month late in arriving; it came at last in
mid-May, when the book should have been ready for distribution.

But, very quickly, the first half of the book was printed (together with 200 extra copies on ordinary paper), the second half of the book set up, proof-corrected and printed (together with the corresponding 200 extra copies); and the final details arranged. On the advice of his friends, Lawrence dropped the sub-title *John Thomas and Lady Jane* which was to have appeared on the title-page; he was also busy with a job he usually strongly protested about, to publishers who wanted to produce books bearing his signature: signing and (in this case) also numbering 1000 sheets to go opposite the title-page, with 10 spares signed but not numbered, in case of accidents. Doing it for his own book was different, though he was glad when the job was done. Only then, for his health's sake, could he escape the growing heat of the Italian summer and leave Orioli in charge. He went to Switzerland, though he would have liked to 'have stayed on till the thing is out, and posted'.[19]

There remained, of course, the considerable work of receiving and banking cheques and money-orders as they arrived, of paying the bills from printer and binder, and of eventually sending the copies out. Orioli continued to forward the cheques (and paying-in slips from the bank) to Lawrence, who kept the record in his account book of money received; he would then leave Orioli to deal with posting the book to the address on the order-form. The first copies went out at last at the end of June; when Lawrence's own copy arrived in Switzerland, he commented:

> I do really think it is a handsome and dignified volume – a fine shape and proportion, and I like the *terra cotta* very much, and I think my phoenix is just the right bird for the cover. Now let us hope she will find her way safely and quickly to all her destinations.[20]

The book was coming from the binders at the rate of 40 a day, and was being posted by registered mail to addresses in England and America. Apart from the cost of postage, the final bill for printing and binding came to exactly 15 000 lire – only £162.

The first real problem with the book, apart from the delays occasioned by the time it took for the typescripts and paper to arrive, came with copies ordered by bookshops. In spite of Lawrence's reluctance to deal with booksellers – he only offered them 15% discount, not their accustomed 25% or (in America) 33⅓% – there had, in the end, been a considerable number of bookshop orders. When, however, the London shops saw what they had ordered, they unanimously cancelled their orders and demanded that the books be removed: by the end of July there were 114 copies to be collected and worrying rumours 'that the police are going to raid the shops'.[21] The problem was solved by friends in London – Enid Hilton, Koteliansky and Richard Aldington in particular – collecting the booksellers' copies, and keeping them until orders came to Florence for another copy to be sent to an English subscriber. The name and address would then be sent back to London, and the copy despatched. What had begun as a nuisance turned out to be a blessing in disguise, as customs officials began to watch for the arrival of potentially offensive parcels from Florence. Most copies for English subscribers arrived safely from Florence, however, before any hint of trouble.

The whole enterprise both angered and exhilarated Lawrence, as evidence of people's reaction came in and he and Orioli found their way round the problems. 'It has been good fun, really, and worth it' he commented in August: 'I feel I've had another whack at 'em – a good satisfactory whack'; 'I feel I've shot it like a bomb against all their false sex and hypocrisy'.[22] He had enjoyed making the book as he really wanted it, and the excitement of doing something which thoroughly offended so many people he disliked. The outsider in literary circles had now really made his mark; as Frieda put it, 'the fighting does his soul good!'[23] He had felt 'rather Gummidgery and "low" and disheartened these last two years – but now I really think I'm picking up, getting my pecker up again, and on the war-path therewith once more'.[24] It was probably good for his health, too, for him to be devoted to such a project, and to win through in the face of so much disapproval. Though individuals at his agents (such as Laurence Pollinger) helped him a good deal with the book's distribution in England, the Curtis Brown agencies in London and New York ('because it may affect *their pockets*', he decided) officially disapproved of it; 'are angry with me for publishing it – say it will damage my reputation', and, he thought:

> probably disliking her, anyhow. But I stand by her: and am perfectly content she should do me harm with such people as take offence at her. I am out against such people. Fly little boat![25]

Things were, however, very different in America. From the start, the US Mail was on the alert, and a large number of the copies destined for American subscribers never arrived: such subscribers lost their money and their books. Orioli and Lawrence tried various devices: holding back copies until telegrams came announcing that the book was getting through; sending the book to post offices in out-of-the-way places. Lawrence suggested a dummy book jacket with 'The Way of All Flesh by Samuel Butler: Giotto Edition *Price One Guinea*' on it, and a replacement cover for a trial posting of the paper-covered edition of 200 – '*Joy Go With You* by Norman Kranzler, The Ponte Press'. But in the end, after many failures and only a few successes at getting copies in to America, it proved more sensible to keep the remaining copies for the European market. Lawrence briefly considered an arrangement with the Vanguard Press in America, for them to reprint and distribute the book; they warned him in particular against the danger of a non-copyright book like *Lady Chatterley's Lover* being pirated. But nothing came of the plan; Curtis Brown New York were very much against Lawrence making a contract with Vanguard.

By the start of September, Lawrence knew that he had made at least £700 out of the book (£70 for Orioli, £630 for himself) out of the sale of only about 560 copies, with the loss of a considerable number in America. In mid-September the book's price went up to $20 and £4 (later to £5 5s) to take advantage of a growing demand and the small number of copies left: no fear now of putting people off with too high a price. By October he was remarking, to some old friends:

> Think of it. I've made eight hundred pounds out of *Lady Chatterley*. I've never had so much money before all at once. What shall we do? I think we'll take a villa in Taormina. Yes, we'll take a villa and live like gentlemen and have a butler.[26]

They did nothing of the kind, of course; Lawrence was far too sensible. But he could afford to help those less well off than himself; Brigit Patmore, who remembered him talking about the butler, was herself struggling to finish a book in order to earn her advance:

> I was working in my room that afternoon when someone knocked ... He came up to the writing table holding a little paper in his hand.

'I want you to take this.'

I looked. It was a cheque for ten pounds.

'*Dear* Lorenzo, I *can't.*'

'Yes you can. It would please me. Things are hard for you just now.' . . . And he went out quickly.[27]

By December he was sure of profits of £1024. He told Secker: 'I have made £1000 over *Lady C.*, anyhow – been spending it, of course.'[28] He and Frieda had given up the rather bleak Villa Mirenda (he had never really been happy there since his illness of July 1927); they were, at the end of 1928, living quite comfortably in a small hotel at Bandol on the Mediterranean coast. It cost them 40 frs. a day, about 6/6, but they could at last afford it.

By the end of the year, however, sales of pirated copies of the novel had begun to take hold, first in America and then in Europe. At least two pirated editions were in existence by November 1928, and others followed in 1929. By the end of December 1928, Lawrence was lamenting that he had not printed more copies of his Florentine edition. The first edition of 1000 copies was practically gone; he only had 200 copies of the paperback second edition, and was fast running out of them; while reports from all sides told him of pirated editions taking advantage of demand for the book – and making him not a penny. By April 1929 he was sure that 'People must already have made two or three thousand pounds out of pirated editions – and I am left with nothing'.[29] One semi-repentant New York bookseller

> sent me some dollars which were, he said, my 10% royalty on all copies sold in his shop. 'I know', he wrote, 'it is but a drop in the bucket'. He meant of course a drop out of the bucket. And since, for a drop, it was quite a nice little sum, what a beautiful bucketful there must have been for the pirates![30]

It was not just the loss of money that concerned him, though it certainly made him angry. A friend commented, a little sanctimoniously, that 'he badly wanted the book to reach the masses – of England particularly. Like Tolstoy he was indifferent to any royalty there might be from such an edition.'[31] Pricing the book first at £2, then at £4, he had not shown any particular care for the masses; and he was by no means indifferent to his royalties. He could not afford to be: but he hated other people profiting from *his* work.

The only thing he could do against the pirates was to publish –
or get published – a new edition of his own. But neither he nor
Orioli wanted the trouble of doing that job again. The obvious
place to go was Paris, where Sylvia Beach had published *Ulysses* in
1922, and where the Frank Harris *My Life* had come out; it was the
centre of the dubious or sexually explicit book trade, and commanded a ready market in British and American tourists. With what the
Florentine edition had earned, Lawrence was prepared to 'put up
the expenses of a Paris edition myself'.[32] He asked Sylvia Beach if
she were interested, and he also tried the notorious Pegasus Press:
'I don't incline very warmly to either, yet *must* have someone.'[33]
One of the problems was to undercut the sale of the pirated
edition, which was selling to the trade at anything between 100
and 300 frs., and retailing at anything up to 500 frs. (nearly £5).

Since however it proved impossible to arrange things by post,
Lawrence went to Paris himself, hoping for 'a little fat book that
will go in your pocket and cost only 50 frs. or 75'.[34] While in Paris
he received, however:

> a belated offer from the European Pirates, who found the
> booksellers stiff-necked, offering me a royalty on all copies sold
> in the past as well as the future, if I would authorize their
> edition. Well, I thought to myself, in a world of: Do him or you
> will be done by him, – why not? –[35]

'The sum due was substantial' reported a friend with him in Paris:
'Lawrence was unusually indecisive'. He went to see the pirate:

> and found the place shut up: it was after office hours. 'I knew
> then,' he sighed, when he arrived back at our hotel, 'I didn't
> want to see the man. I stood there on the pavement with relief
> and was utterly glad the office was closed.'[36]

Lawrence himself put it a little differently: 'When it came to the
point, however, pride rebelled. It is understood that Judas is
always ready with a kiss. But that I should have to kiss him
back –!'[37] Within three weeks he had arranged with the bookseller
Edward Titus to handle the new edition. It turned out that none of
the pirated editions sold for less than 300 frs. a copy, 'so I am
arranging for an edition, small, paper bound, at 60 frs., so that
anybody can get it ... I have written a nice introduction telling

them all that I think of them – one can't do more.'[38] The Paris edition came out in May 1929, in a printing of 3000 copies photographically reproduced from the Florentine edition; it was reprinted over and over again – another 10 000 copies in February 1930, for example – so that within a year it had made as much money as the whole of the Florentine edition.

Within a year, however, Lawrence himself was dead. The book was one of the money-spinners that he left behind for Frieda. It was to her, in fact, that Titus sent the 10 000 frs. the book earned in the six months up to May 1930.

II

The year 1928 had, however, been an extraordinary one for Lawrence as a professional writer: firstly for the runaway success of *Lady Chatterley's Lover* and the method of selling it; secondly for the transformation the novel brought to the Lawrences' finances; and thirdly because, simultaneously with the production of the novel, Lawrence's London agents had at least managed to open up a new popular market for his writing.

He had never really been a good judge of what was popular; like Secker, he had thought *The Lost Girl* would be – and it was not; and he had advised Secker that Lion Feuchtwanger's *Jew Süss* was not worth publishing in translation – but 'Luckily he did it, and saved his life and almost made his fortune'. The book came out in November 1926 and sold nearly 90 000 copies in its first two years. The experience confirmed Lawrence's feeling that 'I'm absolutely no good at judging what the public might like'.[39]

Nevertheless, towards the end of April 1927 he had written two essays, one of which ('Making Love to Music') never got published in his lifetime, but the other ('The "Jeune Fille" Wants to Know') – a year later, and revised – was his first ever genuinely popular publication. Nancy Pearn sold it for £10 to the London newspaper *The Evening News*. Lawrence commented that:

I may as well earn this way – though I must say, I had gooseflesh when I saw that page with me in the Evening News, next to the Lady who knows why she couldn't marry a foreigner, because never a one asked her![40]

However, a week later he was more reconciled to the idea:

> I find it really rather amusing to write these little articles. If Mr
> Olley will tell me what he'd like, I'll try more or less to oblige . . .
> if we can make them go higher than ten quid, good for us.
> Perhaps after all the public is not such a dull animal, or would
> prefer an occasional subtle suave stone to polish its wits against.
> Let us see![41]

The public clearly did prefer it: the paper printed, in all, seven
articles by Lawrence between May and October 1928. When they
started, Lawrence was a rather highbrow and relatively little-
known author; but by October he was the notorious author of 'the
most evil outpouring that has ever besmirched the literature of our
country';[42] and that helped him a good deal, when it came to
expanding his market as an author. As he told Secker in December
1928, 'Lately they've taken to asking me for little articles for the
newspapers. It amuses me, when I feel like it . . . it seems *far* the
best way of making money'.[43]

He also received offers he didn't want to accept; his sister Ada,
with him in January 1929, remembered how 'he received scores of
letters from editors of sensational newspapers imploring him to
write articles for them. He could have made a good deal of
money . . .'[44] But he let the *Sunday Dispatch* (who paid £25, not £10)
print three articles, of the same kind as the *Evening News*: the *Daily
Express* also printed two essays. Whereas the last months of 1927
and the early months of 1928 had seen his production of other
writing – apart from *Lady Chatterley's Lover* – slow down to a trickle,
the success of 'The "Jeune Fille" Wants to Know' provoked him to
take hold of his new market with both hands. As he wrote to
Dorothy Brett in America, the royalties from his commercially
published books were still 'damn little':

> What's the good! It pays me far, far better to write little
> newspaper articles, and the papers want them now. Imagine me
> appearing regularly – irregularly, as a matter of fact – in the
> *Evening News, Sunday Dispatch, Daily Express*! But the *Sunday
> Dispatch* gives me £25 for a 2,000 article, written in an hour and a
> half – and nobody would even publish a story like *None of That*.[45]

Between April 1928 and late 1929, Lawrence wrote twenty-six

short popular articles: only six failed to get into print, and only five appeared in 'non-popular' places. He sold the other fifteen at prices between £10 and £25, making considerably more than the 'little money to go on with'[46] he had expected. They were pieces of writing he could – and normally did – dash off in a morning, often before getting up. They were mostly about sex and relationships, with a distinctively astringent, sardonic, provocative tone. Lawrence had often wanted to write for (and make money from) the popular market, and had found time after time that 'I'm afraid I'm not the stuff prosperity is made out of', that it was 'Not my destiny to be popular'.[47] Now at last his agents had found his market, and he had found his voice: a down-to-earth, man-in-the-street voice; one of the selves he could be. He wrote to the editor of the *Sunday Dispatch*, after they had taken his first two articles: 'I really don't know much about the Sunday morning public: or any other':

> But I'd rather write for the *Sunday Dispatch* than for the high-brow papers and magazines. Though the thought of the godless Sabbath public makes me shiver a bit, I still believe it has more spunk than the 'refined' public. It comes back with *some* sort of response, even if it gives one gooseflesh.[48]

He also offered to 'do some articles along the lines you suggest . . . when you have something you really *want*, tell me, I can always do things better if I know they're really wanted.' His essay 'Do Women Change?' – collected as 'Women Don't Change' – was written for the paper some weeks later; he had remarked in May that he preferred it when magazines suggested titles ('it somehow tickles me more'), and that may well have happened on this occasion. The production of these popular pieces, and his avowed liking for them, pays tribute to the profound ordinariness and simplicity of part of Lawrence's genius; it is hard to imagine any other writer of his standing (apart from Bennett) being able to express himself with such good sense, clarity and point, in such circumstances, without compromising himself. Lawrence naturally ignored the controversial language which caused such trouble for him over *Lady Chatterley's Lover*; but he did a good deal to stir people up to recognise points of view very different from their own. At the very start of his writing career, he had wondered whether he would have a chance in journalism: these essays show that with practice he could indeed have been a journalist.

III

One of the lasting effects of the *Lady Chatterley* adventure was that he was left with a very different attitude towards his money-making potential; not only to what he could earn from the articles which the newspapers wanted, but towards what he could earn from small and private publications. His earliest attempts to publish his work in such a way – *Bay* in 1919 and *Reflections on the Death of a Porcupine* in 1925 – had not been particularly successful commercially (the former made almost nothing and the latter paid Lawrence some $400). The little books made up of single short stories published in 1926 and 1928 had done better; and the Black Sun Press had produced a rewritten *Sun* in 1928, in an edition of only 150 ordinary copies (and 15 on vellum). Lawrence had however sold his manuscript to Harry and Caresse Crosby; they paid him with $100 and 5 gold coins; he got no royalties.

When, however, plans were formulated early in 1929 for an expensive and limited edition of his paintings – the kind of production probably impossible before *Lady Chatterley's Lover* had made him notorious – Lawrence reckoned that the book should make him almost £500. Heinemann also wanted to produce his short story 'The Man Who Loved Islands' in an expensive edition, giving him an advance of £300.[49] His name could now sell an expensive limited edition, especially if it was prefaced to risqué work like his paintings, or *Lady Chatterley's Lover* or his volume of poems *Pansies*, or his short novel *The Escaped Cock* about the resurrected Jesus, written between 1927 and 1928. In April 1929 an editor tried to persuade him to allow the republication of the first part of the latter – 'offering me money if I was "in need" ... He kept repeating over 900 *dollars* till I almost told him nine hundred shits'.[50] But no editors had pressed money on Lawrence before.

He was, however, characteristically ambivalent in his attitude towards his new potential: both puritanical and astute. The plans for the book of paintings – to be sold at ten guineas each – seemed 'madness to me ... how mad people are – there is quite a large vogue in editions de luxe that cost two or five or even twenty-five pounds'.[51] He himself had exploited exactly that market when publishing *Lady Chatterley's Lover*; but he was still enough of a puritan and an opponent of the moneyed classes to be angered by its existence, even while profiting from it. When, early in 1929, he sent to his agents a volume of short, doggerel poems which he

called *Pansies* – he had been writing them for several months – he
suggested that Secker should first publish 'just a limited edition of
500 or so, signed at a guinea or thereabouts'. But he would have
liked this to be followed by 'quite a cheap edition, say 2/6, because I
should like them to be easily accessible to poorer people'.[52] The
two types of publication, like the expensive Florentine and cheap
Paris editions of *Lady Chatterley's Lover*, perfectly corresponded to
the kind of author he had finally become: the esoteric writer who
made his money from the expensive purchase, by well-off people,
of signed and limited editions; and the working-class, ordinary
writer who wrote for popular newspapers and who would have
liked his books sold cheaply.

His manuscript copies of *Pansies* were in fact stopped in the post
on their way to Pollinger at Curtis Brown, and Secker objected to a
number of the poems – 'but I am making him include some, and
put just a blank when a word is improper. I won't have him issue a
perfect hymn-book.'[53] He wrote sternly to Secker about his attitude, and about the Home Secretary Sir William Joynson Hicks,
usually known as Jix:

> If you and the respectable booksellers can't stand the word
> cat-piss, then put two plain dashes for the two monstrous
> syllables. And if 'To pee in the eye of a policeman' is beyond all
> bearing, then 'To — in the eye etc.' But would you scrap that
> good sarcastic little poem for the mere three letters 'pee'. That's
> outjixing Jix. It is quite simple. Where the word merely is
> offensive, put a dash. If there is any poem whose *content* is
> alarming, just tell me exactly which it is. And if this isn't
> agreeable to you, let us not bother about the matter any further. I
> can look for another publisher, without being in the least
> offended. But make the *Pansies* into a good, 'innocuous',
> bourgeois little book I will not, and you shall not.[54]

Not only had Lawrence the authority now to insist on what he
wanted, and to take his book elsewhere if need be; he was also
thick-skinned enough to accept his market, and to compromise. He
could allow Secker to produce an expurgated edition, while he
himself arranged for the almost simultaneous publication of a
complete edition by another publisher. Secker's *Pansies*, with 14
poems missing, came out in July 1929 in both expensive signed
copies (at 2 guineas) and cheaper ordinary copies (costing 10/6);

while an edition including all the poems, costing £2 for the paper covered version (and more for the hard-cover version), was produced in August by P. R. Stephenson, the man who had handled Lawrence's book of paintings. Secker had to accept the rival edition: but could console himself that he was allowed to go on producing the book after his rival's (never reprinted) sold out. Lawrence had always insisted that he would be a good, if long-term investment for his publishers: that was becoming true at last. The only audience not catered for by the various editions of *Pansies*, ironically, was the ordinary audience Lawrence also wanted to get through to, and wanted to reach with his 60 fr. (10/-) *Lady Chatterley's Lover*. 'I do hope you'll bring out a cheap edition, soon' Lawrence told Secker in August 1929, and repeated the request in November.[55] Secker never did, though he reprinted the book twice.

Lawrence was, however, able to get his way with two little books he produced in the aftermath of the row over the exhibition of his paintings in the summer of 1929. The exhibition had been raided by the police, and 13 pictures had stood trial. Lawrence's essay 'Pornography and Obscenity' was published by Faber and Faber at only 1/- in a series in which they also asked the Home Secretary 'Jix' to write in favour of Censorship. Lawrence was quite elated when his pamphlet sold better than his rival's: it sold 6000 copies in three weeks.[56] And although Secker never produced a cheap edition of Lawrence's *Pansies*, Faber and Faber brought out his final little book of poems, *Nettles* – many of them about the police-raid on the exhibition – in a 1/- paperback with a first print-run of 3000, soon reprinted.

Book after book, in these years after *Lady Chatterley's Lover*, thus sold well after years of small editions and poor sales. Lawrence's new-found sense of his commercial potential also lay behind his anger when Caresse Crosby sold yet another limited edition of his work, the Black Sun edition of *The Escaped Cock*, to a New York bookseller on most unfavourable terms: Lawrence wrote to her just a fortnight before he died:

> did you really sell that whole edition for $2250? It seems absurd, for Marks was selling it at $25 a copy, as I know from two sources. He may have had to come down in price, later. But did you sell the whole edition, *including the vellums*, for $2250? If you did, you are not the good business woman I should expect you

to be, and I resent bitterly those little Jew booksellers making all that money out of us.[57]

There had been 450 ordinary copies, and 50 on vellum. Given that the latter would cost a good deal more than the former, the ordinary copies had been sold to Harry Marks for rather less than $4.00 each; while if Marks had sold only half of the ordinary copies at $25 he would still have made himself $5625. We don't know what percentage Lawrence was getting from the Black Sun Press: but even 33⅓% of $2250 was only $750.00, and he may well have got less. With an exchange rate of (now) roughly $5 to the £1, that meant £150 or less: the kind of royalty which, in the old days, he would have been pleased to get for a not particularly successful novel, but which was now absurd. It is not surprising that Lawrence was annoyed. By 1930, just before he died, he had at last become a writer who knew how and where he could get a good return for his work.

There continued, of course, the profound contradiction between the author who allowed himself to appear in expensive limited editions, and the man who denounced those same editions. He told an impecunious friend, Max Mohr, about what he considered as the insanity – and immorality – of the market for which his volumes of paintings was produced:

The book is to be sold at 10 guineas a copy, with ten copies on vellum – Pergament – at 50 guineas a copy ... Well, there were sixty orders for the copies of 50 guineas – those on vellum. Of course only ten are printed. But this shows you the insanity of this modern collection of books. And a good author can't even get his work printed. Makes me tired! I hate this expensive edition business.[58]

He may have hated it, but we can see how glady he profited by it too, he who until so recently had himself been in the position of the good author who could not get his work printed.

10
Providing: 1929–30

All his life Lawrence had been financially careful; he remained strict about small sums of money as much as about large ones. He was not a good business man, because he did not devote himself assiduously enough to making money or to organising his affairs, though, as Frieda once wrote, 'Had he succumbed to the "passion for possessions", he, with his great intelligence directed that way, would have made pots...'[1] But his letters show innumerable examples of his shrewdness and carefulness. He had once remarked to Dorothy Brett that 'I would loathe to draw a cheque if I thought it wouldn't be covered: it's sort of false' (*Letters*, V, p. 426). He paid his bills promptly and – if short of money – tried to ensure that he had few bills. He always paid on the nail for services rendered. A friend typed for him, and received the instruction: 'count the thousands, and I'll pay the current rate. 1/- per 1000, 3d for carbon' (ibid., p. 343). His Florentine doctor, submitting a bill, was prepared to take a copy of *Lady Chatterley's Lover* to be going on with, but Lawrence commented 'Really, I much prefer to pay him. One doesn't want to have those things unpaid'.[2] In 1926 his friend Dorothy Brett went back to the American ranch which Frieda owned, and Lawrence regularly wrote to her with instructions about paying to have ditches cleaned, and on buying food for the horses; and with comments about what she herself should be spending:

Don't get yourself into financial straits, it is such a handicap. (*Letters*, V, p. 421)

If you get stuck for money, let me know. Any expenses incurred for the Ranch, I will pay. But be careful and thoughtful, don't do foolish things, and don't buy unnecessary ones. All our means, of all sorts, are definitely limited (ibid., p. 441)

Be economical, & get your debts paid off – they are a great bore.[3]

His behaviour was a direct consequence of how he had been brought up, and of how he had learned to survive on 'limited' means over the years of his literary career. In 1929 he gave advice to the young American author Edward Dahlberg:

> if you are going to write, manage the business end of it as sensibly as you can. Many young men make their real mess there ... It's up to you to use your wits and your energies *not* to go hungry. I have lived myself on next to nothing, for years, yet I never went hungry ...[4]

But after the success of *Lady Chatterley's Lover*, simultaneously with his own rapid decline in health during 1929, he became particularly concerned about how he – and how Frieda, after him – would be able to live in the future. During his last years he had to pay bills such as he had not previously faced; and that was going to get worse. 'It is not cheap, being ill', he remarked at the end of 1927. At the end of July 1928, for example, his Florentine doctor's bill came to 1345 lire – £14 10s. 'Not cheap!' Lawrence exclaimed; he had not even been ill much. What made things worse was that, after 1928, he and Frieda were no longer able to live in places which depended upon Lawrence doing any physical work for the household. They lived in small hotels or in rented houses with a maid and a cook. Following the *annus mirabilis* 1928, for the moment they no longer had any financial problems. But Lawrence knew that his new-found capacity to earn might not continue for very long; and that he, too, would not live very long. He became very conscious of what best to do with what he had. He had never possessed property, or very much of anything; it was his literary property which was valuable: his books, his copyrights and even his manuscripts. In the late 1920s, he became aware of how much the latter were worth, and started to think of them (very rightly, as it turned out) as a kind of 'nest-egg': 'they may come in so handy some rainy day'.[5] He started to take care to preserve them.

Similar canny advice also went to his relations. He had never been one to bother about the value of his first editions; but he advised his sister Ada, early in 1928, 'I hope you keep all the first editions – they're all worth a guinea & more each now – so one day they'll be quite a nice little sum'.[6] And when he sent a copy of *Lady*

Chatterley's Lover to his other sister Emily at the end of 1928, he told her how:

> It is being sold in the shops now at £5-5-0. But if I were you I wouldn't read it, you'll find it mostly rather heavy. And don't let Peg read it either – just keep it uncut, its value then is higher. –[7]

He had originally tried to prevent either of his sisters knowing about the book, and was in part trying to stop Emily reading it; but he was, too, giving Emily thoroughly sensible advice. Peggy, then 19, however did read her mother's copy, one wet Good Friday afternoon.[8]

He also invested his own savings, though he had problems justifying such investment to himself; his friend Earl Brewster remembered how he 'often expressed himself as ashamed that he had any money saved in banks or stocks'. But the Curtis Brown agency in New York provided him with advice and put him in touch with a broker; he had invested money in Heat and Light companies, and in some railroad stock. He was not, however, to know that 1928–29 was a particularly bad time to invest in American industry; Brewster recalled how:

> when the financial crisis fell upon the New York markets, that winter, he furiously objected to being informed, or to Frieda's even looking to see, if it had affected their investments.[9]

He does not appear to have lost very much; but the fact of the investment (with money earned from *Lady Chatterley's Lover*) is another good example of the ambivalent attitude he had towards money-making, and towards his new-found (if relative) prosperity. He preferred not to care about such things, but he continually found that he had to care. He actually seemed more concerned about the finances of others than his own; he was particularly worried, for example, about the Brewsters, who also had money invested in America. His last letter to Earl Brewster, written three days before he died, characteristically asked, 'How much did those shares bring you, actually? Tell me.'[10]

II

As 1929 went on it became clear that, in spite of the success of *Lady Chatterley's Lover* and of the other limited editions of his work which were coming out, Lawrence's health would not permit him to add to his earnings by writing very much more. 'I shan't die . . . a rich man now', he remarked to Frieda that winter: 'perhaps it's just as well, it might have done something to me'.[11] Frieda thought that extremely doubtful. But Lawrence had stopped writing fiction; his final story ('"Henry"', she said') was started in January 1929 but not finished; his last completed stories, *The Escaped Cock* and 'The Blue Moccasins', dated from July 1928. He was still capable of bursts of energy which allowed him to write, for example, the lengthy 'Introduction' to his book of paintings in January 1929, and the pamphlet *Pornography & Obscenity* in April. But over the next few months he otherwise wrote only short things: some introductions and reviews; some more poems in the *Pansies* vein; the *Nettles* poems; a number of poems about death (rather unusual in addressing the topic directly). He made no attempt to publish the latter. In November 1929 he wrote the last of his popular essays, 'The Real Thing'; and in December he put together, for Secker, a revised collection of his essays which he called *Assorted Articles*. It was as if he were consciously rounding off his writing life. Then, between October 1929 and January 1930 he wrote his last piece of any length: the short book *Apocalypse*, which started as an introduction to a book by his friend Frederick Carter, but which grew beyond all bounds and took on a life of its own. He wrote it as he had often written: for the love of the exploration which writing meant, rather than for the reward which it might bring. That would come, he believed and expected, because he thought his work was good, and he always needed it to be paid for decently. But the reward was only one reason why he wrote. *Apocalypse* was a book which explored man's relationship not solely with the human world, but with the cosmos: the man who was dying wrote how 'I am part of the sun as my eye is part of me . . .'[12]

III

His financial cares now were not for himself, but for Frieda; the saving and securing of his manuscripts, for example, was so as to provide another sort of insurance policy for her. He had always taken care of financial matters, in spite of Frieda's occasional (and rather disastrous) attempts to organise things; now he had, so far as possible, to leave things tidy for her. When he had to go into a sanatorium at the start of February 1930, Frieda remembered:

> With a set face Lawrence made me bring all his papers on to his bed and he tore most of them up and made everything tidy and neat and helped to pack his own trunks, and I never cried . . . His self discipline kept me up . . .[13]

The main problem with his published work was with his American publications, following Seltzer's demise as a publisher; Seltzer's nephews, the Boni brothers, had taken over Seltzer's titles – but neither they, nor Knopf, was having much financial success; what Frieda called 'this priceless unique property' of Lawrence's writing was bringing in 'not 200 dollars a year in America',[14] which seems quite extraordinary. But Lawrence was leaving it to his agents to sort out the mess; eventually, the Viking Press took over the Lawrence titles in America and made a great deal of money. But that money was for Frieda, not for Lawrence; he died on 2 March 1930.

During the years of their travels, however, his will had got lost: when he asked about it three days before his death, Frieda 'told him not to worry about it. He said that in any case she would have everything.'[15] But the fact that he died intestate led to two and a half years of quarrels, recriminations and (in the end) a lawsuit between Frieda and some of the Lawrence family. Lawrence's sister Emily and brother George wanted Frieda to have the income of the estate during her lifetime, so long as the copyrights reverted to the Lawrence family after her death. Frieda – supported by Lawrence's sister Ada, let it be said – wanted both income and copyrights, on the grounds that Lawrence would certainly have wanted her to have them. For two years the estate was administered jointly by Frieda and by George Lawrence; but the dispute culminated in a hearing in London in 1932 which awarded Frieda the estate: capital, income, copyrights, everything. The family were left a number of manuscripts and paintings, in compensation. From that day to this, not a single relative of Lawrence's has earned a penny from the sale of his books; when Frieda died in 1956 she divided her estate equally between her children and her third husband, Angelo Ravagli, so that the continuing income of the estate goes to the relatives of Frieda's children by her marriage to Ernest Weekley (whom she left for Lawrence), and to the relatives of Angelo Ravagli (with whom she frequently betrayed Lawrence before his death).

But what Lawrence earned between 1927 and 1930 was increasingly designed to give Frieda some security, so that she could go on living as he and she had lived together: where she wanted and as she wanted. And in fact she managed to do that to the end of her life, out of the income of Lawrence's estate. When she died, the Lawrence estate was one of the most valuable literary properties in the Western world; and even after the end of the 50 years copyright in 1980, the new edition of Lawrence's work published by Cambridge University Press (publishing for the first time what Lawrence wrote, not what typists and publishers made of him) continues to make money – for its editors, publishers and agents, and for the Weekley and Ravagli relatives. Lawrence several times remarked that the value of his writing would be recognised only after his death. But the fact that his writing made so little money for him, but so much for others, is the final and greatest irony of his literary career; of those years of struggles, of unpopularity, of his writing subsidising his travels and new experiences; of, finally, writing and publishing what he wanted, regardless; of writing, writing, writing.... *Lady Chatterley's Lover* and his other late writings made him the money he had never previously managed to earn; but, as so often before and after, it was mostly others who profited from it.

Epilogue

By no standards had Lawrence been a commercially successful writer. But the progress of his writing career also suggests something else: the process of his own alientation not only from the class from which he came, and from any of the classes into which he might have moved (including that of the London literary world), but from his own readers; it shows (in the words of E. M. Forster) 'the greatest imaginative novelist of our generation'[1] suffering isolation and exile; and his work, too, suffering from that same isolation and exile.

Before the First World War, a novelist like Lawrence was, in the commercial market of the day, able to write his work very much as he wanted it, speaking directly to the largely middle-class audience which he knew would read it; and his work also earned his living for him. The only real pressure he felt – especially during 1912 and early in 1913, when he had just committed himself to the life of the full-time writer – was not to alienate his publisher, and not to attract moral censorship. Heinemann turned down the 'Paul Morel' novel in the summer of 1912 because Lawrence had not been sufficiently careful. Accordingly, Lawrence allowed Edward Garnett to cut *Sons and Lovers* – much longer than the normal commercial novel – for sound commercial reasons; and he was perfectly prepared for Garnett, Duckworth and his printer to tone down the novel's sexually explicit scenes.

In the course of 1913, however, having abandoned yet another novel draft as unpublishable on moral grounds, and having committed himself to writing a commercial novel – a 'pot-boiler' – he found himself able to survive financially without producing another novel immediately. Accordingly he proceeded – through a number of drafts – to create a novel which was as dangerous (morally) as the one he had abandoned; and which was thoroughly 'difficult' by the standards of the age. It also grew extremely long – much longer than the commercially-cut *Sons and Lovers*. And this time he refused to take the advice of his publishers' reader, Edward Garnett, who was severely critical of it. This second novel, which became *The Rainbow* and *Women in Love*, would not concern itself with being successful and would not compromise with its market; it would be thoroughly serious and yet (Lawrence believed) it would also sell and support him.

The literary agents and publishers who pursued his work through 1913 and 1914, following the reputation *Sons and Lovers* had made him, did not know about his change of attitude; and for a while he found them competing with each other for his custom. He acquired J. B. Pinker as an agent, and both a £300 advance and a three-novel contract from Methuen, the same publisher who had signed an identical contract with Joseph Conrad (another client of Pinker), who enjoyed Bennett's commercial success and who had offered Mackenzie a £750 advance. Unfortunately, Lawrence's breakthrough happened on the eve of the First World War; and though he attempted to maintain his uncompromising attitude towards the commercial market until 1915, he then experienced the catastrophe of the prosecution of *The Rainbow*. This was a sign that his most serious work was not only uncommercial, especially in the new conditions imposed by the war; it was also actually anathema to critics and a large number of readers. Following the disaster, Lawrence lost all his new status; he became an almost unpublishable author, and could not get another novel into print for five years. The 'unseen witnesses' (*Letters*, II, p. 602) he wrote of in 1916 were, indeed, almost the only audience he could appeal to. *Women in Love*, published in America in 1920 but finished much earlier, was probably Lawrence's last book to be written out of the belief that, serious and even esoteric as it was, it could still affect profoundly the lives of ordinary people; and it was a much more pessimistic and depressing book than *The Rainbow* had been. Between 1915 and 1919, Lawrence suffered a 'death in belief'; and the belief tended to be replaced by irony, rage and preaching. Not all the time, nor in all his books; but it was a tendency that never really went away.

After the war, we can observe a potential split developing between his 'serious' work (particularly in his novels) and his other work. His short stories, his magazine articles, a travel book such as *Sea and Sardinia* and his novel *The Lost Girl* might all have been wholly commercial; and at moments that was how Lawrence thought of them. Some writers in our century have taken that way out of the dilemma of how to live by their writing: Robert Graves subsidised his poetry writing for many years by writing popular novels. A writer such as James Joyce, on the other hand, never allowed himself to make any such division: for years he precariously supported his writing, himself and his family by language teaching; and after that relied upon the heavy financial subsidies which a number of people – impressed by his genius – were prepared to pay him.[2] He was able to write with no thought at all of his market or of the public.

In the early 1920s, lacking any such subsidy, Lawrence might well have resigned himself to the fact that his kind of serious book would never be popular, would never do more than scrape him a living; that he would have to subsidise his experimental and unpopular writing by more commercially acceptable work. It might have been easier for him if he had decided to do that. But in spite of a book like *The Lost Girl*, he never really tried; and (typically), because of its particularly explicit sexuality, even *The Lost Girl* turned out to be unacceptable to the very market he had hoped would buy most copies – that of the circulating libraries.

Lawrence believed in himself and his writing too much to make such a division. He always believed in his capacity to know the truth and to be the source of it for others – even if those others were the English people he so often scorned, but to whom he remained so strongly attached. He always believed in overturning the boundaries and conventions of accepted middle-class literature; in particular he wanted to write about sexual experience. He believed, too, in his gifted (and given) artist's voice, even when writing popularly. *Fantasia of the Unconscious* is a good example of a book which stands rather uneasily between the 'serious' and the 'popular', and partakes of both. It was characteristic of him to produce it in the early 1920s. It is highly intelligent and bristling with good sense; it is also esoteric, dogmatic and at times outrageous; and, in spite of being written popularly, it was never really successful.

Lawrence went on believing that it was primarily an accident of publisher, agent or public that prevented him from being a successful writer; though by now he was also thoroughly suspicious of 'the public'. His agents believed that it was because of the explicit sexuality of his writing, and begged him to tone it down. Only the fact that, as ever, he wrote an enormous amount kept him going, financially. Putting it crudely, he wrote so much not just because he was a creative genius, but because his books often sold so poorly that he had to write lots of them. For a while in the early 1920s the sheer number of books he had on offer, and the *succès de scandale* enjoyed by Thomas Seltzer in the American market with *Women in Love*, made it seem that Lawrence had at last established himself. But it was not as quite the same kind of writer he had been before 1913, or up to 1916. Neither in optimism nor in his relationship with his audience could he be what he had been before the war. The 'serious' work Lawrence produced in the 1920s increasingly came to be written with a rather narrow, or at least a very reduced, sense of relationship with its readers. And it tended to be drained of the lively wit which characterised his popular writing; it was in danger of communing with itself, and of preaching at its audience rather than subverting it. He always liked to feel that, as an author, he was 'in among the crowd, kicking their shins or cheering them on to some mischief or merriment' (*Letters*, V, p. 201), as he described it in 1925; but that is not a good description of his later novels. Indeed, his last two novels, *The Plumed Serpent* and *Lady Chatterley's Lover*, were in many respects genuinely hermetic: written out of a profound sense of alienation, prophetic in different ways but programmatic in rather similar ones; genuine preachings, of a kind incompatible with very much involvement with or belief in their audience.

By 1925 Lawrence's health was severely damaged; and after his illness in Oaxaca he was never really well again. But he was also no longer able to produce the bulk of work he had formerly created; the bottom had fallen out of Seltzer's business, and Lawrence lost both money and sales. Over the next two years, his income began to drop alarmingly. If it had not been for his breakthrough with *Lady Chatterley's Lover*, and the good sense with which he wrote his late, short popular essays (for the first time accepting in them a wholly commercial market, and writing for it directly), his last years might have been a dreadful catalogue of poverty, hopelessness, illness and rage.

In tracing the history of Lawrence as a professional writer, then, this book also suggests a new way of understanding the change in his writing which most critics observe coming over Lawrence's work during and after the war. For one thing, he consciously wrote most of his shorter fiction to sell; and he produced some books (like *Sea and Sardinia*) particularly to do so – though he damaged the chances of that book by insisting that its publishers include his friend Jan Juta's colour illustrations, which effectively doubled its price and spoiled its market. The kind of work he began to do in his novels, however, was in general more consciously experimental than we generally allow. It was not work with which he really thought he could make his living; that would have to be taken care of by the mass of other forms in which he wrote. And we can see his novels striking out in new (if not always successful) directions, while he resisted his agents' and publishers' pleas to tone down their sexual content. Such experiments were effectively subsidised by the bread-and-butter of his rather more restrained general publishing. But the very division of his work into a serious, rather non-popular sort and an easier, though not really commercial kind, was itself destructive. Only in the last two years of his life – when he almost abandoned the writing of fiction – was Lawrence able to earn his living as the author of select and limited editions, produced only for the wealthy but saying exactly what he wanted. He was simultaneously able to reconcile his sense of alienation from an audience with his capacity to write directly and commercially for the English people in whom (in spite of all his anger with them) he continued to wish to believe. At last he produced some genuinely popular, genuinely commercial work.

But that does not mean that he was, in the end, able to return to where he had been as a writer in the summer of 1913. The world had changed, and he himself had changed; the man who wrote so enthusiastically in the hope that 'English folk would alter' in 1913, and who felt that he could and would change them, was now fifteen years older, and divided from his audience by habit, domicile and illness. He was skilled as a popular essayist; but also constantly referred back to an older, warmer-hearted and instinctive England which was part of his own very personal myth, and had very little to do with the England that had actually existed. When he wrote about the real world, he was as inclined to write *Nettles* – short, sharp and stinging poems – as to dwell upon the capacity of the English for change; and when he did write directly about the English, it tended to be in the same tone of voice as Mellors announcing gloomily 'they're very dead'.[3]

We can, therefore, see Lawrence's professional career not only as a triumph of resilience as he won out against considerable odds; but also as exemplifying the problems encountered this century by the serious writer who has to compromise with publishers needing to make profits, and thus with his own market. Such problems were heightened in Lawrence's case by his natural alienation from the ways of the literary world. He always felt he was, by class, background and inclination, an outsider in it; he preferred (if he could) to form relationships of trust and friendship within it, rather than to make business contacts; and he was regularly disappointed. His appointment of Robert Mountsier and then (if only briefly) of Barbara Low as his literary agents show how much he wished to avoid, if he could, the normal habits of the transaction of literary business; so did the (temporarily) more successful relationships he formed with Edward Garnett and Thomas Seltzer. He would have preferred to keep his distance from the literary world, of which he remained thoroughly suspicious; but as a professional writer, he could not do so. Again, from the very start of his career he had been regarded as a 'working-class genius', with all the disadvantages of waywardness and perversity which accompanied such an appellation. But he was also deeply and genuinely affected by his own removal from the working class into an uneasy classlessness; and by his rage and anger when his own attempts at books that reached out to his English readership were actually rejected – in the case of *The Rainbow*, literally destroyed.

It is natural, therefore, that if we wish to celebrate Lawrence's achievement as a professional writer – and it is a remarkable story – then we should understand, too, how his particular experiences changed him as a writer. This book has endeavoured both to describe the detail and richness of the day-to-day achievement, and to suggest the larger changes which beset the writing itself, as the writer was himself beset.

Notes

Abbreviations

The following abbreviations are employed in the notes:

Cincinatti   Manuscript in the possession of the University of Cincinatti.
Clarke   Manuscript in the possession of W. H. Clarke, Esq.
DHL   D. H. Lawrence.
Lazarus   Manuscript in the possession of G. Lazarus, Esq.
NYPL   Manuscript in the possession of the Berg Collection, New York Public Library.
UT   Manuscript in the possession of the Harry Ransom Humanities Research Center, University of Texas.

The place of publication of books is London unless otherwise stated.

Introduction

1. The Curtis Brown Archives (UT) reveal that on 7 October 1929 Bonbright & Co. – working on DHL's behalf – sold 20 American Superpower shares for $1965 and bought 60 shares in the United Corporation for $2887.50; they retained 10 Chicago Northwestern Railway shares and a total of 33 shares in Commonwealth & Southern Warrants, in Superpower and in Electric Power & Light, worth altogether $3134.25.
2. Harry T. Moore, *The Priest of Love* (Heinemann, 1974) p. 442.
3. Richard Aldington, *Portrait of a Genius, but . . .* (Heinemann, 1950) pp. 315–16.
4. *The Letters of D. H. Lawrence*, Volume I, edited by J. T. Boulton (Cambridge University Press, 1979) p. 510. Future references to the Cambridge edition of Lawrence's letters will be given in short form in the text, e.g. (*Letters*, I, p. 510).
5. Frieda Lawrence, *The Memoirs and Correspondence* (Heinemann, 1961) p. 54.
6. Ibid., Frieda Lawrence, 'Introduction' to *Look! We Have Come Through!* (Brushford: Ark Press, 1971) p. 11.
7. Frieda Lawrence, *'Not I, But the Wind . . .'* (Santa Fe: Rydal Press, 1934) p. 20.
8. Compton Mackenzie, *My Life and Times: Octave Four* (Chatto and Windus, 1965) p. 190.
9. *Letters of Arnold Bennett*, Volume I, edited by J. Hepburn (Oxford University Press, 1966) p. 120.
10. Ibid., p. 147.
11. Ibid., p. 296.
12. Ibid., p. 365.

13. DHL to Aldous Huxley, 27 March 1928.
14. F. Karl, *Joseph Conrad* (New York: Farrar, Strauss and Giroux, 1979) p. 730.

Chapter 1: Early Years

1. E. T. [Jessie Chambers], *D. H. Lawrence: A Personal Record* (Jonathan Cape, 1935) p. 57.
2. Ibid., p. 47.
3. D. H. Lawrence, 'Autobiographical Sketch', *Phoenix II*, edited by Warren Roberts and Harry T. Moore (Heinemann, 1968) p. 300.
4. 'Getting On', p. 6 (Cincinnati).
5. George Neville, *A Memoir of D. H. Lawrence*, edited by Carl Baron (Cambridge, University Press, 1981) p. 42.
6. Edward Nehls, *D. H. Lawrence: A Composite Biography*, Volume III (Madison: University of Wisconsin Press, 1959) p. 601.
7. 'Getting On', p. 6.
8. Emile Delavenay, *D. H. Lawrence: L'Homme et la Genèse de Son Oeuvre*, Vol. II (Paris: Klincksieck, 1969) p. 665.
9. 'Getting On', p. 6.
10. 'Autobiographical Sketch', *Phoenix II*, p. 595.
11. E. T., *A Personal Record*, p. 156.
12. Ibid., p. 157.
13. Ibid., p. 158.
14. Ibid., p. 179.
15. Frank Swinnerton, *The Georgian Literary Scene*, revised edn (Dent and Sons, 1951) p. 299.
16. 'Autobiographical Sketch', *Phoenix II*, pp. 593–4.
17. Compton Mackenzie, *Octave Four* (Chatto and Windus, 1965) p. 190.
18. Ford Madox Hueffer to DHL, 15 December 1909 (Lazarus).
19. 'Autobiographical Sketch', *Phoenix II*, p. 592.
20. In June 1911, when DHL was paid £10 for 'Odour of Chrysanthemums', he remarked that it was 'twice the amount I expected' (*Letters*, I, p. 282); the earlier story probably therefore earned £5.
21. Lydia Lawrence to Ada Krenkow, 8 February 1910 (Clarke).
22. Nehls, I, p. 109.
23. 'Autobiographical Sketch', *Phoenix II*, p. 593; Hueffer to DHL, 15 December 1909.
24. *The White Peacock*, edited by Andrew Robertson (Cambridge University Press, 1983) pp. 149, l. 1; 150, ll. 22–3; Textual Apparatus pp. 150, l. 22; 150, ll. 26–7.
25. D. H. Lawrence, 'Introduction to *A Bibliography of D. H. Lawrence*', *Phoenix*, edited by Edward D. McDonald (New York: Viking Press, 1936) p. 233.
26. Ibid., p. 232.
27. Swinnerton, *The Georgian Literary Scene*, p. 222.
28. 'Introduction to *The Collected Poems of D. H. Lawrence*', *Phoenix*, p. 253.
29. Frieda Lawrence, *'Not I, But the Wind ...'* (Santa Fe: Rydal Press, 1934) p. 53.

30.   'Autobiographical Sketch', *Phoenix II*, p. 593.

Chapter 2: First Year as a Professional Writer: 1912–13

1.   See *Mr Noon*, edited by Lindeth Vasey (Cambridge University Press,
       1984) p. 172, ll. 23–5, for an episode where DHL's recreation of his
       sister-in-law Else provides money for Gilbert and Johanna (his
       recreation of Frieda and himself). In 1923, Frieda recalled that Else
       'has been so well off' (*D. H. Lawrence: Letters to Thomas and Adele
       Seltzer*, edited by Gerald M. Lacy (Santa Barbara: Black Sparrow
       Press, 1976) p. 64.
2.   Hutchinson & Co. to DHL, 17 September 1912, and T. Fisher Unwin
       to DHL, 19 September 1912 (NYPL).
3.   *The Letters of Arnold Bennett*, Vol. I, edited by J. Hepburn (Oxford
       University Press, 1966) p. 188.
4.   See Mackenzie's *Octave Four* (Chatto and Windus, 1965) for his
       experiences with library censorship in 1913.
5.   'Introduction to *Memoirs of the Foreign Legion*', *Phoenix II* (Heinemann,
       1968) p. 312.
6.   'Italian Studies: By the Lago di Garda', *English Review* (September
       1913), vol. xv, pp. 202–34; these were early versions of three essays
       published in *Twilight in Italy* in 1916.

Chapter 3: Success and Catastrophe: 1913–15

1.   The publisher's calculation presumably was that an edition of 2500
       copies retailing at 6/- should, after the bookseller's discount (around
       30%), bring in £500, while their own production costs would not
       have amounted to more than around £200. A 15% royalty on the 6/-
       published price of the first 2500 copies would provide Lawrence
       with £112.10.0, and Duckworth with a final profit of a little less than
       £200.
2.   *Daily News*, 7 June 1913, p. 4; *Times Literary Supplement*, 12 June 1913,
       p. 256; *Academy*, 28 June 1913, p. 815; *Nation*, 12 July 1913, p. 577.
3.   *Sons and Lovers* did not appear in the list of 'the most popular novels
       of the year' published by the *Times Literary Supplement*, 30 October
       1913, p. 483:
       Hall Caine, *The Woman Thou Gavest Me*
       Jeffrey Farnol, *The Amateur Gentleman*
       Mrs Humphrey Ward, *The Mating of Lydia*
       W. B. Maxwell, *The Devil's Garden*
       Florence L. Barclay, *The Broken Halo*
       W. J. Locke, *Stella Maris*
       Baroness Orczy, *Eldorado*
       Arnold Bennett, *The Regent*
       H. G. Wells, *The Passionate Friends*
       Sir Gilbert Parker, *The Judgement House*
       Robert Hitchens, *The Way of Ambition*
       Hugh Walpole, *Fortitude*

4.   A. M. S. Methuen to J. B. Pinker, 4 July 1913 (NYPL). Assuming that Duckworth's production costs had been around £200, and given they had paid Lawrence's £100 advance, this means that the book must have sold rather fewer than 1500 copies (which would have brought in £300) during its first year.

5.   Publication of English novels in America was hedged around with problems at this time; unless, for example, the novel had been printed in America, it had no copyright there (hence Heinemann's concern to get *The White Peacock* printed in America, in spite of it having been set up in type in England first). The publication of Lawrence's first three novels in America had been arranged by his English publishers, but for *The White Peacock* we have no record of Lawrence making any money at all out of the American publication. It seems possible that Heinemann simply pocketed the money from the American edition published by Duffield. Duckworth arranged for Mitchell Kennerley to publish *The Trespasser* and *Sons and Lovers*; as the first was produced from sheets sold by Duckworth at something less than the full trade price, the royalty to Lawrence would inevitably have been small, though in March 1913 Kennerley was arranging to pay (*Letters*, I, p. 542 n. 2), and on 30 June 1913 did so. Kennerley printed (and therefore copyrighted) *Sons and Lovers* himself, but we know only of his initial payment of £35 to Lawrence. This was just the kind of matter which a literary agent could be charged to pursue, and the author's share secured: but Lawrence had no agent until 1914, and his earlier books remained beyond that agent's control.

6.   Norman Boyer to J. B. Pinker, 12 March 1914 (NYPL).

7.   In 1908, for example, Conrad was about £1600 in debt to Pinker. *The Collected Letters of Joseph Conrad*, edited by F. J. Karl (Cambridge University Press, 1983) p. 489.

8.   *Daily News*, 5 October 1915, p. 6.

9.   *Sphere*, 23 October 1915, p. 104.

10.   Ibid.

11.   *Star*, 22 October 1915, p. 4.

12.   A. M. S. Methuen to J. B. Pinker, 18 October 1915 (NYPL).

13.   *The Rainbow*, edited Mark Kinkead-Weekes (Cambridge University Press, 1989) pp. xlv, l; A. M. S. Methuen to J. B. Pinker, 9 December 1915 (NYPL).

14.   *Sunday Times*, 14 November 1915, p. 13.

15.   Ibid.

16.   'Introduction to *A Bibliography of D. H. Lawrence*', *Phoenix*, p. 234.

17.   *Daily Telegraph*, 15 November 1915, p. 12.

18.   Edward Nehls, *D. H. Lawrence: A Composite Biography*, Vol. I (Madison: University of Wisconsin Press, 1957) p. 335.

19.   J. M. Murry, *Between Two Worlds* (Jonathan Cape, 1935) p. 351.

Chapter 4: War: 1915–16

1.   The conjectural date of the spring of 1924 for the story's composition,

176   *Notes*

given in *St. Mawr and Other Stories*, edited by Brian Finney (Cambridge University Press, 1983) pp. xxi–xxii, is incorrect.

2. A suggestion that this was 'almost certainly the story published as "Samson and Delilah"' (*Letters* II, p. 493 n. 3) must be wrong; that story was drafted in a notebook left over from *Women in Love*, and cannot have been written before November 1916.

3. Arthur Waugh (Chapman and Hall Ltd) to J. B. Pinker, 26 April 1917 (NYPL).

4. Frieda Lawrence, *The Memoirs and Correspondence* (Heinemann, 1961) p. 133.

5. *The Rainbow*, edited by Mark Kinkead-Weekes (Cambridge University Press, 1989) p. li.

6. *Women in Love*, edited by David Farmer, Lindeth Vasey and John Worthen (Cambridge University Press, 1987) p. 431, ll. 27–8.

7. Catherine Carswell, *The Savage Pilgrimage* (Chatto and Windus, 1932) p. 80.

Chapter 5: Poverty: 1917–19

1. Austin Harrison to J. B. Pinker, 2 July 1917 (NYPL).

2. Austin Harrison to J. B. Pinker, 7 March 1917; W. L. Courtney to J. B. Pinker, 28 April 1917 (NYPL).

3. Isaac Spalding to J. B. Pinker, 8 October 1917 (NYPL).

4. *St. Ives Times*, 5 October 1917, p. 3.

5. *Letters of Arnold Bennett*, Vol. I, edited by J. Hepburn (Oxford University Press, 1966) pp. 260, 261 n. 245.

6. B. W. Huebsch to J. B. Pinker, 23 December 1919 (NYPL).

7. D. H. Lawrence, *Kangaroo* (Secker, 1923) p. 288.

8. Virginia Roderick to J. B. Pinker, 5 August 1919; *The Rainbow* sold 54 copies, *Twilight* 85 copies, *Amores* 112 copies and *The Prussian Officer* 79 copies – George Doran to J. B. Pinker, 5 August 1920 (NYPL).

9. Warren Roberts, *A Bibliography of D. H. Lawrence*, 2nd edn (Cambridge University Press, 1982) p. 37.

10. Goldring, however, deceived him over *Touch and Go*:

> Goldring got *Touch and Go* out of me, saying it *Touch and Go* would be the first of the 'Plays for a Peoples Theatre'. Then the sly journalist went and put this offensive *Fight for Freedom* [his own play] as the first play – and for sure has damned and doubly damned the lot. I don't *want* to be associated with the *Fight for Freedom* and it's knavish preface. And there is *Touch and Go*, with a preface written specially. Curse the sly mongrel world. (*Letters*, III, p. 469)

> The arrangement with Goldring was Lawrence's first venture at running his business affairs without the help of Pinker; it had clearly not been a success.

Chapter 6: Struggling Through: 1919–21

1. 'Introduction to *Memoirs of the Foreign Legion*', *Phoenix II*, p. 303.
2. *Women in Love*, edited by David Farmer, Lindeth Vasey and John Worthen (Cambridge University Press, 1987) p. xliii.
3. Ibid.
4. Ibid.
5. Ibid.
6. *The Lost Girl*, edited by John Worthen (Cambridge University Press, 1981) pp. 233 l. 35–234 l. 17.
7. Ibid., p. xxxix.
8. Ibid., pp. 386–7.
9. *Women in Love*, edited by Farmer, Vasey and Worthen, p. xliv.
10. *Mr Noon*, edited by Lindeth Vasey (Cambridge University Press, 1984) pp. 118 ll. 6–7, 141 ll. 37–9, 142 ll. 1–2.
11. Ibid., pp. 204 l. 39–205 l. 5.
12. Mountsier Miscellaneous MSS (UT); *Women in Love*, edited by Farmer, Vasey and Worthen, p. xlix.
13. *Women in Love*, edited by Farmer, Vasey and Worthen, p. lii.
14. Ibid., p. liii.
15. Ibid., p. xlix.
16. E. W. Tedlock, *The Frieda Lawrence Collection of D. H. Lawrence Manuscripts* (Albuquerque: University of New Mexico Press, 1948) p. 93.
17. Edward Nehls, *D. H. Lawrence: A Composite Biography*, Vol. II (Madison: University of Wisconsin Press, 1957) p. 93.
18. Ibid.
19. Tedlock, *The Frieda Lawrence Collection*, p. 94.
20. Ibid.
21. *Women in Love*, edited by Farmer, Vasey and Worthen, p. 1.
22. Mountsier Miscellaneous MSS (UT).
23. *Aaron's Rod*, edited by Mara Kalnins (Cambridge University Press, 1988) p. xxxiii.
24. 'Introduction to *Memoirs of the Foreign Legion*', *Phoenix II*, p. 325.

Chapter 7: Living Blithely: 1922–25

1. *Letters to Thomas and Adele Seltzer*, edited by Gerald M. Lacy (Santa Barbara: Black Sparrow Press, 1976) p. 209.
2. Ibid., p. 223.
3. Ibid., p. 184.
4. Ibid., p. 188.
5. E. W. Tedlock, *The Frieda Lawrence Collection of D. H. Lawrence Manuscripts* (Albuquerque: University of New Mexico Press, 1948) p. 97.
6. Mountsier hung on to the manuscripts and typescripts of *Studies in Classic American Literature*, to typescripts of 'Democracy', part of 'The Crown' and *The Lost Girl*, and to Lawrence's manuscript of his 'Introduction' to Maurice Magnus's *Memoirs of the Foreign Legion*.

7. They formed the basis of the collection (now dispersed) of the late Charles Smith of Bermuda.
8. Tedlock, *The Frieda Lawrence Collection*, p. 99.
9. *Letters to Thomas and Adele Seltzer*, edited by Lacy, p. 124.
10. *Reflections on the Death of a Porcupine*, edited by Michael Herbert (Cambridge University Press, 1988) pp. 240 ll. 33–8.

Chapter 8: Economising: 1925–27

1. To Nancy Pearn, 22 March 1927.
2. To Nancy Pearn, 12 April 1927.
3. To Earl Brewster, 25 June 1927.
4. To Martin Secker, 6 June and 2 July 1927.
5. To Martin Secker, 1 August 1927.
6. To Donald Carswell, 5 December 1927.
7. To Martin Secker, 30 September 1927.
8. To Alfred Knopf, 10 October 1927.

Chapter 9: 1928

1. Memorandum Book (Northwestern University); DHL to Curtis Brown, 18 November 1927; to Richard Aldington, 18 November 1927.
2. To Curtis Brown, 18 November 1927.
3. Ibid.
4. Memorandum Book (Northwestern University).
5. DHL to Curtis Brown, 18 November 1927.
6. To Dorothy Brett, 12 February 1928; to Martin Secker, 9 March 1928.
7. To Martin Secker, 11 January 1928.
8. To Curtis Brown, 18 November 1927; to Catherine Carswell, 10 January 1928.
9. To Cynthia Asquith, 5 April 1928; to Edward McDonald, 15 March 1928.
10. To Harold Mason, 11 April 1928; to Laurence Pollinger, 17 March 1928.
11. To Aldous Huxley, 2 April 1928.
12. To Martin Secker, 5 March 1928.
13. See Keith Sagar, *A D. H. Lawrence Calendar* (Manchester: Manchester University Press, 1979) pp. 170–1.
14. DHL to Martin Secker, 24 April 1928.
15. To Curtis Brown, 15 March 1928.
16. To Aldous Huxley, 2 April 1928.
17. To Curtis Brown, 29 March 1928; to S. S. Koteliansky, 18 April 1928.
18. To Aldous Huxley, 27 March 1928.
19. To Pino Orioli, 21 June 1928.
20. To Pino Orioli, 28 June 1928.
21. To Aldous Huxley, 31 July 1928.
22. To Aldous Huxley, 15 August 1928; to Dorothy Yorke, 17 August 1928.

23. To Pino Orioli, 1 August 1928.
24. To Edward McDonald, 9 March 1928.
25. To Juliette Huxley, 17 April 1928; to Dorothy Brett, 5 April 1928; to Laurence Pollinger, 27 August 1928.
26. Edward Nehls, *D. H. Lawrence: A Composite Biography*, Vol. III (Madison: University of Wisconsin Press, 1959) p. 158.
27. Ibid., p. 261.
28. DHL to Martin Secker, 23 December 1928.
29. To Ottoline Morrell, 3 April 1929.
30. 'My Skirmish with Jolly Roger', *Lady Chatterley's Lover* (Paris, 1929) p. III.
31. Nehls, III, p. 313.
32. DHL to Aldous Huxley, 15 December 1928.
33. To Aldous Huxley, 30 December 1928.
34. To Aldous Huxley, 8 March 1929.
35. 'My Skirmish', p. III.
36. Nehls, III, p. 313–14.
37. 'My Skirmish', p. III.
38. DHL to Ottoline Morrell, 3 April 1929.
39. To S. S. Koteliansky, 8 October 1927; to Martin Secker, 15 March 1927.
40. To Nancy Pearn, 13 May 1928.
41. To Nancy Pearn, 21 May 1928.
42. *John Bull*, 20 October 1928, p. 11.
43. DHL to Martin Secker, 3 December 1928.
44. Nehls, III, p. 392.
45. DHL to Dorothy Brett, 24 November 1928.
46. To Dorothy Brett, 23 November 1928.
47. To H. J. Seligmann, 8 November 1928; to Ada Clarke, 1 April 1928.
48. To Bernard Falk, 24 February 1929.
49. To Pino Orioli, 29 July 1929.
50. To Laurence Pollinger, 3 April 1929.
51. To Anna von Richthofen, 19 December 1928.
52. To Martin Secker, 7 January 1929.
53. To Charles Lahr, 18 April 1929.
54. To Martin Secker, 14 April 1929.
55. To Martin Secker, 2 August and 3 November 1929.
56. Warren Roberts, *A Bibliography of D. H. Lawrence*, 2nd edn (Cambridge University Press, 1982) p. 136; DHL to Ada Clarke, 10 December 1929.
57. To Caresse Crosby, 14 February 1930.
58. To Max Mohr, 25 May 1929.

Chapter 10: Providing: 1929–30

1. Frieda Lawrence, *Memoirs and Correspondence* (Heinemann, 1961) p. 95.
2. DHL to Pino Orioli, 31 July 1928.
3. To Dorothy Brett, 25 April 1928.

4. To Edward Dahlberg, 11 January 1929.
5. To Dorothy Brett, 2 March 1929.
6. To Ada Clarke, 3 February 1928.
7. To Emily King, 19 December 1928.
8. Information from Margaret ('Peggy') Needham, April 1988.
9. Edward Nehls, *D. H. Lawrence: A Composite Biography*, Vol. III (Madison: University of Wisconsin Press, 1959) p. 406.
10. DHL to Earl Brewster, 27 February 1930.
11. Nehls, III, p. 439.
12. *Apocalypse and the Writings on Revelation*, edited by Mara Kalnins (Cambridge University Press, 1979) p. 149 ll. 20–1.
13. Nehls, III, pp. 439–40.
14. Frieda Lawrence to Edward Titus, 5 February 1930.
15. Nehls, III, p. 478.

Epilogue

1. E. M. Forster, letter to *Nation & Athenæum*, 29 March 1930, p. 888.
2. Harriet Shaw Weaver supported Joyce financially from 1917 until his death in 1941; see Richard Ellmann, *James Joyce*, 2nd edn (Oxford University Press, 1982) pp. 413, 422, 457, 479–81.
3. *Lady Chatterley's Lover* (1928) p. 363.

Further Reading

I   D. H. LAWRENCE

A: Biographies

E. T. [Jessie Chambers], *D. H. Lawrence: A Personal Record* (Cambridge University Press, 1981).
David Ellis, Mark Kinkead-Weekes and John Worthen, *D. H. Lawrence: A Life*, 3 volumes (Cambridge University Press, forthcoming).
Frieda Lawrence, *'Not I, But the Wind . . .'* (Granada, 1984).
Edward Nehls, *D. H. Lawrence: A Composite Biography*, 3 volumes (Madison: University of Wisconsin Press, 1957–59).
Keith Sagar, *The Life of D. H. Lawrence* (Methuen, 1985).

B: Bibliographies and other reference books

Warren Roberts, *A Bibliography of D. H. Lawrence*, 2nd edn (Cambridge University Press, 1982).
E. W. Tedlock, *The Frieda Lawrence Collection of the Manuscripts of D. H. Lawrence: A Descriptive Bibliography* (Albuquerque: University of New Mexico Press, 1948).
A D. H. Lawrence Handbook, edited by Keith Sagar (Manchester University Press, 1982).

C: Letters

The Cambridge Edition of the Letters of D. H. Lawrence:

The Letters of D. H. Lawrence, 1903–1913, Volume I, edited by James T. Boulton (Cambridge University Press, 1979).
The Letters of D. H. Lawrence, 1913–1916, Volume II, edited by George J. Zytaruk and James T. Boulton (Cambridge University Press, 1982).
The Letters of D. H. Lawrence, 1916–1921, Volume III, edited by James T. Boulton and Andrew Robertson (Cambridge University Press, 1984).
The Letters of D. H. Lawrence, 1921–1924, Volume IV, edited by Warren Roberts, James T. Boulton and Elizabeth Mansfield (Cambridge University Press, 1987).
The Letters of D. H. Lawrence, 1924–1927, Volume V, edited by James T. Boulton and Lindeth Vasey (Cambridge University Press, 1989).
D. H. Lawrence: Letters to Thomas and Adele Seltzer, edited by Gerald M. Lacy (Santa Barbara: Black Sparrow Press, 1976).

D: Works

The Cambridge Edition of the works of D. H. Lawrence:

Aaron's Rod, edited by Mara Kalnins (Cambridge University Press, 1988).
Apocalypse, edited by Mara Kalnins (Cambridge University Press, 1979).
The Lost Girl, edited by John Worthen (Cambridge University Press, 1981).
Love Among the Haystacks and Other Stories, edited by John Worthen (Cambridge University Press, 1987).
Movements in European History, edited by Philip Crumpton (Cambridge University Press, 1989).
Mr Noon, edited by Lindeth Vasey (Cambridge University Press, 1984).
The Plumed Serpent, edited by L. D. Clark (Cambridge University Press, 1986).
The Prussian Officer and Other Stories, edited by John Worthen (Cambridge University Press, 1982).
The Rainbow, edited by Mark Kinkead-Weekes (Cambridge University Press, 1989).
Reflections on the Death of a Porcupine, edited by Michael Herbert (Cambridge University Press, 1988).
St. Mawr, edited by Brian Finney (Cambridge University Press, 1983).
Study of Thomas Hardy and Other Essays, edited by Bruce Steele (Cambridge University Press, 1985).
The Trespasser, edited by Elizabeth Mansfield (Cambridge University Press, 1981).
The White Peacock, edited by Andrew Robertson (Cambridge University Press, 1983).
Women in Love, edited by David Farmer, Lindeth Vasey and John Worthen (Cambridge University Press, 1987).

Other volumes in preparation.

Phoenix, edited by E. D. McDonald (New York: Viking Press, 1936).
Phoenix II, edited by Warren Roberts and Harry T. Moore (Heinemann, 1968).

II SELECTED MATERIAL ON OTHER TWENTIETH CENTURY BRITISH WRITERS

General

Curtis Brown, *Contacts* (Cassell, 1935).
F. Swinnerton, *The Georgian Literary Scene 1910–1935*, revised edn (Dent and Sons, 1951).

Arnold Bennett

Letters of Arnold Bennett, edited by J. Hepburn, 3 volumes (Oxford University Press, 1966–70).
Margaret Drabble, *Arnold Bennett* (Weidenfeld and Nicolson, 1974).

Joseph Conrad

The Collected Letters of Joseph Conrad, edited by F. J. Karl (Cambridge University Press, 1983–).
Cedric Watts, *Joseph Conrad: A Literary Life* (Macmillan, 1989).
Z. Najder, *Joseph Conrad: A Chronicle* (Cambridge University Press, 1983).

Ford Madox Hueffer

Arthur Mizener, *The Saddest Story* (Bodley Head, 1971).

James Joyce

Richard Ellman,, *James Joyce,* 2nd edn (Oxford University Press, 1982).

Compton Mackenzie

Compton Mackenzie, *My Life and Times: Octave Four* (Chatto and Windus, 1965).
Compton Mackenzie, *My Life and Times: Octave Five* (Chatto and Windus, 1966).
Compton Mackenzie, *My Life and Times: Octave Six* (Chatto and Windus, 1967).

Virginia Woolf

The Diary of Virginia Woolf, edited by Anne Olivier Bell, 5 volumes (Penguin Books, 1978–85).
The Flight of the Mind: The Letters of Virginia Woolf, edited by Nigel Nicolson, 6 volumes (Hogarth Press, 1975–80).

Index

Academy, The
  review of *Sons and Lovers*, 31
Adelphi, The, see Murry, J. M.
Aldington, Richard
  helps with *Lady Chatterley's Lover*,
    149
  DHL buying stocks and shares,
    xx
American copyright, 175n.5
American market, 49, 53, 56, 75, 81,
    86–7, 89, 116, 117
  American novel for, 122, 123
  DHL depends upon, 107–8, 114–
    15, 117–18, 122
  DHL gives priority to, 118, 122
  DHL writes for, 118, 133
  see also Huebsch, B., Knopf, A.
    and Seltzer, T.
Arlen, Michael
  DHL discusses money with, 144
Asquith, Cynthia and Herbert, 44,
    72
  ghost story commissioned, 138
Athenæum, The, see Murry, J. M.
Authors' Society, 45

Bank accounts, 37, 116, 121, 125,
    133, 162
  for *Lady Chatterley's Lover*, 147
Barmby, A. W., 125, 126, 131, 132,
    135
Barrie, J. M., 94
Beach, Sylvia (bookseller)
  asked to publish *Lady Chatterley's
    Lover*, 152
  publisher of Paris *Ulysses*, 152
Beaumont, Cyril (publisher)
  Bay, 74, 132
  poems for, 73
  potential publisher of *Women in
    Love*, 73
Bennett, Arnold
  Clayhanger, xxiv
  English Review, the, *xxv*

DHL on, *xxvi*
  lends DHL money, 71–2, 73, 86
  popular writer, 155
  wealth, *xxvi*
Beresford, J. D., 54, 78–9
Bibliography of D. H. Lawrence, xxvi
*Bibliography of the Writings of D. H.
    Lawrence*, 132
Black Sun Press (publishers), 156,
    158–9
Boni brothers, 164
Borg, Michael, 128
Borzoi, The, 131
Brett, Dorothy, 125, 154
  DHL advises, 160–1
Brewster, Earl and Achsah, 112
  stocks and shares, 162
Brooke, Rupert, 81
Burrows, Louie,
  and 1907 story competition, 7
  co-author of 'Goose Fair', 11
  engagement to DHL, 14, 16
Bystander, The, 128

Caine, Hall
  trouble with libraries, 31
Cambridge University Press
    (publishers)
  new edition of DHL's work, 165
Cannan, Gilbert
  collects money for DHL, 89, 95
Carswell, Catherine (Jackson), 63,
    81
  organises typing of part of *Lady
    Chatterley's Lover*, 146
  prize-winning novel *Open the
    Door!*, 90, 95–6
  reviews *The Rainbow*, 43
Carter, Frederick, 163
Casanova's Homecoming, 117
Centaur Press (publishers)
  DHL likes, 132
Chambers family, 3
  Alan, 6

Edmund (father), 7
May, 7, 13
Chambers, Jessie, 2, 19
Eastwood, 4–5
1907 story competition, 6–7
reader of DHL's early work, 3, 6
sends poems to English Review, 8–9, 11
Chatto and Windus (publishers), 63, 94
interested in *Look! We Have Come Through!*, 67
objections, 67–8, 74
terms and publication, 68
reject *At the Gates*, 69
reject *New Poems*, 74
Chesterton, G. K.,
column in *Daily News*, 7
DHL sends writing to, 7–8
Clayhanger, *xxiv*
Collins, Vere, 76
Collins, William (publisher), 67
Conrad, Joseph, 8, 17
and the public, *xxvi*
Methuen, 37
Pinker, 37, 175n.7
Constable (publishers), 52, 63
Crane, Nathalie, 135
Criterion, The, 129
Crosby, Harry and Caresse, 156, 158–9
Curtis, Brown (literary agent), 83, 87–162 *passim*
advises DHL about investments, 162
archives, 172n.1
attitude to DHL, 110, 114, 118, 130
DHL and American branch, 121, 125
DHL and Knopf, 126
DHL takes as agent, 87, 103
disapproval of *Lady Chatterley's Lover*, 149, 150
fears for *Women in Love*, 104
fears for *Aaron's Rod*, 110
not involved in publication of *Lady Chatterley's Lover*, 144
writes to DHL (1913–14), 34

Dahlberg, Edward
DHL advises, 161
Daily Express, The, 154
Daily Herald, The, 104
Daily News, The
G. K. Chesterton's column, 7
R. A. Scott-James literary editor, 17
review of *Sons and Lovers*, 31
'Davison, Laurence H.', 80
de la Mare, Walter
selects poems for a book by DHL, 18
helps DHL, 22–3
de Morgan, William, 10
Dial, The, 120
Dickinson, Sir John
criticises Methuen over *The Rainbow*, 46
Doran, George (publisher)
Pinker's contact in the USA, 56, 86
rejects *The Rainbow*, 44
Douglas, Norman, 88, 89
and limited editions, 144–5
Duckworth, Gerald (publisher), *xxiv*, 17, 19, 23, 25, 62, 69, 94
The Trespasser, 18, 22, 26
'Paul Morel', 26
Sons and Lovers, 27, 30, 34, 166, 174n.1
poor sales, 30–2, 34–5, 38, 175n.4
Kennerley's edition, 35
DHL takes *The Rainbow* from, 36–8
The Prussian Officer, 38
Twilight in Italy, 38, 42, 50–1, 60
Love Poems, 52
Amores, 52–3, 60, 67
'The Sisters', 59–60, 63
rejects *Look! We Have Come Through!*, 67
abandons DHL, 67
The Rainbow and *Women in Love* negotiations, 90–1
rejects *The Rainbow*, 91
DHL's attitude to, 21, 22, 34, 52, 59–60
Duse, Eleanora, 100

Eastwood, 4–5, 13, 19
Egoist, The, 33
English book market, the, 108–9,
    112, 116, 117–19, 168
English Review, 18, 51, 69, 83
    Hueffer, *xxv*
    Harrison, *xxv*
    Jessie Chambers, 8–9
    DHL's poems, 11, 17, 67, 75
    'Goose Fair' and 'Odour of
        Chrysanthemums', 11, 15–16
    DHL loses support of, 23
    'Honour and Arms', 25, 33, 39
    'Samson and Delilah', 62
    prints Italian sketches, 29, 33
    prints 'The Reality of Peace', 66
    prints 'Love' and 'Life', 72
    prints American essays, 75–6, 79,
        81
    prints 'The Blind Man', 102
Estate, the D. H. Lawrence, 164–5
Evening News, The, 153–4
Evening Standard, The, *xxv*

Faber and Faber (publishers)
    'Pornography and Obscenity'
        and *Nettles*, 158
Feuchtwanger, Lion
    Jew Süss, 153
Fisher Street
    meetings in, 41, 48
Florence
    DHL in, 88, 89, 139, 140–2, 144–6,
        146–8
    DHL meets Arlen, 144
    doctor, 160, 161
    publication of *Lady Chatterley's
        Lover*, *xx*, 55, 144–53
Forster, E. M., 166
Fortnightly Review, The, 66
Forum, The, 25
France, Anatole
    DHL as second, 130
Freeman, G. S., 77
Freud, Sigmund
    preface to *A Young Girl's Diary*,
        117

Galsworthy, John, 17

Garnett, Edward, *xxi*, 13, 19, 21, 28,
    31, 34
    advises and helps DHL, 16–18,
        22–5, 29, 34–5, 121, 171
    at The Cearne, 17, 29
    cuts *Sons and Lovers*, 26–7, 30,166
    critical of 'The Sisters', 34–5, 166
    DHL's disagreement with, 35
    hopes to keep DHL with
        Duckworth, 36, 121
    relationship ends with *The
        Prussian Officer*, 38
George, Walter, 44
Georgian Poetry, 33, 67, 69
Gertler, Mark, 55
Glasgow Herald, The
    review of *The Rainbow*, 43
Goldring, Douglas, 96
    Touch and Go, 83, 176n.10
Götzsche, Kai (Danish friend), 123
'Grantorto', 80
Graves, Robert, 167
Gray, Cecil, 70
Green Hat, The, 144

Hardy, Thomas, 1, 8
Harper's Bazaar, 114, 138
Harris, Frank
    My Life, 144, 152
Harrison, Austin, 72, 83
    English Review, 11
    cuts 'Odour of
        Chrysanthemums', 12
    offended and relents, 23, 29
    supports DHL in wartime, 51, 66
    'The Reality of Peace', 66
    rejects 'The Mortal Coil', 66
    accepts poems, 66–7
    accepts essays, 72
    accepts American essays, 75–6
    'The Blind Man', 102
Hearst's International
    buys 'The Captain's Doll', 116,
        117, 120
    never publishes, 117
Heinemann, William (publisher),
    10, 21, 32, 69
    DHL's agreement with, 10–11, 17
    cuts in *The White Peacock*, 12–13

royalties for *The White Peacock*, 10–11, 13–14, 21
unsure of 'The Saga of Siegmund', 15, 18, 19
rejects 'Paul Morel', 26, 166
hopes to print 'The Man Who Loved Islands', 156
Heseltine, Philip, 54–5
attacks *Women in Love*, 104–6
private income, 59
Hicks, Sir William Joynson ('Jix'), 157, 158
Hilton, Enid
helps with *Lady Chatterley's Lover*, 149
Hudson, W. H., 16
Huebsch, Benjamin (publisher), 84, 91, 94, 102
The Rainbow, The Prussian Officer, Amores, Twilight in Italy, 53
issues *The Rainbow* slowly, 56
Look! We Have Come Through!, 75
royalties, 81, 88, 176n.8
New Poems, 82–3
Studies in Classic American Literature, 84–5
angry over *Women in Love*, 85–6
The Lost Girl, 90
new edition of *The Rainbow*, 92, 121
royalties, 117
Hueffer, Ford Madox
assists and prints DHL, xxi, 11–12, 19, 35
Bennett, xxv
criticisms of DHL, 12, 14–15
English Review (1908–1910), xxv, 8–9
influence on DHL, 11–12
Jessie Chambers sends poems, 8–9
letter to Heinemann, 10–11
meets DHL and reads *The White Peacock*, 9–10
Hutchinson (publishers), 24, 128–9
Hutchinson's Story Magazine, 127, 128
Huxley, Maria
types part of *Lady Chatterley's Lover*, 146, 147

Illnesses, DHL's, 17–18, 53–4, 79, 114, 130–1, 136–7, 142, 143–4, 149, 151, 160, 161, 163
Inwood, Alfred (London Editor of *Sheffield Telegraph*)
DHL asks for advice, 5

Jaffe, Else, 57
advises Frieda and DHL, 26
and Alfred Weber, 22
loans money, 22, 174n.1
James Tait Black Memorial Prize
The Lost Girl wins, xiv, 112
James, Henry, 8
Jew Süss, 153
John Bull
review of *Lady Chatterley's Lover*, 154
review of *Women in Love*, 104, 110
Journalism, 5, 14, 16, 17, 153–5
Joyce, James
short of money, xxi, 167
subsidies for, 168, 180n.2
Juta, Jan, 169

Kennerley, Mitchell (publisher)
royalties from *Sons and Lovers*, 33, 35–6, 39–40, 52, 95, 121, 175n.5
The Widowing of Mrs Holroyd, 33, 52
The Rainbow, 41, 44
Love Poems, 52
The Trespasser, 175n.5
Knopf, Alfred (publisher) and Blanche, 126–7, 135, 143
St. Mawr, The Plumed Serpent, 126, 131
Memoirs of the Foreign Legion, 128
'Accumulated Mail' in *The Borzoi*, 131
DHL sees in New York, 132
and private editions, 135–6
concerned about lack of new DHL book, 142
expurgated text of *Lady Chatterley's Lover*, 145–6
and success, 126–7, 132, 164

Koteliansky, S. S., 72, 73, 79, 81–2, 83, 85, 96, 139
  helps with *Lady Chatterley's Lover*, 149

Lawrence, Ada (sister), 1, 126, 154
  after DHL's death, 164
  and *The Tempest*, 2
  DHL advises, 161
  offers to pay DHL's rent, 70–1, 74
Lawrence, Arthur John (father), 4
  response to *The White Peacock*, 13
Lawrence, D. H.
  as popular and unpopular writer, *xxiv–xxvi*, 25, 42, 90, 93–5, 107, 109, 111–12, 127, 132, 151, 153–8, 168, 169–70, 174n.3
  as professional writer, *xxii–xxiii*, 5, 22, 29, 57, 76, 80, 94, 158–9, 168–71
  his relationships with agents and publishers, *xxiv*, 10–11, 23–5, 35, 37, 72, 83, 85–7, 95, 101–3, 119–21, 124–7, 138, 143, 149, 157
  his sense and shrewdness, *xx–xxiii*, 26–7, 33, 55–6, 74–5, 94, 144–5, 160–2, 164
  the special importance of his novels to, 64, 90, 111, 116, 134, 139, 141
Lawrence, D. H. (works)
  Aaron's Rod, *xiv*, 134; started, 71; Turin used in, 89; problems with, 76–7, 89, 101; finished, 109; Seltzer, Secker and, 109–11, 115–16; libraries and, 115–16; importance, 109, 123
  'Accumulated Mail', *xvi*, 131
  'Adolf', 79
  'All of Us', 73
  All Things are Possible, see Shestov, L.
  Amores, *xii*, 38, 65; terms, 52–3; revised, 54; published, 52; remaindered, 67
  Apocalypse, *xix*, *xxiii*, 163
  A Propos of Lady Chatterley's Lover, *xix*

Assorted Articles, *xix*, 163
At the Gates, 69
Bay, *xii*, 73–4, 75, 132, 156; published, 80
Birds, Beasts and Flowers, *xv*, 96, 101, 122
'Blind Man, The', *xiii*, 102
'Blue Moccasins, The', 163
Book reviews, *x*, *xvi*, 139
'Border-Line, The', *xvi*, 127
Boy in the Bush, The, *xv*, 134; originally 'The House of Ellis', 123; Seltzer considers, 123
Bunin, I. A., DHL translates *The Gentleman from San Francisco*, *xiv*
'Burns Novel, The', 28
Captain's Doll, The, *xiv–xv*, 108, 122
'Captain's Doll, The', sold to Hearst, 116; DHL worried about Secker publishing, 118–19, 121
'Certain Americans and an Englishman', *xiv*, 118
'Christening, The', *xi*
'Christs in the Tirol', *x*
'Clouds', 79
Collected Poems, *xviii*, *xix*, 142
Collier's Friday Night, A, 10, 17
'Crown, The', *xii*, 42, 54
'Daughters of the Vicar', 16, 17, 38
David, *xvii*, *xix*, 131
'Do Women Change?', *xviii*, 155
'Dull London', *xviii*
'Elsa Culverwell', 28
'England, My England', *xii*
England, My England, *xiv*, *xv*, 108
Escaped Cock, The, *xviii*, 156, 158–9, 163; profits, 159
Etruscan Places, *xix*, planned as popular book, 136, 139, 141; essays printed, 141, 143; unfinished, 142
'Fanny and Annie', 80
Fantasia of the Unconscious, *xiv*, 109; popular and serious, 168

'Fireworks in Florence', 140
'Fly in the Ointment, The', *x*, 33
'Flying Fish, The', 130
'Fox, The', written, 78; sold, 80;
    rejected in USA, 81;
    collected, 108
'Fragment of Stained Glass, A',
    ix, 7
'French Sons of Germany', *x*
'Future of the Novel, The', 120
Gentleman from San Francisco, The,
    see Bunin, I. A.
'Glad Ghosts', 138, 139; as book,
    xvii, 140
'Goose Fair', *ix*, 11
Grazzini, A., DHL translates *The
    Story of Doctor Manente*, *xviii*
'Hail in the Rhineland', *x*
'"Henry", she said', 163
'Her Turn', *x*
'Honour and Arms', *xi*, *xxv*, 25,
    39, 40; retitled 'The Prussian
    Officer', 38
'Hymns in a Man's Life', *xviii*
'If Women were Supreme', *xviii*
'In Love?', 139, 140
'Indians and Entertainment', *xvi*,
    127
'Insurrection of Miss Houghton,
    The', written and
    abandoned, 28–9; in wartime
    (1916), 57–8; used (1920), 90;
    see The Lost Girl
'Introduction to These Paintings',
    163
'Is England still a Man's
    Country?', *xviii*
'"Jeune Fille" Wants to Know,
    The', *xvii*, 153–4
John Thomas and Lady Jane, 147–8;
    see Lady Chatterley's Lover
Kangaroo, *xv*, 134; written, 116,
    122; Mountsier and, 119;
    published 119, 122
Lady Chatterley's Lover, *xvii*, *xviii*,
    xx–xxi, *xxii*, *xxv*, *xxvi*, 55, 134,
    138–9, 143–53, 155, 156, 158,
    160, 161, 169, 170; 'English
    novel', 140; first version,
140–1, 144; second version,
    141, 144; third version, 144–
    5; schemes for publication,
    144–5; expurgated for Secker
    and Knopf, 145–6; profits,
    145, 150–1, 153, 156, 163, 165;
    pirated, 151–2; expensive
    and cheap editions, 151–3,
    156–7; copy for DHL's sister
    Emily, 161–2
Ladybird, The, *xiv*, 119, 138
Last Poems, *xxiii*, 163
'Laura Philippine', *xvii*
'Lessford's Rabbits', 12
'Lesson on the Tortoise, A', 12
Letters of D. H. Lawrence, The, *xix*
'Life', *xii*
Little Novels of Sicily, see Verga, G.
Look! We Have Come Through!, *xii*,
    xiii; compiled, 65; sent to
    Pinker, 66; accepted, 67–8;
    royalties, 68, 75
Lost Girl, The, *xiii*, *xiv*, 134;
    written, 90; offered to
    Secker, 93–4; title 'Bitter
    Cherry' considered, 94; as
    commercial novel, 95, 153,
    167, 168; libraries and, 93,
    96–9, 168; DHL cuts, 97–8;
    Secker cuts, 98, 106; sales,
    99; wins James Tait Black
    prize, 112; *see also*
    'The insurrection of Miss
    Houghton'
'Love', *xii*
'Love Among the Haystacks', 16
Love Among the Haystacks, *xix*
Love Poems, *x*; reprinted, *xi*, *xv*, 52
'Making Love to Music', 153
'Man is the Hunter', 140
Man Who Died, The, see *The
    Escaped Cock*
'Man Who Loved Islands, The',
    139, 140
'Master in his own House', *xviii*
Mastro-don Gesualdo, see Verga, G.
Memoirs of the Foreign Legion,
    DHL's Introduction to, *xvi*,
    89, 112

Lawrence, D. H. – *cont.*
 Memorandum Book, *xx*
 'Mercury', 140
 'Miner at Home, The', *x*, 18
 'Monkey Nuts', 80
 Mornings in Mexico, essays
  written, 129; as book, *xvii*,
  140, 141
 'Mortal Coil, The', *xii*, 62
 Movements in European History,
  xiii; written for money, *xxii–
  xxiii*, 76, 77, 79; completion
  delayed, 79; published
  under name of 'Laurence H.
  Davison', 80
 Mr Noon, 134; address to the
  reader in, 100–1; abandoned,
  101
 'Myself Revealed', *xviii*
 My Skirmish with Jolly Roger, *xviii*
 Nettles, *xix*, 158, 163, 170
 New Poems, *xiii*, 73–4, 82, 88
 'Nightingale, The', *xvii*, 140;
  American and English
  publication, 141
 Noah's Flood, 131
 'None of That', 154
 'Odour of Chrysanthemums', *ix*,
  11–12, 173n.20
 'Oh! for a new Crusade', *xviii*
 'Old Adam, The', 16
 'Once – !', 33
 'Over Ernest Ladies', *xviii*
 'Overtone, The', 51, 175n.1
 Paintings of D. H. Lawrence, The,
  xviii, 156, 159
 Pansies, *xviii*, 156–8, 163
 'Paul Morel' started, 15; lack of
  progress with (1911), 16;
  almost finished (1912), 18;
  revised in Germany for
  Heinemann, 22; revised in
  Italy for Duckworth, 26; *see
  also Sons and Lovers*
 Plumed Serpent, The, *xvi*, *xvii*, 134,
  135, 138, 169; novel of
  America, 122; written as
  'Quetzalcoatl', 122–3;
  rewritten, 129–30; finished,

 130, 134; revised, 131;
  royalties, 131; title, 130;
  damages DHL's health, 134,
  137
 'Poetry of the Present'
  (Introduction to *New Poems*),
  xiii, 80, 88–9
 Pornography & Obscenity, *xviii*,
  158, 163
 'Prelude, A', *ix*, 7
 Prussian Officer, The, *xi*, *xii*, *xvi*,
  38; reviews of, 41
 'Prussian Officer, The', *see*
  'Honour and Arms'
 Psychoanalysis and the Unconscious,
  xiv, *xv*; American and
  English editions, 107, 109
 'Quetzalcoatl', *see The Plumed
  Serpent*
 Rainbow, The, *xi*, *xii*, *xvi*, *xxvi*, 36,
  39, 48, 94, 109; royalties from
  36–7, 38–9, 40–1, 42, 50, 51,
  79, 116; DHL rewrites, 40, 58;
  published, 42; reviews, 42–3;
  sales, 43; advertising
  withdrawn, 44; seized, 44;
  court case, 45–6, 58;
  lesbianism in, 43, 58, 92;
  destroyed, 46, 171; questions
  in Parliament, 47; DHL
  wants to publish privately,
  47, 55; lasting effect of ban,
  48–9, 54, 57, 58–9, 63, 68, 104,
  166; material excised from,
  50, 57, 58; *see also* Huebsch,
  B., Methuen, A. *and* Secker,
  M.
 'Rawdon's Roof', 143; as book,
  xvii
 'Real Thing, The', 163
 'Real Trouble about Women,
  The', *xviii*
 'Reality of Peace, The', *xii*, 66
 *Reflections on the Death of a
  Porcupine*, *xvi*, 131–2, 156
 'Return to Bestwood', 140
 'Rex', 79
 'Rocking-Horse Winner, The',
  xvii, 138, 139

'Saga of Siegmund, The', finished, 14; criticised by Hueffer, 14–15; Garnett sees, 17; accepted by Duckworth, 18

St. Mawr, xvi, 126, 128

'Samson and Delilah', *xii*, 62, 176n.2

Sea and Sardinia, xiv, xv, xvii, 101; American and English editions, 107, 121; as 'popular' work, 109, 167, 169

'Second Best', *x*

Selected Poems, xvii

'Sex Locked Out', *xviii*

'Shadow in the Rose Garden, The', *xi*, 33

Shestov, L., DHL translates *All Things are Possible, xiii*, 81–2, 83

'Sick Collier, A', *x*

Signature, The, 42, 48

'Sisters, The', started, 29, 58; as 'pot-boiler', 29, 95; revised, 33, 34–5, 166; *see also The Rainbow and Women in Love*

'Smile', *xvii*, 138

'Snapdragon', 33

'Soiled Rose, The', *x*, 23, 25

Sons and Lovers, x, xv, xxiv, 12, 20, 41, 48, 77; finished, 26; cut by Garnett and Duckworth, 26–7, 166; published 28, 30–2; reviews, 31, 41; royalties, 28–9, 30; Duckworth's profits, 32; poor sales, 30–2; 34–5, 174n.3; good reputation, 30–2, 167; Kennerley publishes in USA, 33, 35–6, 39–40, 52, 95, 121, 122; *see also* 'Paul Morel'

Story of Doctor Manente, The, see Grazzini, A.

'Strike-Pay', *x*

Studies in Classic American Literature, xv, 94; begun, 69; continued, 73; sent to Pinker, 75; accepted by

Harrison, 75; finished, 76; revised in America, 118; published, 122

'Study of Thomas Hardy', 39, 42, 51, 54

'Suggestions for Stories', 130

'Sun', 138; as book, *xvii, xviii*, 140, 156

'Surgery for the Novel, or a Bomb', *xv*, 120

Thimble, The', *xii*, 51

'Tickets Please', *xiii*, 78, 79, 80–1

Tortoises, xiv

Touch and Go, xiii, 83; written, 78; unperformed and unprinted, 80; 'Plays for a People's Theatre', 176n.10

Tresspasser, The, x, 18, 129; literary quality, 20; royalties, 22, 26–7; *see also* 'The Saga of Siegmund'

Twilight in Italy, xii, xvi, xvii, 38, 42, 51, 174n.6; terms, 50–1

'Two Blue Birds', 139

Verga, Giovanni, DHL translates, *xv, xvi, xvii*, 114, 142

'Vin Ordinaire', *xi, xxv*

Virgin and the Gipsy, The, xix, 138, 141

'When She Asks Why', *see* 'The "Jeune Fille" Wants to Know'

'Whistling of Birds', *xiii*, 79, 80

White Peacock, The, ix, 3; early drafts, 6; Hueffer reads, 9–10; contract, 10–11; cuts, 12; royalties, 10–11, 13–14, 21, 69, 175n.5; publication and reviews, 15; literary quality, 20

'White Stocking, The', *xi*, 7, 34

Widowing of Mrs Holroyd, The, xi, xiii, published by Kennerley, 33

'Wintry Peacock', *xiv*, 96, 108

'Witch à la Mode, The', 16

'With the Guns', *xi*

'Woman Who Rode Away, The', *xvi*, 128

Index

Lawrence, D. H. – *cont.*
  Woman Who Rode Away, The, *xvii*,
    142
  'Women Don't Change', *xviii*; *see*
    'Do Women Change?'
  Women in Love, *xiii*, *xiv*, *xxvi*, 39,
    56, 65, 94, 109, 134, 167;
    begun (as 'The Sisters'), 58;
    first draft finished, 59–60;
    typed, 60–1; completed and
    revised, 61–2; rejected, 63–4,
    70, 76–7; plans for private
    editions, 69, 73; further
    revision, 69–70; safety of TS.,
    71; characters in *Touch and
    Go*, 78; plans for publication
    by Seltzer, 84–6; published,
    96, 103; court case in
    America, 117; success of
    popular edition, 117, 122;
    Secker's plans, 90–3; proofs,
    98; cuts, 99–100; published,
    103; reviews, 103–4, 110;
    attacked by Heseltine, 104–6;
    new edition, 106–7; royalties,
    107, 122; *see also* 'The Sisters'
  'You Touched Me', 80
Lawrence, Emily (sister), 2
  after DHL's death, 164
  copy of *Lady Chatterley's Lover*,
    161–2
Lawrence, Ernest William
  (brother), 1–2, 4
Lawrence, Frieda (née von
  Richthofen), *xxii*, *xxiii*
  DHL meets and goes away with,
    18–19, 21
  lawsuit for estate, 164
  money, 28, 123, 164
  separation from DHL, 123–4
  supported by DHL's
    posthumous earnings, 153,
    164–5
  see also Weekley, Ernest
Lawrence, George (brother), 1, 2, 4
  after DHL's death, 164
Lawrence, Lydia (mother), 2, 3–4, 13
Lawrence, T. E. ('Aircraftsman
  Shaw'), 136–7

Libraries, sales and problems, 27–8,
  41–2, 93, 96–8, 99, 115–16,
  174n.4
Limited and private editions, 74,
  132, 135–6, 140, 144–5, 156–9,
  170
*Literary Digest International Book
  Review*, 120
Literary property, 82, 158–9, 161–2,
  163–5
Living Age, The, 102
Lorna Doone, 10
Low, Barbara (as literary agent),
  102–3, 171
Lowell, Amy
  gives DHL typewriter, 39, 60–1
  gives money, 63, 75, 89, 95
  pays royalties, 122
  tries to help with Kennerley, 39–
    40

Mackenzie, Compton, *xxiv–xxv*, 10
  advises DHL, 88–9, 93
  Carnival, *xxiv*
  influence on Secker, 89, 91, 92
  The Passionate Elopement, 15–16, 88
  Poor Relations, *xxv*
  Sinister Street, *xxiv–xxv*, 89
Magnus, Maurice, 89, 112, 128
Manchester Guardian, *xxv*, 39
Mansfield, Katherine (Mrs J. M.
  Murry), 42, 47, 54, 57
Marks, Harry (bookseller), 158–9
Marsh, Edward, 33, 39, 48, 52–3, 81,
  117
McDonald, Edward D.
  *Bibliography of the Writings of D. H.
    Lawrence*, 132
Melrose, Andrew (publisher), 90
Methuen, Algernon (publishers),
  31, 34, 38–9, 40–1, 92, 94, 103
  anxious about *The Rainbow*, 41–2,
    43–4
  bill for changes, 42
  co-operate with suppression, 44
  court appearance, 45–7
  demand return of advance, 51,
    117
  DHL's contract with, 60, 63

The Rainbow terms, 36–7, 38, 41
  reject *Women in Love*, 63
Metropolitan, The, 39–40, 96, 108
Meynell, Viola, 40
Mohr, Max, 159
Moore, Harry T.
  DHL buying stocks and shares,
    xx–xxi
Morrell, Philip and Ottoline, 44, 47,
    52–3, 54, 117
  Hermione in *Women in Love*, 64,
    104
  Times Literary Supplement review
    of *Women in Love*, 103
Morrison, Nelly
  types part of *Lady Chatterley's
    Lover*, 145–6
Mountsier, Robert (as literary
    agent), 87–121, 128, 171
  claims to have sold 'The
    Captain's Doll', 116
  DHL breaks with, 120–1
  DHL disagrees with, 101–3, 109,
    119
  DHL leaves details to, 95
  dislike for Seltzer, 95, 119–20, 126
  insists on DHL's American
    market, 108
  keeps DHL's MSS, 120, 177n.6,
    178n.1
  Our Eleven Billion Dollars, 120
Muir, Edwin, 131
Murry, John Middleton, 42, 47–8,
    54, 57, 70, 137
  Adelphi, 124, 125, 129, 137
  Athenæum, 79–80
  takes 'Whistling of Birds', rejects
    other pieces, 79
Muskett, Herbert, 44
My Life, see Harris, F.

Nation, The
  accepts poems, 17
  'The Miner at Home', 18
  review of *Sons and Lovers*, 31
  'Smile', 138
Needham, Margaret ('Peggy'), 162
Neville, George, 3
New Age, The, 138

New Statesman
  prints poem and story, 33
New York Herald Tribune, 139
New York Society for the
    Suppression of Vice
  raid on Seltzer's office, 117
New York Times, The, 128
Nottingham High School, 4, 5
Nottingham, University College, 4
  magazine rejects poem by DHL,
    6
Nottinghamshire Guardian, The
  1907 short story competition, 6–7

Olley, Mr (*Evening News* editor), 154
Orioli, Pino (bookseller), 55
  and Douglas, 144
  co-publication of *Lady Chatterley's
    Lover*, 144–50, 152
  profits, 144–5
Our Eleven Billion Dollars, 120
Oxford University Press
    (publishers), 76

Palmer, Cecil (publisher)
  plans private edition of *Women in
    Love*, 69
Paris
  centre of dubious book trade,
    152; *see* Beach, S. *and*
    Pegasus Press
  publication of Harris's *My Life*,
    144
  publication of *Lady Chatterley's
    Lover*, *xx*, 152–3
Parliament and *The Rainbow*, 45, 47
Peacock, Walter (literary agent), 83–
    4
Pearn, Nancy (periodical specialist
    at Curtis Brown), 135, 139, 140,
    153
  DHL grateful to, 138, 143
  DHL leaves decisions to, 138, 141
Pegasus Press (publisher)
  DHL asks about Paris *Lady
    Chatterley's Lover*, 152
Pinker, J. B. (literary agent), 39–87,
    102

Pinker, J. B. – *cont.*
  approaches DHL on behalf of
      Methuen, 31, 34–5, 36, 103
  Bennett, *xxvi*, 167
  Conrad, 167, 175n.7
  DHL accepts as agent, 37, 167
  DHL angry with, 72, 82–3, 84–6
  DHL breaks with, 85–6, 120
  DHL considers return, 102
  DHL on, 86–7;
  Garnett sends story by DHL, 24–
      5
  Mackenzie, 167
  settles DHL's account, 89
  subsidies DHL, 38, 40, 60, 61, 86
  wealth, *xxv*
Poetry
  Harriet Monroe, 34
  prints poems, 33, 39, 75–6, 80, 120
Pollinger, Laurence (at Curtis
      Brown), 157
  helps with *Lady Chatterley's Lover*,
      149
Pound, Ezra, 9, 33
  contacts with magazines, 33–4

Radford, Dollie, 54, 70
'Rainbow Books and Music, The',
      54–5
Ranch in New Mexico
  DHL works on, 125, 131, 132
  owned by Frieda Lawrence, 125,
      160
Rauh, Ida
  play for, 130–1
Ravagli, Angelo (third husband of
      Frieda Lawrence), 164–5
Rhys, Ernest (editor of Everyman
      series), 9
Roberts, Warren
  Bibliography of D. H. Lawrence, *xxvi*
Royal Literary Fund, 39, 72
Royal Literary Society, 72, 75, 77
Russell, Bertrand, 41, 42

Schnitzler, Arthur
  Casanova's Homecoming, 117
Scott-James, R. A., *see Daily News*

Secker, Martin (publisher), 118, 132,
      138, 143, 153
  offers to publish stories, 15–16, 38
  offers to publish novel, 23–4
  New Poems, 74, 84
  Shestov, 84
  considers *Women in Love*, 84–5, 90
  influenced by Mackenzie, 89, 91
  considers *The Rainbow*, 90–1
  The Rainbow and *Women in Love*,
      91–2
  publishes *The Rainbow* (1926), 91–
      2
  fears for *Women in Love*, 92–3,
      98–100, 104
  changes in, 99–100, 115
  terms, 99–100
  publishes, 103–4
  Heseltine's attack, 104–6
  The Lost Girl, 93–4, 153
  proofs, 95
  libraries refuse, 96–7
  changes in, 97–8, 115
  Sea and Sardinia, 109
  Aaron's Rod, 109–10
  changes in, 115–16
  'The Captain's Doll', 118–19
  The Ladybird, 119, 122, 138
  Kangaroo, 122
  Memoirs of the Foreign Legion, 128
  St. Mawr, 136
  The Plumed Serpent, 129–30
  royalties, 131
  cheap edition of DHL's books,
      135
  David, 135
  better relations with DHL, 136,
      138
  Lady Chatterley's Lover, 138–9, 140,
      141, 145–6
  Pansies, 157–8
  Assorted Articles, 163
  sells rights in DHL's work, 128
  DHL's attitude to, 94, 98–100,
      106–7, 109–10, 118–19, 122,
      136
Secker, Rina, 136
Seltzer, Adele, 120, 123, 125, 126–7,
      132–3

Seltzer, Thomas (publisher), 94, 101, 102, 116, 120–5, 171
   interested in *Women in Love*, 84
   sends advance, 85, 95
   DHL agrees to publication, 90
   retains TS., 85, 90–1, 93
   private edition, 90–1, 96, 111
   proofs and publication, 95–6, 103
   royalties, 103, 107, 115, 117
   cheap edition, 117
   scandal of, 168
   The Lost Girl, 95
   waits for copy, 98
   publication, 98
   royalties, 107
   DHL prefers books to Secker's, 107–8, 115
   Venice novel, 107–8
   Unconscious books, 109, 115, 122
   Aaron's Rod, 109–11
   wants cuts, 110–11
   publishes, 115, 122
   royalties, 115
   'The Captain's Doll', 116, 120
   office raided, 117
   court cases, 117, 124, 135
   Kangaroo, 119, 122
   wants *Sons and Lovers*, 121–2
   The Captain's Doll, Studies in Classic American Literature, Birds, Beasts and Flowers, Mastro-don Gesualdo, 122
   Sea and Sardinia, 107, 121, 122
   DHL with in New York, 123, 132–3
   The Boy in the Bush, 123, 126
   Little Novels of Sicily, 126
   losses, 124, 135
   DHL anxious, 124–5, 125–7
   fails to pay royalties, 124–7, 129, 131, 133, 135
   declines *Memoirs of the Foreign Legion*, 128
   fails to keep DHL's books in print, 135, 169
   titles transferred to Boni brothers, 164
   DHL attitude to, 95, 118, 119–20, 124–7

Servants, 57, 61
Shaw, Bernard, 44
Shearman, Montague, 72–3
Sheffield Telegraph, see Inwood, Alfred
Sidgwick and Jackson (publishers), 52
Skinner, Mollie, *see The Boy in the Bush*
Smart Set, The
   prints stories, 33–4, 127
Some Imagist Poets, 122
Sphere, The
   review of *The Rainbow*, 42–3
Star, The, 139–40
   review of *The Rainbow*, 43
Stephenson, P. R. (publisher), 158
Sterne, Mabel, 112, 117
   presents ranch to Frieda Lawrence, 125
Stocks and shares,
   DHL buys as investment, *xx, xxii,* 162
Strand Magazine, 51, 62, 69, 128
   'Tickets Please', 78, 79, 80, 81
Sunday Dispatch, The, 154–5
Sutro, Alfred, 39

Tax, 142, 144
Teacher, DHL's career as, 4, 5–6, 16, 19
Times Literary Supplement, The, 77–8
   review of *Sons and Lovers*, 31
   review of *Women in Love*, 103
Times, The, 77
Tipografia Giuntina, 145, 146–7, 148
Titus, Edward (bookseller)
   Paris *Lady Chatterley's Lover*, 152–3
Tolstoy, Count Leo Nicolai, 8, 151
Travel, 129
Typing, 34, 40, 81, 160
   DHL's, 39, 60–1

Ulysses, 152
Unwin, T. Fisher (publisher), 24
Vanguard Press (publishers), 150
Vanity Fair, 129
Viking Press (publishers), 164

Vogue, 138, 140

Walpole, Hugh, 94
War, the First World, 38–9, 41, 43,
    44, 50–87 *passim*, 89, 119
    printing and publishing before,
        during and after, *xxii, xxiv–
        xxv*, 48–9, 91
Weber, Alfred
    Else Jaffe and flat, 22
Weekley, Ernest (first husband of
        Frieda Lawrence), 18–19, 165
    costs of divorce, 39, 40–1
Wells, H. G., 8, 9
    Ann Veronica, 15
Westminster Gazette, 21, 22
Woman, 128
Wright, Willard Huntington
    editor of *Smart Set*, 34

Yeats, W. B., 9
Young Girl's Diary, A, 117